Children of the Empire

Children of the Empire
The Victorian Haggards

VICTORIA MANTHORPE

VICTOR GOLLANCZ

LONDON

First published in Great Britain 1996
by Victor Gollancz
An imprint of the Cassell Group
Wellington House, 125 Strand, London WC2R 0BB

A catalogue record for this book is
available from the British Library.

ISBN 0 575 06311 4

Typeset by Rowland Phototypesetting Ltd,
Bury St Edmunds, Suffolk.
Printed in Great Britain by
Butler & Tanner Ltd, Frome, Somerset

For William Hugh Vernon Salazar Haggard
born 1985,
and all his cousins

Contents

List of Illustrations

Acknowledgements

First, my thanks to Mark and Nada Cheyne, who have done so much to help pave the way for this book. Our association began with the production of *King Romance*, a television biography of Sir Henry Rider Haggard for Anglia Television, and continued through research for Shozo Nagaoka's translation of Baroness d'Anethan's memoirs. As I began to realize that Rider was part of a much larger story, Mark and Nada provided every possible help and encouragement towards recovering the whole.

Second, my thanks to all the other members of the Haggard family and their connections, who have so kindly given me access to private papers and answered my persistent queries: Hester Bain, Jill Tucker, Margery and Humphrey Kemball, John Haggard, Peter Lyster, Melville Haggard, Gill Corley Smith, Virginia Leirens Haggard, John Valentine Haggard, Michael Vernon Haggard, Adrian Webb, Dorothy Cheyne, Jennifer Smyth, Geoffrey Haggard, Bridget Muir, Amyand Haggard, Robert Chirnside and Richard Green. I hope the result will provide some satisfaction.

Next, my thanks to those individuals who have contributed to the work: both Patrick Colvin of Woldringfold and Mrs Charles Fox provided information about Lady Archer; Chris Coquet offered material from his collection; Major J. S. Crisp kindly showed me Kirby Cane Hall; Geoff C. Dixon, Land Agent for the Ministry of Defence, provided a photograph of Oran House; Andrea Duncan undertook professional research into Alfred Haggard and the Indian Civil Service; Felicity Elsmore made enquiries to The General Council of the Bar; Dr Erzincli-oglu sent details of his great-great-grandfather General Yusuf Shuhdi Pasha's friendship with Colonel Andrew Haggard; Hélène Haw interpreted Jack Haggard's astrological charts and provided extensive notes on nineteenth-century astrologers; Don Mackenzie of Lammas restored and reproduced photographs; Anne Manthorpe of Norwich undertook research and transcription; Ross Manthorpe of British Columbia discovered details of Andrew Haggard's life in Cowichan; Shozo Nagaoka of Kamakura, Japan, shared his research into the lives of Baron and Baroness d'Anethan; Mrs Lilian Sanders, the Honorary Archivist at Ledbury Parish Church, found Bazett's grave and gave access to the church records; Mrs Stebbings of Shipdham supplied a rare photograph of Shipdham Hall; Janet Thatcher provided material on the Jacksons of Catterick; Colonel Whatmore shared details of Colonel Andrew Haggard's career; Ian Weekley offered access to his reference books after Norwich Central Library was destroyed by fire.

Of the many institutions whose staff have been so generous with their time, I should like particularly to thank: The Royal Anglian Regiment, The Institution of Civil Engineers, Eton College Collections, the Royal Commonwealth Society Library, The Haileybury Society, The King's Own Scottish Borderers' Archives, Lincoln's Inn Library, the National Maritime Museum, The Norfolk Record Office, North Walsham Library, The Shropshire Light Infantry's Archives, St Andrew's Hospital, Northampton, St Leonard's-on-Sea Local Studies Archive, Tonbridge School, The Union Jack Club, and Winchester College.

Finally, I should like to thank Peter Beard for all the help he has given in amassing and analysing information over a period of years; he transcribed Andrew Haggard's Sudan diary, undertook military research, and read the manuscript. His contribution has been essential to the finished work.

Victoria Manthorpe
Scottow, Norfolk
July 1995

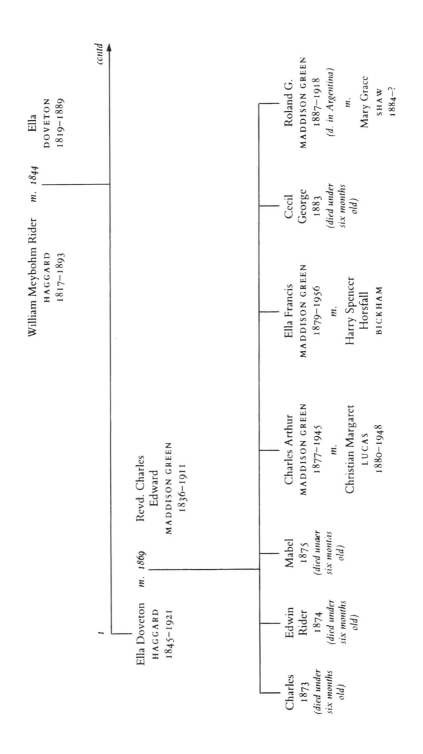

contd

William Meybohm Rider   *m. 1844*   Ella
HAGGARD   DOVETON
1817–1893   1819–1889

1

Ella Doveton   *m. 1869*   Revd. Charles
HAGGARD   Edward
1845–1921   MADDISON GREEN
                          1836–1911

Charles
1873
*(died under
six months
old)*

Edwin
Rider
1874
*(died under
six months
old)*

Mabel
1875
*(died under
six months
old)*

Charles Arthur
MADDISON GREEN
1877–1945
m.
Christian Margaret
LUCAS
1880–1948

Ella Francis
MADDISON GREEN
1879–1956
m.
Harry Spencer
Horsfall
BICKHAM

Cecil
George
1883
*(died under
six months
old)*

Roland G.
MADDISON GREEN
1887–1918
(d. in Argentina)
m.
Mary Grace
SHAW
1884–?

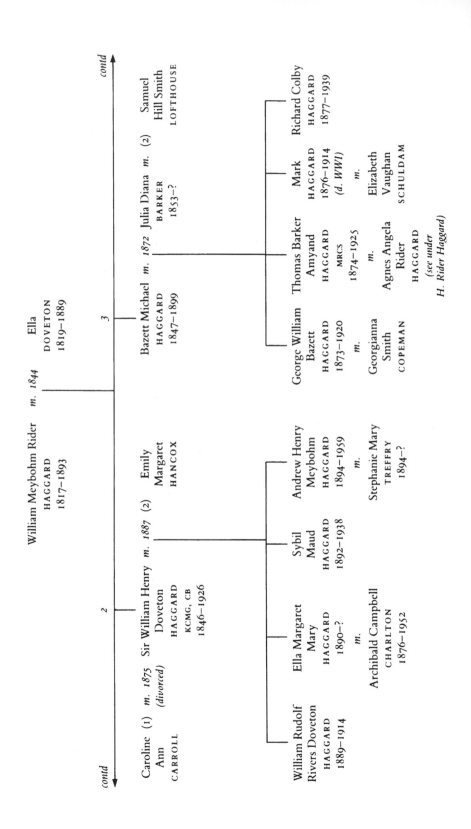

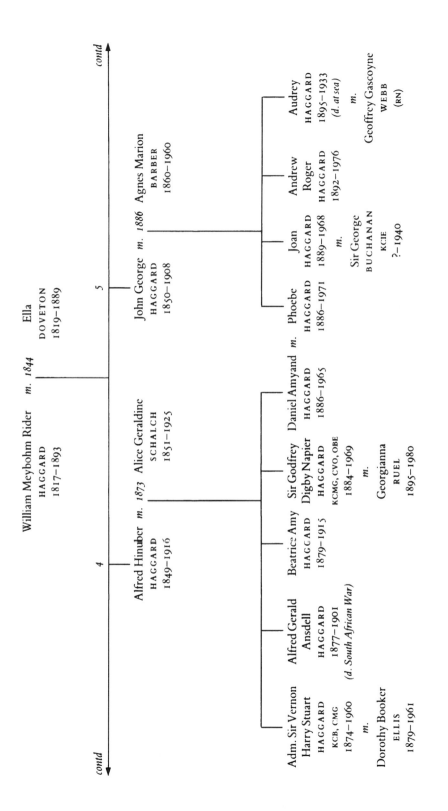

William Meybohm Rider   *m.* *1844*   Ella

HAGGARD   DOVETON

1817–1893   1819–1889

contd   4   5   *contd*

Alfred Hinuber   *m.* *1873*   Alice Geraldine

HAGGARD   SCHALCH

1849–1916   1851–1925

John George   *m.* *1886*   Agnes Marion

HAGGARD   BARBER

1850–1908   1860–1960

Adm. Sir Vernon

Harry Stuart

HAGGARD

KCB, CMG

1874–1960

m.

Dorothy Booker

ELLIS

1879–1961

Alfred Gerald

Ansdell

HAGGARD

1877–1901

(*d. South African War*)

Beatrice Amy

HAGGARD

1879–1915

Sir Godfrey

Digby Napier

HAGGARD

KCMG, CVO, OBE

1884–1969

m.

Georgianna

RUEL

1895–1980

Daniel Amyand   *m.*   Phoebe

HAGGARD   HAGGARD

1886–1965   1886–1971

Joan

HAGGARD

1889–1968

m.

Sir George

BUCHANAN

KCIE

?–1940

Andrew

Roger

HAGGARD

1892–1976

Audrey

HAGGARD

1895–1933

(*d. at sea*)

m.

Geoffrey Gascoyne

WEBB

(RN)

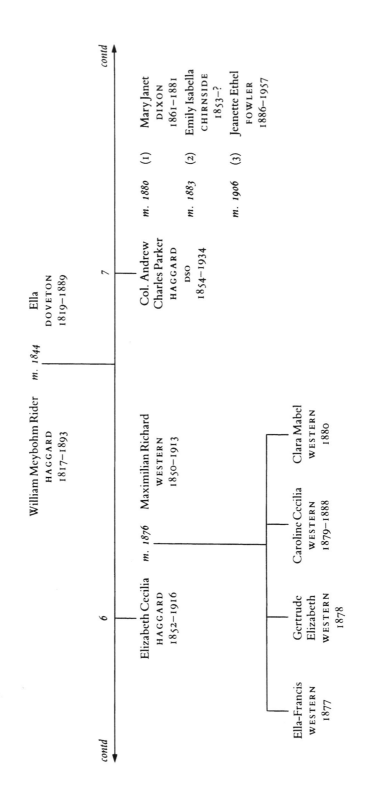

contd

William Meybohm Rider   *m. 1844*   Ella
HAGGARD   DOVETON
1817–1893   1819–1889

6   7

Elizabeth Cecilia   *m. 1876*   Maximilian Richard   Col. Andrew
HAGGARD   WESTERN   Charles Parker
1852–1916   1850–1913   HAGGARD
                                                             DSO
                                                             1854–1934

                                                             m. 1880   (1)   Mary Janet
                                                                               DIXON
                                                                               1861–1881

                                                             m. 1883   (2)   Emily Isabella
                                                                               CHIRNSIDE
                                                                               1853–?

                                                             m. 1906   (3)   Jeanette Ethel
                                                                               FOWLER
                                                                               1886–1957

Ella-Francis   Gertrude   Caroline Cecilia   Clara Mabel
WESTERN   Elizabeth   WESTERN   WESTERN
1877   WESTERN   1879–1888   1880
                    1878

contd

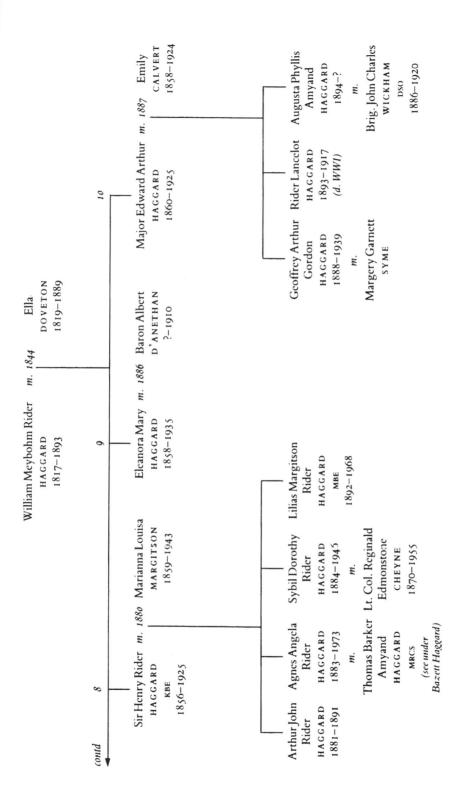

contd

8

William Meybohm Rider
HAGGARD
1817–1893

m. 1844

Ella.
DOVETON
1819–1889

9

10

Sir Henry Rider   m. 1880   Marianna Louisa
HAGGARD   MARGITSON
KBE   1859–1943
1856–1925

Eleanora Mary   m. 1886   Baron Albert
HAGGARD   D'ANETHAN
1858–1935   ?–1910

Major Edward Arthur   m. 1887   Emily
HAGGARD   CALVERT
1860–1925   1858–1924

Arthur John
Rider
HAGGARD
1881–1891

Agnes Angela
Rider
HAGGARD
1883–1973
MRCS
(see under
Bazett Haggard)

m.

Thomas Barker
Amyand
HAGGARD

Sybil Dorothy
Rider
HAGGARD
1884–1945

Lt. Col. Reginald
Edmonstone
CHEYNE
1870–1955

Lilias Margitson
Rider
HAGGARD
MBE
1892–1968

Geoffrey Arthur
Gordon
HAGGARD
1888–1939

m.

Margery Garnett
SYME

Rider Lancelot
HAGGARD
1893–1917
(d. WWI)

Augusta Phyllis
Amyand
HAGGARD
1894–?

m.

Brig. John Charles
WICKHAM
DSO
1886–1920

Introduction

Not every family has a story. Dignified lines plod on for centuries without offering a single individual of interest. Not so the Haggards. The story of Sir Henry Rider Haggard was first told, by himself, in *The Days of My Life* and, since his death in 1925, five biographies have followed. But the Haggards have another story, and the time is running out for its telling.

Rider Haggard was one of ten siblings who came to maturity as the British Empire was reaching its zenith. Because Rider was so famous, their story has been over-looked. Yet his brothers were as much involved with the Empire as he was – their opportunities and careers were dependent on the expansion and maintenance of the colonial world. Between them they spanned the Army, the Royal Navy, the Diplomatic Corps, the Indian Civil Service and the Colonial Service, with exploits which ranged from the Sudan to South America. Now their children have passed on and also many of the grandchildren; what remains of the evidence is in pieces and fragments, distributed among a wide net of descendants. Theirs is a good story, worth the telling, and one which reflects both the vitality and confidence of the British Empire, and its intrinsic weaknesses.

Not only Rider but many of his brothers and sisters were writers. Colonel Andrew Haggard wrote twenty-eight novels and histories; Major Arthur Haggard wrote five novels, and various pamphlets and articles on military life; Alfred Haggard wrote learned papers on political and social issues, as well as translating from the Classics; Baroness d'Anethan, born Mary Haggard, wrote eight romances and an autobiography of her life in Japan. Lieutenant John Haggard, whose writing never went into print, left a superb legacy of long, detailed accounts of his travels to some of the most appalling corners of the globe; John's wife and sister-in-law

were both writers. Will Haggard, the eldest brother, produced a translation from Persian which was a noted aid to learning the language; he
poured the rest of his linguistic talents into the diplomatic bag. Bazett
Haggard became Robert Louis Stevenson's last great friend in Samoa,
inspiring a satire of historical idiosyncrasy. Jack, Ella, Alfred and Mary
all wrote poetry as a pastime.

The diaries of their mother, Ella Doveton, reveal her to be a highly
intelligent young woman with a flair for literary analysis, and a keen
reader of novels in which she looked for clear thinking, sensitivity and
romantic imagination. She was devoutly Christian, giving much thought
to the sermons she heard and read. She was also soft spoken, a good
conversationalist and a sympathetic listener. By contrast (and this accounts
for many of the contradictions found in their children), her husband
William Meybohm Rider Haggard was notoriously argumentative
and sanguine. That his birth place, in 1817, was St Petersburg added an
exotic flavour to his salty personality. Like his father and grandfather
before him, he was famous for his loud voice, which he used to
impress and bully. It was said that you could find William Haggard
anywhere in Norwich by standing in the marketplace and listening.
William quite deliberately taught his boys to shout loud and long. One
might almost think that they have shouted down the century to be
heard.

Rider Haggard was born in 1856 – he was an exact contemporary of
Sigmund Freud – and when he grew up his name became synonymous
with tales of adventure and romance in Africa. *King Solomon's Mines*,
published by Cassell in 1885, made him famous overnight, and was
quickly followed by the original but disturbing best-seller *She*. His success
as a popular writer was unprecedented, but eventually he tired of writing
romances and sought more substantial work as a public servant. This
work was largely concerned with agriculture, on which his views tended
towards the radical, and with the British Empire, on which they did
not. Indeed, his name is now associated with an ideology of active
Imperialism.

His fame has spread not only through his books, which continue to
fascinate seventy years after his death, but also through the many films
made of his work. His style, which relies heavily on imaginative scenes
and incidents, has been particularly seductive to film makers. In addition,
the genre he used so well – the adventurous quest set in an exotic location
– has been developed successfully by many other writers and scriptwriters.

His vision of savage communities, alien worlds cut off from time and history, has been cultivated in hybrid forms for science fiction stories and comics. His work remains today an important source for much popular culture.

But the reason Rider attracts attention as an individual is because of a dichotomy between his character and his work. The question is how could a Norfolk country squire, an upholder of the fabric of county life, an Englishman to the last drop of his decent blood, also have an imagination which gave both Freud and Jung pause for reflection in their studies of the subconscious? How does such a man produce a new, modern female archetype, as he did in *She* with the character Ayesha? What does this say about the real nature of femininity, or Imperialism, or the oppressiveness of Victorian chivalry to women? Did the repression of female intellect and sexuality lead to a deep-seated fear of the feminine to produce the savage, amoral *She*, or was it the Eternal Feminine which rose up through Rider in protest at the simpering Victorian cliché? Or was he simply terrified of female sexuality? One of Jung's protégées, Cornelia Brunner, spent ten years plumbing the depths of Rider's imagination in order to define generic psychological truths for her study, *Anima as Fate*.

The other question that perplexes people of the late twentieth century is how could such a virulent and unreserved advocate of Imperialism have such a sensitive, intuitive personality; how could a man who described scenes of savagery and bloodshed in his books, a man who enthusiastically rallied the Canadians to enter the First World War – how could such a man have so little resistance to personal grief, or be so concerned about the death of his dog and the killing of game birds?

One reason the questions continue to beg answers is that Rider's personality has been mystified. Mystique has a popular appeal and, although it may have increased his book sales, it no doubt contributed to his lack of credibility in more serious literary echelons. Rider had a preoccupation with immortality which was the keystone of the success of the novel *She*, but which became a rather less attractive motif in later books. As one of his nephews testified, 'Rider believed that he had lived before: as an ancient Egyptian, as a Zulu, as a Norseman . . .' Statements like this grab at the imagination, and Rider himself wrote quite clearly: 'Personally I can't believe in extinction – far or near! Our iron would not be forged in all these mortal fires merely to be thrown hissing into a black pool of oblivion. The waste would be too scandalous and Nature (or Super Nature) never wastes. Every effort leads to an effect. Nor do we accumulate so much experience, most of it painful, for nothing. It *must* be reabsorbed into the absolute . . .'

The fact that Rider was not only willing, and unselfconsciously willing, to write about the riddle of life and death, in language that was accessible to everyone, in some way explains the potency of his influence. But in rediscovering the story of his brothers and sisters it becomes clear that a preoccupation with the nature of the hereafter was not his sole preserve. Nor was he the only one to have an unusual psyche. The family as a whole becomes an interesting phenomenon.

Rider's success in his lifetime cannot be underestimated, and his long-term contribution should not be devalued because he never could or never would hone his literary talent. He wrote one of the first novels to be set in Africa; he wrote four novels about the Zulus and their history, believing as he did in a future for their nation. That has certainly been vindicated by history. He created the genre of 'faction', in which fictitious and factual characters mingle in historical stories. And because he had experienced colonial life as a magistrate, farmer and solder, his novels are imbued with a reality that is impossible to manufacture. Rider was no bloodless scribbler, but a man who knew Shepstone and Chelmsford, had seen the *impi* dance, who could outspan an ox wagon, shoulder a gun, and ride for days across the veldt.

His series of Egyptian novels played far more on the public fascination with the cult of the dead. The pyramids were only just coming under the scrutiny of Victoria archaeologists, but Rider was able to transport his readers back in time to the days of the Pharaohs. Once again his background helped him. His mother had returned from India by sea to Aden and then overland through Egypt, where she had seen the ancient monuments of Thebes and Luxor. She retained a lifelong interest in ancient Egypt, and the family's neighbour in Norfolk, Lord Amherst, had a private museum of Egyptian treasures at Didlington Hall, which had also inspired the archaeologist Howard Carter. So, while one is not in a position to deny the possibility that Rider had been an Egyptian priest in a previous life, one can be fairly certain that he absorbed a great deal of Egyptology as a child. Several of his brothers and sisters were equally interested.

Rider was an unmitigated Imperialist. The class system had successfully separated the activities of gentleman in the colonies from those of traders and entrepreneurs – except most notably in the person of Cecil Rhodes, who was not quite a gentleman and towards whom Rider had mixed feelings. Rider believed that in British law and British administrative skill lay the seeds of a better world. He saw lands like Canada and New Zealand as empty lands crying out to be cultivated by good British stock. In Africa the horrors of the slave trade, the barbaric practices of natives and the hopelessly unjust tribal customs could be phased out by association with British culture under British rule. Darwin's theories, in confluence with European expansion, had in general given rise to an idea of scientific, if not divine, justification for Imperialism. Rider saw for himself that there was often little to distinguish morally between whites and blacks. In fact, he thought the warrior Zulus were a rather superior people, their virtues coinciding neatly with the British military caste, though they were, nevertheless, further down the chain of 'civilized' development. In his time Rider was described as a sociologist – for which we might now read 'anthropologist'.

The story of the Haggards shows that Rider's initial work, which won him his reputation, was underpinned by the nature and structure of his family and by many of their own adventures. He drew on the anecdotes of his well-travelled brothers to create his wild tales, and, when criticized for the bloodthirsty nature of his books, he could reply that he was only retelling the truth. As the family's letters from all parts of the world reveal, it was an unforgiving and often cruel environment in which they struggled for their livings. In England the argument between Imperialists and anti-Imperialists raged unceasingly, even while General Gordon drew his last breath. Within the Haggard family the careers of the seven sons illustrate as many shades of response to the Empire – from enthusiasm to ruinous revolt. Given the choice, most of them would have lived and died in Norfolk, to be buried in the soil which bred them.

When the Empire was at its height, the men who built it were glorified beyond their human possibility, and they seemed entirely unable to laugh at themselves. In the post-1945 reaction to Imperialism, people connected with the vision of the British Empire were quite suddenly derided or reviled – often without any understanding of their work. This was particularly true of figures who could be seen to have feet of clay in the glare of Freudian thought. It was quickly forgotten that, to the Victorians, the slave trade was a wrong which it was absolutely essential to right if mankind was to maintain any kind of self-respect. This policy made Britain many enemies – including the Uitlanders, many Arabs and South

Americans, as well as those Africans who were themselves slave traders. For the colonial servants, the mundane work of keeping the peace, maintaining the trade routes and keeping the courts working under conditions of considerable physical and psychological hardship required a tenacity that is easy to undervalue in an age of telephones and antibiotics.

No more than ourselves could the Victorians guess at the censures of history. The Haggards, as they emerged from childhood, were swept into the cavalcade of Imperial progress to play their various parts with all the energy and dash of their excitable natures.

━ I ━

Gathered Here Together

The Reverend Charles Maddison Green was just four days short of his thirty-third birthday when he stood in the nave of West Bradenham church, waiting to take Ella Doveton Haggard as his lawful wedded wife. It was a hot Tuesday in July of 1869, and his equilibrium was severely tested by the suppressed giggles of Ella's brothers, as they gloated over his nervous discomfiture. But Charles was bred in a robust school of Christianity, and neither then nor in the future were the Haggards able to unbalance his sense of propriety.

The parish church of St Andrew's at West Bradenham was built of local flint in the early Gothic style, but had been extensively restored by the Haggards in the previous decade. Three fine stained-glass windows in the west end of the nave, and one in the chancel, commemorated members of the Haggard family. With the proliferation of memorials which have been added since, one might be forgiven for thinking West Bradenham Church was a family chapel. The Haggards would not have disapproved. Their religious devotion was inseparable from their culture.

The church is situated on an open rise of land with the graveyard high up on one side and sloping down the hill on the other. On the southern side, the land sweeps on to the Rectory, a substantial house with stables and outhouses lying quietly among the village fields; to the north lies the road and the Bradenham estate. On 20 July 1869 the villagers, who then numbered some 380, had erected triumphal arches along the route from the church to Bradenham Hall.

A breeze fanned the jostling crowds in the churchyard but inside the sun caught the glass of the clerestory, toasting the well-to-do crowd beneath. All the notable families for miles around were seated in the pews – the Barkers of neighbouring Shipdham Hall, with their confidently beautiful daughter Julia; the Masons and Blomefields of Necton

Hall – friends of the Haggards for generations; the Mottrams, the Hills, the Walkers, the Keppels of Lexham, the Girlings and the Ravenshaws and endless friends and relations from Brighton, Brinsop, Richmond and Bath.

A parson's son himself, Charles Maddison Green had been brought up in a modest rectory at Burgh Castle near Great Yarmouth. He had studied at Cambridge and, in the wake of Tractarianism, was of the High Church persuasion. During his second appointment, as a chaplain at Warwick, he had met the Haggards who were staying temporarily at Leamington. His suit to Ella Haggard had not been assured. She had told her brother Alfred that she did not intend to accept the proposal, but something had changed her mind.

At twenty-five, Ella had left the schoolroom long behind and, as the eldest of ten siblings, she had had responsibility thrust on her from an early age. Ella was used to helping with a busy household, she was well-educated, well-travelled, and literary in her tastes, and would make a splendid parson's wife, if she cared to. She had decided to take her chance.

Of the seven Haggard boys, only six were present at Ella's wedding, and it was the three youngest who paid Charles such scant respect. Andrew was a sensual fifteen-year-old oscillating between high spirits and sullenness; Rider, at thirteen, was dreamy-eyed and pathetically slow; and little Arthur, only eight, was twinkling and ready for fun. The older boys were groomsmen: Will, the heir, aged twenty-three, a Wykehamist just down from Oxford and entering the Diplomatic Corps, was strong featured, bumptious and jokey; Alfred, twenty, intellectual and moody, had been part of the first intake at the new Haileybury College, and was destined for the Indian Civil Service; and Bazett, twenty-one, amusing and light hearted, was in his third year at Trinity Hall, Cambridge.

In the church porch waited the bridesmaids, swathed in white muslin with mauve satin sashes: Cecilia Haggard, small for her seventeen years, but also for seventeen brash and curt even to rudeness, and young Mary Haggard, eleven, sporty, haughty and strident; Charles's sister Elizabeth, a brace of Haggard cousins, and Miss Mildred Snell and Miss Atherton made up the complement of attendants. Will was particularly taken with Miss Snell, and a noticeable amount of flirting took place among the tombstones. The Haggard boys were prone to flirting, and at least one Mama forbade her daughter to dance with them. They were virile, like their father.

At fifty-two, William Meybohm Rider Haggard was a lion – proud, overbearing and handsome, a barrister by profession, a squire by occupation, and a gentleman by status and style. The condition of rural Norfolk was so unremittingly static and so self-regarding in its values that it was possible for a man with a modest estate to be, in his way, a king. Rider said his father ruled West Bradenham like a king, but there was 'no more popular man in the County of Norfolk'. This unlikely opinion is supported by Alfred's comment that his father had the common touch.

The Haggards had inherited their substance from generations of careful merchants and bankers and, early in the nineteenth century, had bought Bradenham Hall.[1]

William Meybohm Rider Haggard Esquire, Justice of the
Peace, Deputy Lieutenant and for thirty-six years Chairman
of the Quarter Sessions for the County of Norfolk.

Although they had some early family associations with Norfolk, the Haggards had been until recently established in Hertfordshire, unlike many of their neighbours, who had owned estates in Norfolk for several centuries, or their labourers and tenants, whose lineage – if it could only be traced – would go back to the Norsemen and Danes.

Sir Bernard Burke, the Herald, had hit upon the lucrative idea of producing a new catalogue of family histories, a list of the untitled, unofficial aristocracy of the shires, the Landed Gentry. The Haggards did not immediately penetrate its red leather bindings, but they were soon to provide sufficient details of their lineage to be included. The Reverend Gray's preface to the 1862 edition of the catalogue was the first to admit that 'from time immemorial' it had been the tendency in Britain for self-made men to buy estates and try to establish themselves in the County. He explained that, while this practice was advantageous and showed generosity of spirit, it was still necessary, by genealogy and heraldry, to distinguish between people who were closely associated with *trade*, and the true Gentry.[2] The Haggard family itself had only relatively recently abandoned its mercantile banking business, and William Meybohm Haggard was adamant that none of his sons should enter trade.

Spurred by Burke's creation of a hallowed galaxy, the Haggards, father and sons, spent a good deal of time and quite a bit of money in digging their family roots out from the mists of medieval Denmark, and in researching their coat of arms. The single device of a six-pointed star, a mullet, has a resemblance to the Star of David, an association made rather more awkward because William's mother, Elizabeth Meybohm, was indeed a Jew of German or Russian descent.[3] Fortunately, with Disraeli leading the Imperial crusade, anti-semitism had not yet completely gripped the upper classes. The important thing was Gray's proclamation in *The Landed Gentry*: 'We are zealous in asserting that England is the very first nation under the sun, that the English aristocracy stands pre-eminent above that of every other country, and that the English gentle-man is the most perfect type of the civilized, educated, honourable, and manly character.'

As the owner of Bradenham Hall, William Haggard was also governor and employer of the villagers of West Bradenham. He took this role seriously, holding public service to be his inalienable duty. As a Justice of the Peace and Master of the Quarter Sessions, and an active member of the West Norfolk Conservative Association, he was able to cultivate the friendship of influential people such as his neighbour and MP Lord Walsingham, and took pleasure in the acquaintance of great men.

The village itself was small but busy, straddling a stream where a ford allowed a crossing. There were several pubs, and most of the inhabitants turned their hands to a number of occupations: the blacksmith sold beer, the innkeeper of 'The Star' supplied poultry, and so on. John Adcock was the host of the 'King's Head'; his relatives, Sam and William Adcock, worked Manor Farm, and Sam fulfilled a very important role at the Hall as factotum and the butt of the Squire's humours. The carpenter at East Bradenham was also a wheelwright and an undertaker. It gave people a turn sometimes to go into his shop on an errand and come face to face with a neighbour laid out in a box. John Thacker was a baker, and the Thackers also farmed some fields at East Bradenham, as well as being labourers. Martha and Samuel Thacker were the parents of Alfred, the stable boy at the Hall. He had been born in the same year as Mary Haggard, but it was ten years before his parents brought him to the vicar for baptism. When he grew up to resemble Andrew Haggard it made some people wonder. Most villagers married within the district, except one or two brave souls who took up with folk in Shipdham, two miles away. People like the Thackers had been in Bradenham for generations – and they are still there now that the Haggards have gone.

In his time, William Haggard had also been a Captain of the East Norfolk Regiment of Militia (a call to arms which had captured the public imagination after the Crimean War). Lecturing to the Camp at Colchester, he enjoined his audience to aspire to 'the English spirit of vigorous thought, of resolute action, of painstaking and successful industry' and a 'gradual return to ancient Saxon privileges'. Intuitive, but not very subtle, William Haggard subjected his reason to his sentiment. As proof that the amateur soldier could be trained to be reliable, he triumphantly offered an incident in which 700 militiamen were instructed not to return enemy fire: they all obeyed, and '500 fell dead before the enemies guns in the space of twenty minutes, without returning a single shot!' When he resigned from the Militia, Haggard applied for permission to continue to wear the uniform – a request which was denied. But he was often referred to as Captain Haggard for long afterwards.

It was said in the family that the Haggard stock had been undermined by intermarriage with the excitable Amyands, causing an unstable temperament and an inclination to sexual passion.[4] Their dear friend Colonel Mason called the Haggards 'harum scarum', and said they left too much to the servants and didn't take enough responsibility for themselves. They were, in a way, spoiled by the financial acumen of their forbears and the growing social stratification of the mid–Victoria period. But they had a 'don't–give–a–damn' streak in their characters, as well as having learned the intransigence of Norfolk, so that beyond a certain point they would not be pushed.

William Haggard's social position and personal power over a modest Norfolk estate granted him immunity from criticism – even from criticism of his rumoured indiscretions. Alfred Thacker's paternity was attributed either to William or to his brother James. It was quite common for an employer, if he were inclined, to treat his maidservants as little more than whores. On the other hand, whispers of glamorous paternity were popular among the working and labouring classes, sometimes to disguise less desirable mistakes. As he grew to manhood, Alfred Thacker developed an important role in the family story, and his letters to the Haggards, while not lacking in deference, are unusual.

William Haggard played the squire like an eighteenth-century gentleman, displaying a peculiar mixture of dominant and nervous principles. The night before Ella's wedding, his excitability peaked at the thought of receiving the Bishop of Worcester. Then he panicked about the weather, and Alfred Haggard was detailed to organize a theatrical performance of *The Rivals*, for the entertainment of the wedding guests if it should rain. When the weather changed suddenly for the better, the Squire turned his attention to inspecting the batteries which were being erected in the grounds to fire salutes throughout the celebrations. The noise, like his legendary voice, would thunder across West Norfolk. It was typical of Mr Haggard's brand of patriotism that, when his eldest daughter walked down the aisle, he had the organist strike the first chords of *God Save the Queen*.

Unlike her tall, red-haired brothers, Ella Haggard was petite, but very strong and forthright. She had inherited her looks from her mother, along with many of her mother's virtues. Mrs Haggard had been born Ella Doveton; her father, Bazett Doveton, was a lawyer in the Indian Civil Service. In the heat of India, Mrs Doveton had suffered from nauseous, thundering headaches and recurring illnesses, and young Ella Doveton had to a large extent been brought up by her poetry-loving aunt in England. She had been sent to a boarding school in Chelsea, where she was harshly treated but had learned her lessons well. Her brother Bazett had been bullied to death at Rottingdean School, still

Ella Haggard, née Doveton, eldest daughter and co-heiress
of Bazett Doveton of the East India Civil Service.

only a child. When she went back to India to be with her parents, she left a younger sister behind in England.

Once out in India she had enjoyed the attentions of many beaux, riding out to the Breach or Flagstaff Hill, attending cheerful, informal dinners and dances with neighbours, singing and playing the piano. She read voraciously, her favourite author being Bulwer Lytton.[5] She had enjoyed her popularity as a charming and sensitive companion, and many a young man had set his cap at her. In fact she had been engaged to be married, but the knot was never tied, a disappointment which took a long time to heal. Afterwards, and since her parents were planning to return to England, she determined not to choose a husband in India.

In her diary she described one particular evening in Bombay – 3 September 1838 – when, at a dinner party, she argued in favour of

Whiggism, and also of the equal rights of man. She also admitted to a belief in the equality of women, but would not press the point, believing that time alone would bring justice. She later confessed to her diary a 'great affection for hereditary distinctions', which she attributed to the pleasure she took in histories. After the lively dinner, a native fortune-teller had arrived. When her turn came, Ella Doveton was told that, as regards love, she 'would remain long indifferent' but 'should have a son, an honour to his family, and the admiration of the world'.

The first part of the prediction proved to be true. She did not marry until 1844 when she was twenty-five, seven years after the fortune-telling. She had been co-heiress to her father's fortune and, after she took William Haggard of Bradenham Hall as her husband, her sister Caroline had married William's brother James so that all the Doveton money was absorbed by the Haggards. William and James had one sister, Fanny, whose husband, William Fowle, was the Vicar of Brinsop.

Mrs Haggard had borne William eleven children, their first child, Ella, arriving in Rome while they were still on their tour of the Continent in 1845. One had been stillborn; of the rest she must sometimes have wondered which, if any, of her sons would 'bring honour to the family and become the admiration of the world'. Since, even to his face, Rider was spoken of pityingly, her hopes must have rested on one of his brothers.

Charles Maddison Green, the Vicar of Lyonshall, may also have wondered what the Haggard children would mean to him in later years. But if he faltered, there is no record of it, and it was just as well that he, unlike some of the Haggards, was not burdened with psychic presentiment. His practical good sense was required to sort out a mistake the Bishop made in the ceremony which was quite beyond the incumbent Reverend Morgan. Charles's competence sustained them all.

Squire Haggard was a generous man when he could be, and on Ella's wedding day 'the entire poor of the parish were feasted', and everyone was to go up to the hall to inspect the wedding breakfast and admire the grounds. Later there would be a supper for all the guests. While the tenants came to congratulate and gape, young Alfred Haggard, acting as Master of Ceremonies (a natural progression from his role as Stage Manager in the family dramatics), issued seating instructions and prepared to call the names of the guests as they entered the Hall.

Of a modest size and style when compared with many of the neighbouring houses, Bradenham Hall boasted a pediment and pilasters which

The south face of the Hall at West Bradenham, Norfolk. The Hall
was bought by the Haggards in 1818. Its dining room, which
witnessed so many eruptions, is on the left of the central door.

raised the redbrick Georgian façade above the purely domestic style.
Facing south, its twenty-foot drawing room and dining room enjoyed
the light from large, long windows. At the back of the house a study,
kitchens, pantries and cellars formed the working heart of the home. On
the first floor were 'five good chambers', and above were extensive attics
where some of the boys and servants slept. Outside there was a wash
house, laundry, double coach house, barn, stables, game store, and out-
buildings. Beyond were orchards and two walled kitchen gardens. Set
in the centre of a lawn, the house was surrounded by plantations of
magnificent oak trees, on land which had not been ploughed since
Domesday. The oaks were the Squire's pride and joy, and many of them
had been given names.

The house itself was spacious and pleasant, full of three generations
of Jacobean and Georgian furniture. The walls were hung with superb
family portraits, extending back to the Haggard days as merchants and
bankers in St Petersburg and to the Dovetons in India. The library held
thousands of books, and the landings and hallways were filled with good

English chests, maps and etchings, clocks, lacquer and ormulu in profusion, 'a good collection of armour', and contemporary bric-à-brac that
had already begun to include exotic items from all parts of the globe.
And it was a house that was always alive with children and their attendant
nurses and governesses. By and large, it was a happy family home.

The outbursts and bullying of William Haggard would eventually bear
desperate fruit, but in all their many travels and all their enforced sojourns
abroad in the service of the Empire, the children remembered Bradenham Hall with hugely sentimental pleasure. It was the emblem of their
family life, their childhood days together when hope was a natural
birthright. In later years it was a consolation amid their failures and
disappointments.

Twenty-five years after Ella's wedding to Charles, Alfred wrote to
her, 'I cannot forget the day of the original wedding with all its mirth
and brightness'. The wedding breakfast was laid out with a centrepiece
of a peacock in full fan and carved ice blocks. All was laughter and jollity
and light – they loved facetious humour and silly jokes. The bride's
uncle, James Haggard of Bournemouth, toasted the bride and groom,
and Green replied with a happy speech. William Haggard proposed the
health of the Bishop, after which Bazett and Alfred, spurred on no doubt
by the sparkling atmosphere and their own youthful enthusiasm, took
the floor. Bazett championed the cause of the bridesmaids and declared
cheerfully that, henceforth, he would devote himself to the fairer sex.
Alfred (whose heart, the family knew, was already at the mercy of Miss
Eba Heyward) proposed the health of the groomsmen: 'an unprotected
male appealing on behalf of unprotected males'. A final flourish, and
suddenly it was time to rise. Ella hurried away to change her dress, but
time was short and 'it was found that the posters would have to gallop
the whole way to catch the train'.

Amid laughter and cheers, the happy couple reappeared as hurried
farewells were made. Good wishes, kisses and chaff cascaded on to the
bride and groom; '. . . crack goes the postillion's whip, the wheels rattle
on the gravel, lilies fly in through the window, handkerchiefs wave, a
cheer rises, old shoes buzz, (mine, I carefully threw where I could find
it again), the horses gallop off and vanish in the plantation and through
an arch inscribed with Faith, Hope and Charity', remembered Alfred.
The couple just caught the train, and it was later found that Charles had
left his Cook's Guide behind.

At Bradenham, the festivities continued for several days, with various lunches, croquet, dancing and entertainments being provided both at the Hall and at neighbours' houses. Squire William, with his brother James, paid for all the servants to be taken by omnibus to the ruins of Castle Acre priory for a picnic. Mrs Haggard, writing to her newly wed daughter, noted that 'the chief amusement of the younger people has consisted in sitting under the trees by day, and on the steps of the house by night, singing or telling stories, varied on Thursday last (a very hot one for the purpose), also walking to the churchyard at midnight to see the moonlight and look for ghosts'.

For young Henry Rider Haggard, poised in the doorway between childhood and adolescence, the innocent evening amusements inspired a much deeper experience. Going to bed late in a tiny, makeshift room beside the first-floor library, his imagination turned on the rustling sounds, and he wondered if he was hearing Lady Hamilton's ghost – for members of the Nelson family had once lived in the house. After falling into a troubled slumber he suddenly awoke in terror. An enormous ferret with flaming eyes had been chasing him down a tunnel, which decreased in size making escape impossible. He awoke, as so often happens in dreams, at the moment of crisis, just about to be caught, and realized that in his dream he himself had been a rat.

He stared at his hands in the moonlight; they were no longer claws but pale white fingers, pale as death, pale as the bodies in the carpenter's workshop. And like those bodies he too would rot and decay beneath the weight of the turf in the churchyard. That night, he dreaded death so much he wished for it to take place at once, so that his terrors would cease. It was those terrors that haunted his literary work.[6]

Only eight years had passed since the demise of Prince Albert had devastated the still-youthful Queen Victoria. She had taken up mourning as a way of life, and set a morbid tone; effigies, statues and vast, ornate memorials to the Prince Consort sprouted throughout the land. The Queen insisted that everything in her husband's apartments should be left exactly as it was when he died. Worse still, for many years she clung on to him as though he still lingered, by giving the servants orders to lay out fresh clothes on his bed every evening, to strew fresh flowers beneath his pillow and even to put hot water in his wash stand. This macabre theme, which stole darkly through society, was fed with Gothic fantasies. In the same year that Prince Albert died, Dickens treated the avid readers of *Great Expectations* to the chilling, thrilling spectacle of

Miss Havisham's rotting wedding breakfast. The Romantics had done their work well.

In Norfolk, the Court had arrived soon after Albert's death in the person of the Prince of Wales. In 1862 the Prince had bought Sandringham House, and was intent on its improvement for use as a sporting estate. Sandringham (north-east of King's Lynn) lay only fifteen miles from West Bradenham, and the royal presence brought the mixed blessing of Social Distinction to the county. The life of leisure to which the Germanic Prince of Wales was devoted was a far cry from the poverty and deprivation to which industrial society had succumbed. The Liberals were bent on reform, and were about to bring in the first Elementary Education Act. Gladstone had just been returned to office, and Charles Wentworth Dilke, a rising star of the Liberal party, had won the new parliamentary seat of Chelsea, having recently published his book *Greater Britain*. William Haggard, active Tory and an ardent Imperialist, scarcely needed the inspiration of Dilke's observations from his world tour. But to Liberal and Tory alike, Dilke handed Imperialists the acceptable tools of idealism. His concept of 'the grandeur of our race, already girdling the earth' went far beyond the destiny of domination; he saw that 'our possession of India, of the coasts of Africa, and of the ports of China, offers the possibility of planting free institutions among the dark-skinned races of the world . . . the power of English laws and English principles of government is not merely an English question – its continuance is essential to the freedom of mankind.'

These were the ideals which set the stage for the expansion of the British Empire in the latter half of the nineteenth century. The tone was evangelical, while duty, courage, public integrity and moral certitude were the essential qualities of the colonial servant. It was an idealism which encouraged the sons of country squires and clergymen to go out to the dark and dusty places to hold them for England – and it was an idealism which sustained them through danger, corruption, loneliness, sickness and despair. It was also an idealism so lofty that it blinded many of them to the fundamental moral issue of Imperialism.

The raising of the men who would do the work of Empire was developed, in the true Spartan spirit, by the public schools. There is a certain irony in that the one man whose name is synonymous with the boyish ideals of Empire, and whose books inspired two or three generations of colonial civilians and soldiers, never attended a public school. But, as young Rider Haggard grew up, the new spirit of the Empire was surging through England, bringing with it the realization of extending opportunities. Up and down the country, the destiny of dozens of County families was to lie with Imperial expansion. On the face of it, the Haggards were well-suited to their times. Their background in banking and law was a solid foundation for an understanding of the mechanics of Empire, and their sense of duty was deeply instilled. But their argumentative skills, so useful in the pursuit of the law, were often ungoverned by intellect, and had degenerated into no more than a quarrelsome family trait.

To Mrs Haggard, the health and fortunes of her children were her constant preoccupation. However, late at night, when she finally had time to sit down at her desk, she would take up her pen to administer the care and information with which she succoured her children. In an age when married women had no right to their own inheritance, no woman could vote, and only a tiny minority of women were educated, her husband's word was law. But the evidence is strong that Mrs Haggard successfully influenced him. Even at the time of Ella's wedding, she was trying to persuade the Squire to defer Rider's formal education; she could not think that the dull, slow boy was ready to leave home. In the event, he only went as far as Ipswich, to an inexpensive school.

This decision, made out of necessity as well as, perhaps, for his own good, was one which made Rider feel singled out as less worthy than his brothers. Anxious that he should be educated with the sons of gentlemen, the Squire had made some attempt to get him into a choir school at Cambridge, but at Ipswich he would have mixed with a wide variety of boys and this may well have widened his sympathies.

The choice of school represents one very important element in the Haggard history. The Squire was running out of money. Like every other landed family, the Haggards were suffering from the catastrophic decline in the profitability of farming. When agriculture was abandoned to the forces of Free Trade in the 1870s, it could no longer sustain the standards of the gentry. Unfortunately, Mr Haggard had invested all his and his wife's money in land, buying when prices were high in a surge of dynastic enthusiasm. His debts were substantial, and the only reason that little Arthur was able to go to a public school was because of a legacy. From this time forward, it would be essential that the boys pursued careers outside Norfolk, and probably outside England.

When the older boys were young there had been less financial strain; Will and Bazett had been sent off to prep. school in Tonbridge, and then on to Winchester, of which city Mr Haggard's uncle was the Recorder. Will had done well enough and gone on to Oxford and, though his choice of a career in the Diplomatic Service was an expensive one, he would, in time, be in a position to help his brothers. Will liked to see himself as a grand man, and he cultivated a look like the Prince of Wales. He was a strapping fellow and full of go, though not perhaps as sensitive as he might have been. The affair with Mildred Snell ended in the shame of a broken engagement, and a frisson fell between the families for a while until they brought poor Mildred back from her little holiday in Paris. Will's passions were so easily fanned, while Mildred, though beautiful, was cold as ice.

In contrast to his robust brother, Bazett's delicate constitution had already interrupted his schooling. Bazett – Baggs as the others called him – wasn't searching for fame, only fortune. He had such exuberant tastes, was so interested in the arts, and was so delightfully sociable that it was impossible not to respond to his engaging charm and good humour, despite the scrapes he had already got himself into. He enjoyed his life in London, where he studied at the Inns of Court. Judging from his rudimentary business advice to his father, he was not perhaps overly astute and, having missed out on some of his schooling, may well have been undereducated for a career at the Bar.

If Mrs Haggard did indeed wonder which of her sons would have an illustrious future, she must surely have thought that Alfred was the most likely candidate. He was intelligent and ambitious and, above all, he was bound for India, which was the only reliable place for a colonial servant to make his name. British interests in Africa were only sustained in support of their interests in India, and it was too early to see the potential for profit that Africa would represent. Nor was it possible to see that, in pursuit of his ambition, Alfred's star would eventually take him to the Dark Continent where he would cross swords with Cecil Rhodes himself.

There was another family for whom Africa was to be of singular importance. Indeed, the history of modern East Africa is incomplete without reference to Frederick Jackson and his nephew Geoffrey Archer. That the Jacksons should become known to the Haggards is scarcely surprising in the tight social milieu of the period, but the effect of their association is certainly remarkable.

Six months before Ella began her life as a country parson's wife, John Jackson, of Oran House near Catterick in Yorkshire, died of tuberculosis at the age of forty-three. An expert on bloodstock, Jackson had made a fortune as a bookmaker – a fortune which he left to be administered for the benefit of the four daughters from his first marriage, Eliza, Alice, Laura and Lilly, and his young son Frederick from his second. Mrs Jackson and her children moved south, and in due course the Jackson family history was to march beside that of the Haggards. Between them they would affect not only the history of Kenya and Uganda but, through Rider and Lilly, the developing ideas of the psyche in the western world.

The Reverend Charles Maddison Green and Ella Maddison Green,
née Haggard, in their early married years at Lyonshall, Herefordshire.

~ 2 ~

No Wind Along These Seas

When Ella and Charles Maddison Green returned from their honeymoon in Switzerland, they went to live in the small, white rectory, near the church on the old castle mound in Lyonshall. Ella put aside her fine leather shoes, and pushed her little feet into heavy walking boots. As a parson's wife she must ride or tramp the lanes of the hilly rural parish: every child's illness and every family's hardships would be her business.

Although Lyonshall was only a village, one of the new railway lines connected them to their county town of Hereford, and thus to the rest of the world. Ella kept in touch with her relatives, with a constant chatter and gossip of letters shuttling back and forth. She was a long way from the wide horizons of Norfolk, but her paternal aunt and uncle lived a few miles away in Brinsop, and such was the Haggard children's affection for Ella as almost a second mother that, rather than losing her, they formed a second focus for their family here on the Welsh borders.

Ella was not the first child to leave the nest. By the time of the wedding Mrs Haggard had for several years been receiving letters from her middle son, John George Haggard, always known as Jack. Why it had been decided to send him to sea is unclear. He had been at Guildford Grammar School, where he had been very unhappy: 'I do not like this school any better and never shall,' he wrote. The boys nicknamed him Jack Carrots for his red hair, and he was bullied and taunted until the masters eventually put a stop to it. He did, however, manage to visit the Great Exhibition at the Crystal Palace.

At thirteen he was sent for tuition to a naval crammer in Southsea, where he was even more unhappy. Jack took his walks near the seafront, where he met an old sea captain with whom he struck up a slight, chatty acquaintance. When the friendship was discovered by his tutor, it was immediately forbidden. He wrote home: 'It is very lonely indeed there is nobody here but myself and I have no one to speak to except four old women and Cooper and I only see them at meal times and so the Old Gentleman was the only person I had to speak to.' A few days later he asked: 'May I come home on the first of July for it is so very lonely.'

Jack had a number of physical problems during this time, including great pains and strains in his ankles, heels and knees. Perhaps ill-fitting boots were the cause. The numerous attentions of a dentist also brought great suffering: 'The other day he made them [the teeth] ache when he was putting in a powder so he took a sharp knife looking thing with an ivory handle twitched it under my gum and cut a piece out of it. It did not hurt me much but there was something in feeling the keen edge which turned me very bad, he did it both sides of my mouth and then got me a glass of wine.' Ironically it was to be his teeth, or lack of them, which eventually ended his Naval career.

That career began in 1864 when, at the age of fourteen, he entered Dartmouth Naval College on HMS *Britannia*. His first report in 1865 said he was 'very slow and uncertain in his work'. He appears to have run away on one occasion, just before a crossing of the Channel. He may have fled to his Uncle James in Bournemouth, because it was he who delivered him back to the ship. Eventually, however, he seemed to settle.

Mrs Haggard could not know of, and perhaps scarcely guess at, the endemic brutality of the Navy. Jack's letters to her are different from those addressed to his father, but the details she did receive can hardly have been reassuring. On one occasion all the cadets had broad arrows cut across their noses by the Paymaster, when they were in transit on HMS *Liverpool*, although John wrote home that 'you hardly felt it being done'.

Soon after he arrived on HMS *Caledonia* in 1866, Jack was detailed to supervise the flogging of a bluejacket. The cat-o'-nine-tails was a dreadful implement, scouring out flesh and blood in its inexorable arc. Jack wrote in his new logbook: 'Monday May 7th. Punished J. Winstanley B.I.C. with 24 lashes as per warrant.' Bullied and beaten at school, cold and hungry at the crammer, the Royal Navy simply gouged a deeper scar of hardship and cruelty. For Jack there was to be no going home.[1]

It was not long before he himself was to recommend the use of the 'cat' on Irish bluejackets who had thrown an Armstrong gun down a hatchway, in revenge for their treatment by officers. Tenderness was not part of the vocabulary of the Senior Service, and morale was often low.

Nelson's victory at Trafalgar had established the invincibility and the prestige of the Royal Navy, which was so rarely challenged that few ships saw action, and the dearth of promotions led to jealous rivalry. Jack kept himself aloof from his messmates and, in the crowded, cramped conditions in which 125 men lived with a total lack of privacy, he led a lonely, detached life.

It was, however, a life of some interest to a boy. The skills of seamanship and navigation under sail and steam were a challenge to any young man; the excitement and romance of exotic lands – about which Jack could have known almost nothing until he experienced them first-hand – stimulated his interest. The Navy's role as a peacekeeper was essential: gunboat diplomacy requires visible gunboats. As the Empire extended through exploration and commerce, so the naval bases proliferated. A network of coaling stations and strategic islands enabled the Navy to patrol the coastlines, stemming piracy and curbing the slave trade, and ensuring the Pax Britannica. Tours of duty lasted for four years – a long time for a lad in his formative years to be away from home and exposed to malignant influences: homosexual practices were rife, and venereal disease was virtually unavoidable.

At the age of seventeen Jack made his first crossing of the Equatorial 'Line', the occasion for the rites of Neptune. The night before, on 21 December 1867, Jack and his fellow initiates were treated to some traditional theatricals, in which Neptune and Amphitrite arrived on board seated on a shell-shaped chariot drawn by eight 'bears'. The King of the Sea entered into a charade with the Captain, asking about the new faces. 'Neptune' then predictably observed that they were all far too bushy for the hot climate and promised to return and thin out their beards on the morrow. As the theatricals disappeared amidst the glare of blue lights, the company was stunned by 'about three ton of water coming down from a height of about 70 feet on our heads'.

The next morning Neptune returned and the novices were sent below to await their turn. Jack related matter-of-factly:

I was taken up to the Topgallant Forecastle and made to sit on the edge of it with our backs to a large sail full of water about 3 feet or 4ft. 6 ins. deep in which were the bears who were ready to receive you. You are then blindfolded and your face lathered all over with a compound of softsoap and whitewash with a little oatmeal . . . and asked all kinds of questions and accused of all kinds of sins which you have never committed in order to make you open your mouth that they may shove the brush in. Neptune's barber then asks Neptune what your character is (he of course being supposed to know everyone's character). If good you get the smooth razor (No. 1) if fair you get a razor which hurts a little (No. 2) if a bad character you get No. 3. an awfully rough piece of hoop iron which jags your flesh, and what is called the smelling bottle, a cork with about a dozen needles stuck in it which is shoved up your nose; this is what the obstreperous marines and some others got. After you have been shaved your heels are suddenly tripped up and you are precipitated about six feet into the sail full of water, where you are nearly drowned and are hauled out nearly insensible; and just as you get above the sail a hose is played in your face, swabs thrown round your neck and when you are nearly dead they leave you alone to recover. Whilst all this is going on of course hoses are being played on everybody, men and officers running about naked except a pair of white trousers. About 2 o'clock it was all over and everybody turned in that night pretty well done up.

This kind of horseplay made for a rough passage into manhood. A First Lieutenant took a dislike to Jack after overhearing him slanging him to his fellow midshipmen, and Jack was the object of much bullying. The Navy's reputation for drunkenness caused his parents considerable anxiety, and they made careful enquiries. With the careless humour of adolescence, Jack replied that they need not worry since drunkenness was so common that he scarcely noticed it anymore. 'A man never returns sober from shore', and many were so dead drunk that they had to be hauled up the side of the ship. Within this context it does not appear that Jack himself drank excessively.

In the Victorian Navy, the cadets needed at least a subsistence allowance from home in order to survive. Their own meagre pay of ten shillings a month might be forfeit before they could receive it. If not, they would blow it all on a 'spree' just as soon as they reached port. Jack wrote home often for money for clothing (a huge twenty-two shillings for a cap lost overboard), for food and for pocket money. However, he made some kind of progress. To his great pleasure, he earned the respect of the foretopmen, who chaired him round the deck on Christmas Day while the band played, proving that he 'was successful in [his] endeavours not to use any of those petty tyrannies which a Midshipman is so capable of exercising if he chooses'.

Jack's ship, HMS *Satellite*, had made its way round the Cape of Good Hope and, via Aden, across the Indian Ocean to Singapore and on to Hong Kong. Then they headed west again for the Nicobar Islands,

John George Haggard – always called Jack. In this studio portrait he is wearing his Midshipman's uniform and is probably aged sixteen – *c.* 1866.

situated on an age-old trade route in the Bay of Bengal. The islanders were in the habit of pirating merchant ships, and although the Nicobars were not yet British islands, *Satellite* and HMS *Wasp* had been given the task of meting out punishment.

The latest offence involved a brigantine sailing under British colours which had been boarded by pirates, and all except three of the native crew killed. These three had seized their moment and escaped to Penang to tell the tale.

HMS *Satellite* approached the densely foliated islands and anchored just off the village of Trinket, where the brigantine had been attacked. From the ship they could see some of the native huts, built on stilts with palm-thatched roofs. On the beach, tall, flexible bamboos with grassy tassels marked the settlement. The villagers, anticipating what was in store, fled into the interior. Two cutters and a galley were sent ashore and the sailors 'ransacked all the houses bringing away all the spear, God [*sic*], fishing apparatus, killed all the dogs, pigs, fowl, (and hadn't we a bouse out of fresh grub next day) and after doing all possible harm they set fire to the village and burned it to the ground'. Jack added in his letter: 'It was a splendid blaze, I don't think I ever saw a finer one.' After this they weighed anchor and moved on to Little Nicobar Island.

Here, Jack had his first close view of the natives: 'They have large holes in their ears through which they put, when they arrive at the age of manhood, pieces of wood about three inches long and about one and half or two in circumference, one fellow had two English cotton reels.' After some ineffectual questioning, 'We sent the pinnace and two cutters and jolly boat to destroy all the canoes and things off the beach, to ransack the houses taking care to bring out all spears and other arms and to kill the dogs which are very fierce.'

Some of the Nicobar villagers who had been captured were 'by intimidation' forced to admit that they had taken four merchant ships over the last few years, and that there was still an English girl on the island. The prisoners were sent off to find the girl, who was to be exchanged for a native Captain. Jack adds: 'I suppose we shall then burn all the villages and most likely the Sepoys will be sent to put an end to some of the savages.'

The following day, 25 July, when the messengers did not return, the sailors burnt all the villages on one side of the island, ransacking and shooting the livestock. They also burnt about thirty canoes which Jack could not help but notice were beautifully constructed. In searching the village huts they found children's petticoats, and French and English books and other things which showed that the crews of the merchant ships had been captured and murdered.

Jack himself was not on shore duty, but went off with a Lieutenant from a Sepoy regiment and had 'splendid fun' on the far side of the island, with the burning parties from the *Wasp* and the *Satellite* coming towards them in a pincer movement, firing on the livestock and game.

Jack and the Lieutenant were in for the kill when the firing parties closed together,

> then for the next five minutes it was awfully exciting spearing the brutes, what with blood and brains flying about, pigs shrieking, men shouting and shashing [*sic*] with their heavy cutlasses it was certainly the most exciting and disgusting scene I ever had anything to do with, though I did not think about its being disgusting then. Very few pigs escaped . . . they were fearfully hacked about, you would see one nearly cut in two, another with his head gone, a third with two of its legs cut off, another entirely disembowelled and so on, for they did not use firearms because it was such close quarters. At the end of it I found myself in the most beastly condition. I did what I could in the way of plundering, I got some beads and carved coconut shells for calabashes . . . we have seen numbers of savages leave the island so we are going to burn and destroy the other islands too. I cut the tusks out of one of the wild pigs . . . I don't care if we live here for six months as we live like fighting cocks. We go and take what we want.

The little girl, when she was found, turned out to be French Creole, and had been living with the natives for six years since she was two, so, as Jack observed, 'I think it is a pity that we have got her.'

After many days of systematically burning the Nicobar villages, the crew turned its attention to surveying Hoko Bay and, by the beginning of August, Jack remarked: 'I shall be uncommon glad when we get clear out of this part of the world and go back to Singapore as I am well tired of it.'

A birthday message from Jack to a brother concluded by saying, 'I wish you every happiness possible and that you may live in Norfolk for the best part of your life, for that is my idea of the height of happiness; it is the greatest ambition I have. I hope, one of these days, I hope not far off, to go home to Norfolk and stop there.'

Jack expected to sail for Japan to witness the opening up of the port of Osaka. He was looking forward to the spectacle of fleets from England,

France, Holland and America assembled in the Inland Sea. Instead, he was surprised to find HMS *Satellite* heading for Bombay and then for Abyssinia. They reached Aden in late October, and Annesley Bay on the Red Sea soon after.

Some years before, King Theodore of Abyssinia had imprisoned the British Consul and about thirty Europeans. A mission sent to release them in 1866 was itself confined to the capital, Magdala. This open abuse was intolerable, and seen as a direct challenge. Sir Robert Napier, at the head of the Bombay Army, was despatched to secure the release of all the prisoners.[2]

It was an extraordinarily well-supplied campaign. Elephants, horses, ammunition, stores and kit were needed for the inland march. Captain Tyron, the Director of the Transport Service, ordered a large convoy of both merchant and naval ships (198 sailing ships and forty-eight steamers) to be sent to Annesley Bay to deliver and manage supplies for the Army. The Bay was too shallow for the big sailing ships, which had to anchor off shore and discharge their supplies on to native boats. 'It was the last great fleet of deep-water sailing ships,' and presented a fabulous spectacle.[3]

The congestion which followed has been attributed to excessive preparation. Captain Tyron was later to report: 'I consider that there never was an expedition in which the captains of the transports endeavoured to do their duty better.' This was the official line, but Jack's letters convey a different picture.

Appalled by the inefficient methods of unloading and maintaining the massive quantities of animals and stores, Jack wrote home in November about the squalor and confusion:

> . . . more mules, horses, camels and donkeys coming ashore every day and the same amount of water for them to drink. They have discovered water about 8 miles from the beach and yet they don't send the poor starving animals there . . . The officers put in charge of them are too idle and lazy to have them looked after, when there are hundreds of muleteers to do the work, and then the watering is so badly managed and the most disgusting scene I ever witnessed.

Jack displayed the typically English preference for animals over humans when he saw a Persian muleteer stand by and watch an animal trampled to death. His red-headed temper erupted, and he caught the man and beat him soundly with a stick, after which a party of bluejackets took over and flogged the fellow with a 'cat'.

Preparations for the Abyssinian Relief Expedition seemed tailormade to keep Jack in a constant state of agitation. No doubt the heat and crowding were a spur, but his basic decency and common sense were outraged by 'the really wicked laziness of the soldier officers; nearly all the work has been done by Chinese carpenters and our men. I may say all except the pier which is being made by negroes.' Yet an Egyptian frigate had anchored in the Bay to watch the proceedings, and in true Victorian military fashion, 'They are going to give a grand dinner to all officers here before the expedition starts and she (the frigate) is heaped up on the forepart of her maindeck to the very beams with cases of champagne.'[4] There was never any love lost between the Army and the Navy, the latter considering the former to be foppish and indolent.

These new experiences matured his judgement and, now that he had time to reflect on the Nicobar episode, he wrote: 'I daresay that you have seen that the *Libra* and the *Wasp* had been again sent to the Nicobar Islands by order of the Admiralty. They are if possible to exterminate the natives as they go. The Admiralty are of the opinion that in killing pigs and fowls we did not commit murder enough.'

This new maturity also showed in his intolerance of officers for whom he had no respect. He described his First Lieutenant as a foolish, vindictive man who was probably 'a shilling short in the pound'. Argumentative in the face of injustice and foolishness, Jack's inability to control his temper was a stumbling block for his career.

By mid-December, Jack's thoughts had turned again to Bradenham, and he wrote with great feeling to his father: 'I should like very much to be at home this Christmas, this is the second I have passed out of England, but two more and very likely three will pass before the ship will return. I am now heartily tired of foreign parts and won't go far from England again unless I am forced.'

Realistically, he knew that he would barely notice Christmas Day, because he had been assigned to the watering party whose responsibility it was to pump a hundred tons of water ashore for the animals and troops. At last the arrangements had been improved: 'When General Staveley came with the 33rd he found out that the animals were not only dying for want of water but from actual starvation. There were hundreds of tons of grub 500 yards from the water. Would you believe it that things were so badly managed that out of the hundreds of natives in the English employ none had been told off to feed the beasts . . .'

From his next letter, written in January 1868, one can sense the frustrations which turned irascibility into violence. A row had erupted among the watering party, and Jack and his men had had an all-out fight with the natives. The Navy won, taking nine prisoners, all of whom Jack 'had well flogged without trial'. The Captain assured Jack that he had done the right thing, and then took him off the watering detail. Jack enthusiastically reported: 'I believe the tussle did the men more good than all the fresh beef and vegetables they serve out and it showed them that fists are better weapons of defence and offence than sticks.'

By 20 April, Jack wrote home that Magdala had been taken and King Theodore killed, but the sailors, who had been sleeping in cabins which heated up to 120°F, no longer cared about Magdala, the hostages, or King Theodore; they just wanted to weigh anchor. But, instead of leaving Abyssinia, Jack went on an excursion a hundred miles inland to Senafe with two other fellows. They borrowed five army mules and took advantage of the hugely excessive supplies of food and drink which had been issued to the various military stations along the route – plenty of bread, rice, tea, sugar, chocolate, lime juice, rum and porter.

> When the troops first came here there was no road at all and in some places the animals could not pass, well the soldiers have made a splendid road that a carriage could drive up. Wherever they came to a large boulder or rock they had to build the road right over it . . . Perhaps in fact the only advantage of the expedition is that it is a perfect prodigy in road making and shows what men can do when they are put to it. It is certainly a wonderful achievement but all the rest of it is bosh and they would have done well if they had let the captives sweat where they were.

At the end of May he confided to his younger brother, Andrew, that the soldiers were getting Indian Batta money and Field Allowance, unlike the sailors, and also that 'everybody here cheats the government right and left, sending in claims for extra pay in the most shamefaced [shameless] manner.' Even his captain had been granted freight money on treasure brought down from Suez.[5]

At last the transports began mending their sails and stoking up, ready to leave. By August HMS *Satellite* had arrived at Siam, where Jack was included in a party of Naval officers who accompanied the Governor of Singapore and the English consuls to a reception at the King's Palace. Unfortunately, Jack found the sight of the court servants crawling at a run in the presence of the Prime Minister so 'awfully ludicrous' that he burst into a roar of laughter, 'for which I got a scowl from my skipper'.

At Whae Waer, he had his first opportunity to see an eclipse: 'the sun was so exceedingly bright that there was but little darkness until nearly total. The effect was very extraordinary and was so sudden that it made people feel funny and queer, the Captain's dog howled and the Captain's cat went nearly mad.'

From Siam, *Satellite* had sailed on to China and Japan and, in the winter of 1868–9, made its way across the Bering Sea to Canada where they put in to Esqimault, the Royal Naval base on Vancouver Island which Jack thought a wonderful place with a lovely climate and friendly settlers. He was especially pleased by the absence of the formality which dominated society in England and, if he could have seen a way to make a decent living, Vancouver was probably the one place he would have chosen to make his home. It was during that summer that Ella and Charles were married, and Alfred's account of the wedding was doubtless meant for Jack. It was not until the autumn of 1869 that he cruised down the Pacific coast to Mazatlan on board HMS *Tenedos*.

The ship was on its way to protect silver smugglers escaping the Mexican authorities, who levied a prohibitive tax on all exports. The silver mines were owned by Englishmen who did not care to pay the levy, and the Navy gave them a helping hand in shipping out the ingots. Mostly, little boats manned by Mexicans came out to the ships with their cargo, but sometimes men from the Navy took the chance to go ashore themselves, hoping no doubt for loot. If they were caught they would be sent to the mines as slave labour, with no hope of escape.

Jack heard of a recent case of 'a boats' crew and two officers up there now, they have been there for years and will never be heard of again', but he didn't care. It says much for the boredom of seafaring life that he thought he might risk the action: 'I shall certainly volunteer, anything to relieve the monotony.'

Jack was no longer a boy but a man, and one that had seen more in his young life than many a mother would wish for her son. While he had had enough of the Navy within two years, the British Public thought it a great thing to be a sailor policing the Empire.

Relieving the monotony was the main purpose of yarning, for which sailors were famous. Andrew and Rider probably lapped up Jack's adventure stories, relishing the bloodshed and gore like every little boy who ever read *Robinson Crusoe*.[6] The roots of Rider's bloodthirsty novels are in Jack's letters. One can detect in the letters the note of uncritical observation of savagery and brutality that is the hallmark of many of

Rider's adventure stories. It is the voice of the boy: in many ways power-less, in many ways still amoral, and yet also attempting some kind of decency. Jack and his fellow cadets would spend some of their spare time discussing the finer points of gentlemanly behaviour, and he wrote home for a copy of Walford's *English Country Gentleman* to settle the arguments.

From this early correspondence, the story of a European child captured by natives reappears in *Alan Quatermain* and *The Ivory Child*. In the eclipse at Whae Waer is the suggestion of the life-saving portent predicted by Captain Good in *King Solomon's Mines*. Jack's account of his journey into Abyssinia was the first taste for any of the Haggards of African safaris, but it contains the essential ingredients – two or three chaps setting off into the interior looking for adventure. Rider Haggard was to find his own material for his Mexican novel, at dreadful personal cost, but the romance and terror of the silver mines had already been established for him. Not least of the inspirations was the character of Jack himself, of whom there are many glimpses in Rider's African novels.

On his second tour of duty, once again aboard HMS *Tenedos*, Jack was part of a scientific expedition to observe the 'transit of Venus' from a position off the Sandwich Islands. But his long night watches had already given Jack an interest in the stars; unable to escape the miseries of the naval day, he searched for the underpinning of human existence in the nocturnal maps of heaven.

3

And All the Trees Are Green

In the Spring of 1870, Ella Maddison Green lost her first baby, and Alfred Hinuber Haggard lost his first love. When Eba Heyward grew bored with his conversation and jilted him, he ceased to idolize the fairer sex and decided that the only hope of salvation for silly women lay in the teachings of John Stuart Mill – they should all be educated and given the vote. (Alfred also read Darwin, but that was not something to be discussed in polite society.) As an alternative, he suggested in the case of one sulky young lady of Richmond that he would like to 'put her up against a tree, and flick at her from eighteen yards with a cow hide whip.'[1]

Seventeen months younger than Bazett and fourteen months older than Jack, Alfred's most passionate urge was ambition. He had followed his two elder brothers, Will and Bazett, to Winchester, but in 1862 he was transferred to Haileybury College in Hertford, as part of the first intake.[2] This new public school replaced the college which had been maintained by the East India Company, but continued with the tradition of preparing boys for colonial service. Few careers could rival the Indian Civil Service for professional prestige: Alfred would go out to India and follow his Doveton relatives, who had eaten of the Imperial fruits.

India! It sang out to Alfred like a siren in a sapphire sea. But it was not so easily achieved; the Indian Civil Service (ICS) was unrivalled in its intellectual and social élitism. After leaving school, Alfred would be called to the Bar so that he would have a grounding in the legal work he would have to undertake. Day after day, month after month, he studied at Lincoln's Inn, and crammed in the evenings for the ICS exams which would eventually open the channel towards his dreams.

Meanwhile, his lodgings at 93 Gaisford Street in London's Kentish Town brought him face to face with the social conditions which he despised. In a letter to Ella he wrote: 'Confound and sink this rotten old country with its pauperism in the upper classes – pauperism in the middle and lower classes; disease starvation and misery staring one in the face on all sides.'

By the time he was twenty-one he had already decided that his tastes were Epicurean and his character egotistical. He wanted to live well, as an English gentleman should, and he didn't want to wait until he was middle-aged to do so. He thought of himself as a man of learning, at ease in the classical world and understanding the Roman inspiration for the Pax Britannica. Only India could deliver the prestige, power and income which would satisfy his aspirations.

From his boyhood he had heard his mother and aunt talk about Bombay and the family's long association with the East; of how the Bazetts, of the banking firm Bazett, Colvin & Co., came to live on St Helena because it was on the sailing route down to the Cape and out to India. They were polished, well-read men, who married into the Harper and Doveton families of India. The Dovetons of St Helena and Bombay tended to be military men or lawyers, clever and learned, and Sir William Doveton, a great uncle of Mrs Haggard, was a Member of Council of St Helena when Napoleon was on the island.

Long after she had returned to England, Mrs Haggard continued to think and write about India, and the Indian Mutiny of 1857 which had so shocked the whole nation roused her Imperial spirit. She wrote a narrative poem about the catastrophic Kabul Campaign of 1842, called *Myra, or The Rose of the East*. Romantic, savage and vengeful, the year of the mutiny was an apt time to publish the picturesque verses.[3]

In her unequivocal introduction, Mrs Haggard commented on the current 'drama now enacting in our Eastern possessions' which included 'deliberate massacres and unexampled atrocities' for which 'RETRIBUTION must and will be exacted – when the strong arm of England has been put forth, effectually to crush the vipers she has nourished in her bosom.' In the aftermath of the mutiny, attitudes to the Indians tightened and changed. The Anglo–Indian society, which Alfred would be joining, would be more self-contained, more detached from native life than the society his mother had known thirty years earlier.

In May of 1870, Alfred passed his preliminary exams. He had been placed twenty-first on the list and, overcome with the glamour of his prospects, went down to Bradenham for a break before embarking on a further two years of study.

At Bradenham of course the usual excitement reigns and keeps us forcibly alive. I am always late for prayers and come down in the middle of breakfast, and so am able to confine my tongue to eating during that meal by which restraint I save myself a good deal of bother and enjoy myself much as Lucretius who loved to stand by the seashore and see the vessels tossed by the wind. I could wish that they were not tossed, but as they are so I enjoy my own repose.

His brothers and sisters were growing up fast. Rider was fourteen, and Alfred noticed approvingly that he was 'most earnest in whatever he takes up'. What Rider was taking up at the moment was rook shooting. 'He killed 50 yesterday much to his pleasure, though not to mine for I love the shiny-backed birds, and prefer them to any amount of pheasants fed to gratify man's sporting tastes, a remnant of our original barbarism.'

Alfred's views on shooting were at odds not only with those of the rest of his family and class, but also with their Royal neighbour's at Sandringham, who had replaced the English countryman's style of shooting the fields with the Continental battue. Alfred was well aware that his opinions would not go down well in India. How often he must have gazed at his mother's emblematic oil painting of Colonel Harper, tiger hunting from atop an elephant, the gorgeous silks and howdah shadowed by storm clouds.

'I intend however to go in for sport this autumn,' he wrote, 'though I feel no enthusiasm for it, because I believe it is a necessity in India, and I must somehow try to form a liking for killing feathered fowl. Besides the tigers must be killed and practice is necessary to become enough of a shot.'

He had already been pronounced medically fit and had chosen to work in the presidency of Bengal, the seat of government, 'where I shall be boiled parched or stewed in a very short time.' The Governor-General only stayed in Calcutta for half the year, removing to Simla during the monsoons. The civilians (Civil servants), however, were obliged to continue with their work for much of the rainy season. As he detached himself from the general mêlée of family life – to the library to write to Ella, or simply to lounge on a sofa and gaze out at the great beech tree on the lawn – Alfred feasted his dreams:

I am laying all sorts of plans of how I shall live out there. How many servants I shall keep and how many horses; what my livery will be (sky blue and white I think, with great big buttons with the crest upon them). I propose to enjoy a gallop on my elephant before breakfast, and a trot

on my camel after tea. I also propose a pony carriage drawn by two
Royal Bengal tigers.

When he came out of the clouds he had the opportunity to talk with
a person who knew India well. His sister Cecilia (Cissy) had invited a
friend from school to stay for a few days. 'A small woman, Miss Schalch
. . . made herself very agreeable. She is very plain but very pleasant and
took things coolly in which she and I agreed was the best thing to do.
We had a couple of rides together and I never saw such pluck as she
showed on horseback.' Alice Schalch's family was well established in
Calcutta, to which great city she would be returning.

Will had been posted to Switzerland and, with the outbreak of the
Franco–Prussian War, was kept at his desk in Berne writing despatches
and sending telegrams. Although Britain was not directly involved she
had, through loyalties to Belgium, 'a finger in the pie', as Mrs Haggard
put it. She wrote to Jack at some length to put him in the picture with
her no-nonsense, pro-German, summing up of political events. But like
most people she looked across the Channel in horror as the Prussians
marched on Paris, and the 'slaughter on both sides' was 'fearful'.

Oblivious to disasters, Bazett set off to visit Will, who had discovered
the exhilarating new sport of mountain climbing. Alfred was sour with
resentment at Bazett's lighthearted passage through life, but, despite his
lack of seriousness, Bazett had already embarked on his career and made
his début as a barrister in Norwich. Ever the pedagogue, Alfred remarked:
'His voice is good, his manner unconstrained and, if he gets to know
his law well, he will make a good thing of the bar, for he would believe
thoroughly in the goodness of a cause he adopted and would therefore
be successful as a pleader.'

Bazett's jaunts and jollities made Alfred feel the pressure of his work
more acutely. He entered a dismal phase where he feared he would fail
his Final exam. Many of his friends had already left for India, and the
malaise of loneliness and anxiety was so demoralizing that he had even
begun to have doubts about his shimmering goal: 'the necessity of leaving
England for the best part of my life is not pleasing.' He sank into a
despondency which resulted in a nervous illness, and possibly severe
migraine, during which he escaped to Norfolk for five weeks.

That Christmas was one of the last for which so many of the children
were together – perhaps the last time that their father would toss coins
down from the top of the stairs for the younger children to chase in the

Bazett Michael Haggard, photographed in a Norwich studio,
probably in his thirties when he was practising as a barrister and living
at Kirby Cane Hall.

hall below: it always amused him to see them scrambling over each other in their rush to bag the most treasure. They were growing too old for games, though not for charades or plays. In the New Year they presented two theatricals for their friends. The first was *Dearest Mama, A Comedietta in One Act*, followed by an adaptation of Wilkie Collins's *The Woman in White* called *Count Fosco, or the Brotherhood*. The Haggards and the Barkers were joined in their theatricals by a Mr Lofthouse, who was later to play another, more serious, role in their lives.

As Alfred struggled through the last months of his studies, his older brothers were already getting into their stride. Bazett took the plunge and became engaged to Julia Barker. Vain and self-centred, she looked forward to a smart and comfortable life with her charming beau. Her father, having happily inherited Holt House and Shipdham Hall through the fortuitous demise of several wealthy Norfolk families, was most anxious that she should live in the style to which he had accustomed her. Although Julia (or Judy as she was known) would eventually inherit substantial sums, he meant to make sure that the Haggards did their part.

Charles and Ella Maddison Green were holidaying in Cannes when they heard news of Bazett's engagement. Mr Haggard was going to sell a farm he owned in Essex, which would fetch about £6,000 for the settlement, and had proposed an allowance of £200 a year. Charles was in the middle of shaving as Ella read him the letter. Charles paused to look at her, blade in air, soap on jaw. After a minute he remarked that he could not see how his father-in-law could possibly maintain his responsibilities to the rest of his family if he made such an allowance. In later years Charles recalled that moment with absolute clarity – caught, like his razor, in a shaft of Mediterranean sunlight.

It was quite true that Mr Haggard was encumbered with heavy responsibilities. The precocious Andrew was soon to leave Westminster (where he had been in unspecified trouble) for the Army, which would entail expense; Rider had to be found a place; Arthur was going to Shrewsbury, and there were two girls still to be matched. Nevertheless, marriage settlement arrangements were made, the family solicitors consulted, and all was made good. After a fashionable wedding at St George's, Hanover Square in London, on 16 December 1872, the Bazetts (the Haggards referred to themselves when married couples as plurals of the brothers' names) moved into 11 Sussex Gardens, just off the Edgware Road. It was a neat little Georgian house which would do for Town. Of course, they wanted a country house as well.

In the summer of 1872, Alfred began the long journey to India, travelling through France and Switzerland with his father. When they reached the St Gotthard Pass they were joined by Rider and Andrew, who had walked up from Lake Lucerne where the rest of the family was on holiday. Here farewells were said, and Alfred, alone in a diligence, proceeded on the road to Brindisi. He must have thought of Hannibal on his elephant as he watched the waving figures fade and the Alps loom up about him, distant India not to be seen for months, his dear family not to be seen again for years.

The current situation in India was not altogether a happy one. On a visit to the penal colony on the Andaman Islands, Lord Mayo had been assassinated by a Muslim convict. A new Governor-General, Lord Northbrook, had been rapidly appointed and had arrived in Calcutta in April of 1872.

It was a time of great unrest amongst reformist Sikhs and puritanical Muslims. After a Sikh attack on a small Punjabi town, the British squashed the uprising in no uncertain terms: forty-nine prisoners were blown to pieces, having been tied to the muzzles of British cannon. Lord Northbrook, a shy, reserved man with strong administrative talents, was a Whig by both temperament and political persuasion. Although he had great respect for Indian leaders and a desire to reduce racial prejudice, he was not a man to hurry through destabilizing reforms. Perceiving that India had been suffering from over-government, he set his sights on reorganizing the administrative and educational systems. Above all he was determined not to sacrifice India 'for the gratification of England'. He brought with him his kinsman, Evelyn Baring, as his private secretary, and he was destined to be disliked by the English civil servants and welcomed by the Indian educated classes.[4]

Calcutta, the City of Palaces, with its vast layout, its magnificent white Palladian public buildings, esplanades of elegant façades, and wide streets of trading houses, must surely have impressed Alfred as he approached from the steaming mud flats of the Hooghly River. Calcutta was a monument to the success of commerce, and the proliferation of clubs was dedicated to the exclusive comfort of the white male. Government House soothed the effects of the hellish climate with marble floors and high, white, gilded reception chambers. Alfred, being Alfred, would not have been able to ignore entirely the wretched hovels of the natives, descending into seething stews which rivalled anything he could have seen in London.

But he was not long in Calcutta. Arriving in October of 1872, he soon took up his post as Assistant Collector and Magistrate in Bankura, eighty miles north-west of the capital. The size of the country, the lack of communications and the judicial responsibility meant that a Magistrate became practically a pro-consul in his district. Alfred's training could not prepare him for the unnerving reality of touring vast distances between isolated villages, dispensing life-and-death justice, and then simply moving on. There was no comparison of responsibility or circumstance between this and what a young man of equivalent education would have been undertaking in England.

Cautiously, Alfred responded to the new routine: 'Camp life is very pleasant undeniably, one is up early in the morning takes a light meal and goes out shooting. One then returns, bathes, breakfasts does office work in the open air beneath the shade of a tree, rides, dines, plays cards, sleeps.'

Almost immediately, Alfred's work in the court made him anxious. He was not at all sure whether his judgements or sentences were correct or appropriate. He was sensitive to the fact that he might be imposing great hardship on innocent men. He was acutely aware of his inadequacy in not knowing the languages of the people, and longed to bridge the gap between the Europeans and the Orientals – an attitude which cannot have appealed to many of his colleagues. In fact he was quite unprepared for the overriding status of the European, 'of his powers for evil, of the vast superiority which is his over the people of the country. There are few people in the whole district for instance who would venture to sit down in my presence without being bid to do so. I think that we govern as much by fear as anything.'

On the other hand, the natural landscape of lush jungle and flowering shrubs enchanted him, as did the early-morning blue haze and the distant purple mountains. The living arrangements, when at last he set up his own bungalow, began to match his dreams. Although he had only four rooms and two bathrooms and an exterior cook house, the servants, 'who sleep and live where they can', included a valet, butler, groom, grass cutter, cook, sweeper and water carrier, 'and one or two other menials'.

Shooting in earnest involved panthers and bears being driven out of the jungle into open glades by an almost unbelievable number of two thousand beaters. With a friend, he shot a mother bear as she charged him to protect her cubs, but 'I am sorry to say that when we tossed for the skin he won it so I have no trophy.'

Social life was limited entirely to the eight Europeans who lived in or visited the community. At Christmas he was given leave 'to deliver my introduction to the Governor-General which Sir Henry Wolff sent me', and to stay with the Schalchs.[5] Happily, Schalch was 'a great man out here and has a good chance of being next Lieutenant Governor if he lives on'. Sadly for both Schalch and Alfred, he did not. But the Christmas excursion was nevertheless a success: Alfred became engaged to Alice Schalch.

When the news arrived in Bradenham there was an explosion. It was received wisdom that any man who married young scuppered his chances of promotion. Alfred's father was beside himself, and wrote at once a scathing letter which, of course, took weeks to reach its mark.

On 29 July 1873 Alfred wrote to his sister that he was furious. His father had threatened to disinherit him and was browbeating him as though he were still a boy. Alfred blamed Bazett for the immediate cause of the row. He had let out details of his wedding plans to all and sundry at Bradenham! It was either stupid or deliberately mischievous. And they all knew Bazett was the favourite.

Alfred felt honour-bound to answer his father's charges, and to protest at his father's assessment of his prospects if he married. And then the Squire was upset by the tone of *that* reply. And when it came down to it, the nub of the quarrel was the date of the wedding. Alfred needed a wife, and he would rather marry Alice Schalch sooner than later. Several weeks on, Alfred still felt himself smarting from his father's reprimand.

Haggard must surely have known by now where Alfred's priorities lay: 'Work Labour Strife – Pursuit – Winning are the only things that make life tolerable.' All the same, several more 'furious letters' had followed which 'rated him like a child'. Reluctantly, Alfred delayed the wedding until December. The Squire relented and tried to make amends; he suggested that he himself should write to Alice to bring the date forward. Too late. It was already set, and damned inconvenient it was; Alfred would have to undertake the expensive and uncomfortable journey to visit her in Darjeeling in the interim.[6]

Alfred candidly told Ella that Alice was by no means perfect, but she was unselfish and friendly, which would do much to compensate for his own shortcomings. She would make friends for him, cheer his melancholy and warm his loneliness. If he was moody she would be loving and kind. She would counter his carelessness with a comfortable, attractive home. And luckily for Alice, he liked her family!

Alfred had finished his letter and taken a bath; he was just having his feet washed when a servant brought in the post, and he immediately read the latest letter from Ella. She noted that Bazett had sent no congratulations to Alfred on his engagement, remarking that Bazett 'has his trim cut out for him pretty'. On the whole, the news from England was good. Judy was expecting a baby, and so, thank goodness, was Ella. But what on earth, he wondered, did she mean about Cissy? Improved in health, but 'likes the companionship of young gentlemen'! This understatement hid the fact that Cissy was becoming sexually preoccupied – an awkward disposition for a Victoria lady, even amongst the uninhibited Haggards. Perhaps she was like some of her brothers.

Cissy's behaviour had for some time been a topic of family discussion. Alfred thought she was bullied at home and taught to think of herself as stupid – to the detriment of her self-respect and temper. To Ella he confided his recommendation that preaching and reproof should give way to gentle persuasion. Cissy was subject to tantrums and odd abruptness that could no longer be excused by childhood or illness.

Alfred must have received more detailed news of the family when he met up with his brother Andrew, although no details of the occasion remain. Andrew had joined the King's Own Borderers, and the regiment was on a tour of duty in India. The racy young subaltern soon found himself in 'that excellent sporting station Jubbalapore [Japalpur]', where he was devoting himself to his favourite occupations – fishing, shooting and polo.

Alfred and Alice married on 15 December 1873 and, after a short honeymoon, he brought his bride back to Bankipore for a few days before taking up his new appointment at Mozuferpore [Muzzaffarpur] in January. Suddenly, Alfred found himself in the front line of one of the most controversial policies of Lord Northbrook's administration.

In the wake of a drought, famine was anticipated in northern India, particularly in Tirhoot. Northbrook was determined to demonstrate that it was possible to prevent disaster. Secretly, to keep prices stable, he bought and stored up grain from Burma, confident that he could distribute it through the new railway system. Meanwhile, he allowed the continued export of rice from Bengal to protect its markets for the future. It was a policy which left him open to misjudgement and criticism.

Alfred commented that the attitude of the Europeans to the famine was like Nero fiddling, as they continued to attend an annual race meeting which attracted indigo planters and officials. As well as an occasion for extended festivity, the meeting was one of the few opportunities for the two groups to meet together in a convivial atmosphere. Amid the balls and the hunting, Alfred's new wife proved to be something of a success, and he happily wrote home: 'In truth she is a wife to be proud of to my mind – rather a contrast to me I fear who shall remain Don Dismalis till the end of the chapter – but she is so agreeable and charming in her manner that she will well make up for my deficiencies and will attract friends who could never find me out.'

Meanwhile, there was a drought over an area of forty thousand square miles, affecting eighteen million people. The rice from Burma was brought in by train, but had then to be distributed by bullock carts. The indigo planters were paid, and paid more than handsomely in many cases, for the use of their carts. The local officials had the task of organizing the distribution, and in Tirhoot they made the mistake of trying to do everything themselves without reference to the Indian elders. The Lieutenant Governor, Sir George Campbell, and Northbrook thought this was madness, and directed that henceforth Indians should be widely used to help with the famine relief work – after which great efficiency ensued.

While the work was going on, the newspapers argued over the methods and policies. The Indian newspapers supported Northbrook, but the Anglo–Indian press carped and criticised. Although he had been in India for so short a time, Alfred was chafing at the bit. He decided to gain some status – and some money – by writing for the press. He wrote an article about the famine in Lahore for the Anglo–Indian paper *The Pioneer.*

Whether or not Northbrook's six and a half million pound Famine Relief programme was justified, Alfred had begun a critical course which set him at odds with his superiors. He had asked why there was famine at all in India. There were several possible contributing factors – the changing means of distribution, the increased birthrate after the sup-pression of the Mutiny, the nature of capitalism, and, of course, the nature of British administration which taxed in money instead of in kind, thereby impoverishing the lower orders. It was this last cause to which Alfred attributed all famines in India.

Alfred's sensibilities had been rendered frighteningly vulnerable by his own genealogy. In the family it was vaguely known that their maternal great grandmother was of mixed descent, the daughter of a begum. The earlier, illustrious Dovetons of the East India Company had happily fathered half-caste children, whom they recognized and supported, but by the mid-nineteenth century there was a wholly different attitude to mixed blood. It was an anathema.[7]

Alfred was deeply worried, and wrote to his sister Ella.

> There is a little flaw in our genealogical table which I implore you will *never mention to any living soul* . . . I think you know to what I allude. *For mercy's sake don't allude to it in any answer to this letter.* Andrew told me you laughed about it to him as though it were a subject of no importance but he had not been five days in this country before he felt he would tear his tongue out sooner than breathe the secret to any one else.

Believing himself to be touched by the tar brush completely destabilized Alfred's situation, particularly since he was finding himself temperamentally at odds with his superiors.

Alice may not have been aware of this skeleton in the family closet when a new little Haggard arrived on the scene. Vernon Harry Stuart Haggard was born on 28 October, soon after their arrival in the Buxar sub-division where Alfred took up a new appointment. Alice immediately became entirely absorbed in motherhood, finding her little son absolutely perfect, an opinion from which she never wavered for the rest of her life. Alfred observed her complete satisfaction and found himself also quite delighted with the boy – as long as he was seen but not heard.

Untroubled by the colour of his great grandmother, buoyed up by the prestige of an English gentleman and armed with impenetrable self-regard, Will enjoyed his increasing status in the Diplomatic Corps. In July of 1874 he was posted to Washington. The British Minister, Lord Thornton, had been very successful in diffusing the tensions between England and America brought about by the recent Civil War and fishing disputes with Canada. Will, with his jovial confidence and affable charm, impressed the social élite of Washington.

At home Ella, tragically, had again lost a baby, and Charles was so unwell that they undertook another trip abroad, although they had settled into a new rectory, built to Charles's specification.[8] There was deep concern about Cissy's future. Probably in response to a suggestion that she join a 'fishing-fleet' to India, Alfred somewhat callously replied: 'Can't anyone find her a husband at home?' Arthur, who was showing promise at Shrewsbury, found himself in the same year as Frederick Jackson, the only son of the deceased John Jackson of Oran. It would not be long before the two friends went up to Cambridge together.

Jack was kicking against the traces. He had only just been promoted to the rank of Lieutenant, and was languishing in a career which he had outgrown. A threat to his mess arrangements had triggered a torrent of frustration:

> Ever since I joined the service I have had to wash, bathe and dress in public, amongst the men, with filthy dirty water washing round my bare feet, and blue-jackets by accident scrubbing your bare calves in the dark in mistake for a stanchion, but I'm sick of it all, and I don't care about being kicked out of the only little place we have to ourselves, and having to mess among ship's company outside, with my basin or plate on my knees, because I happen to be last down to dinner and there is no room inside. I'm sick of it all. Why can't they house us, treat us and pay us like gentlemen. This is not my feeling only. Ask the first small craft gunroom officer you come across. Ask Amyand.[9]

But Jack had had his chance. Realistically, the Haggard parents concentrated on Rider's future. It was decided to send him to London to take French lessons, and then to a crammer for the diplomatic exams which was run by Mr Scoones, a family connection. Scoones, who tutored two generations of the family, liked to say that the Haggards developed slowly and late. Rider was no exception; and London was so diverting.

He discovered the new fad of Spiritualism, and he and a chum used to enjoy going to these sessions and catching out the medium who, like as not, would be a charlatan. It was all a ripping joke, like country house games. Mrs Guppy was one of their favourite mediums who, amid a series of intrigues, was accused of using her seance rooms as an 'introducing house', a common clandestine activity for a clairvoyant. However, Mrs Guppy was not entirely a fake, and Rider's intuitive nature opened a chasm of possibilities. His psychic abilities were noticed, but he shied away from this tawdry application.

He was, however, ripe for experience and romance. One hot evening at a summer party in Richmond, Lilly Jackson swept confidently into the ballroom. Gliding radiantly between the guests, she paused. On the edge of her eyeline was a tall, lanky youth, whose auburn hair singled him out from the gaggles of boyish swains. He had a glint in his eye which might one day speak of passion. He turned fully towards her and she felt a tingle of satisfaction at his reaction. The lines of Tennyson's

Lilly Jackson in maturity; this undated photograph was taken at
Brighton. Her father, John Jackson, 'Jack of Oran', was a man of
'great physique and indomitable energy and character'.

poem might have whispered on the summer air: 'she saw helmet and
the plume, she saw the water-lily bloom', but it was Rider who looked
down to Camelot.

She offered a hesitant smile to the room but, instead of responding,
Rider simply stared. Did he still see her at all? Lilly turned towards the
older gentlemen who were waiting to mark her card. She was twenty-
one, and time was already snapping at her heels. She did not glance at
Rider again, but moved on.

Something in Rider never did move on. The mirror did indeed crack
from side to side. He did not know Lilly's identity but he made frantic
efforts to discover her name – comically, through a tradesman. Once he

knew who she was he made the connection with her family, and Arthur's friend at school. Lilly was immensely flattered by his admiration and seething ardour, and allowed herself to encourage him. But he was very young and still had his way to make in the world.

In the spring, Rider joined a family trip to Tours in France, staying in separate lodgings so that he was not tempted to converse in English. But Mrs Haggard heard of the proposed appointment of Sir Henry Bulwer, a Norfolk neighbour, to be the new Governor of the Transvaal.[10] She decided to ask him to take Rider with him to South Africa as a Private Secretary. Leaning heavily on the friendship of the families, letters were written and proposals made. Bulwer, having three or four other applications already before him, and needing an experienced man in the position, replied tactfully that he did not know whether Rider 'would think it worthwhile to come with me as an unpaid assistant secretary'. In a subsequent letter he was careful again to point out that he himself had only a quasi-official appointment, which might be rescinded at any time. However, it was an opportunity for Rider to gain some experience.

According to Mrs Haggard's letter to Sir Henry Bulwer of 24 June, Rider was holding himself in readiness for a summons should Bulwer's plans become more settled. Privately, Rider was prevaricating. Sitting alone in the evenings at his lodgings he was deprived of any conversation – his hosts, ironically, were unwilling to talk with him. He had been annoyed to learn that one of his friends had told Miss Jackson 'about this Natal business'. Rider's friend (or rival?) reported Lilly's comment that it was 'extremely foolish' of Rider to change his mind so often. Rider wrote at length, first protesting that it was unlikely that he would go to Natal, but then weighing up his prospects: 'Of course I risk something, I may draw a blank, and I may draw a prize, and I do not see why with the aid of work I should not draw a prize. Look at Sir H. Bulwer himself, how did he begin, and look what he is after 15 years service.' Rider finished a little sadly, 'I suppose that you are thoroughly enjoying the season. I often think of you all, as I sit here of an evening and smoke my solitary pipe.'

Mrs Haggard's patience with her amorous sons was sorely tried. Jack, who had accompanied them to Tours, had met two English sisters on holiday. While he no doubt cut a dashing figure, the seasoned sailor was utterly smitten by Miss Etta White's physical charms. His mother was decidedly vexed, and wrote to Alfred that she wished the Misses White away in India, 'where no doubt their fine faces and figures would soon find them a husband!'

Within days, and quite suddenly, Rider's future was settled. The parents decided it all. He was to accompany Sir Henry Bulwer as an unpaid factotum and to leave for South Africa forthwith. Rider hastened back to London. Bazett organized the purchase of guns for him, while he chased round town buying clothes and making hurried farewells. With Sir Henry, he boarded the *Windsor Castle* at Dartmouth. In his parting letter to his mother dated 23 July 1875, he noted that he had spent fifty pounds on his kit but, with a Parthian shot, consoled her that this was twenty-five pounds less than Andrew's recent expenses.

— 4 —

Home-Born Ills

Included in Andrew's necessary kit for a young officer was a trout rod from Mr Farlow's Fishing Tackle Establishment in London's Strand. The sporting pursuits of a gentleman all came very dear for a chap in Andrew's position. With little private money at his disposal, even his mess bills were difficult to cover. But transferring to India opened up new vistas.

In the East, like every other young officer, he would be spoiled by the sense of moral supremacy which permeated all grades of the Army; spoiled also by the profusion of cheap servants, minimal military duties in hot weather, the pleasant social life of the clubs, and, if his reputation held true, by the lively grass widows of the hill stations.[1] The fishing rod was destined to come into good use in the 'Nerbudda [Narbada] River' in the Central Province where he was so happily stationed. It was of some advantage and comfort to have a brother already in India; Alfred was now Joint Magistrate at Buxar, a station on the East India Railway, some 350 miles away.

However, just as Andrew had begun to enjoy himself, the rapid withdrawal of the King's Own Borderers from Jubbalapore was precipitated by a splendidly melodramatic plot known as the Baroda Incident. The Gaekwar Malhar Rao was at loggerheads with the British Resident, Colonel Robert Phayre, when in November of 1874 arsenic was discovered in Phayre's whisky. A Residency servant confessed to the crime, but there was suspicion that he was under the instructions of the Gaekwar. An alternative explanation was that Phayre himself had planted the arsenic to bring the Gaekwar into disrepute. The Indians feared that the British would annex Baroda which was a much valued place of employment, despite the Gaekwar's rule. Northbrook did, indeed, depose the Gaekwar after an unorthodox meeting of the Executive Council at Simla. In a politically sensitive moment, the Borderers were moved out with only two and a half hours' notice. Andrew later wrote, 'I suppose it was one of the quickest moves of a regiment on record, and I had to leave two nice ponies and all my other odds and ends behind me. It was with a sorrowful heart that I did so.'

Embarking from Bombay, the Borderers were sent to Aden for a year, a prospect which scarcely delighted them, since 'Aden . . . is supposed to be only separated from the lower regions by a sheet of brown paper', and on their arrival they found it was worse than they had anticipated. 'When one is young, however, provided one be gifted with a cheerful disposition and good health, one can be happy anywhere. Thus, in spite of very hard work, caused by a dearth of subalterns, and of intense heat, I soon found that I could enjoy myself immensely in that "desolate, desolate, spot".'

While the other fellows were 'grumbling and growling' Andrew joined his friend, Cunninghame Grahame Makellar, who had been out in China and had 'somehow or other acquired an intimate knowledge of that distinctly hazardous art in the tropics – boat sailing'. Together they escaped the dust and dirt for the open waters and burning skies of the Gulf of Aden. When Makellar died of dysentery, Andrew was left with his boat. In this most dreary period, apparently useless for his career, Andrew sowed the seeds from which he would reap his later glory. Never one to sit idle, he had already made an attempt at the basics of Arabic grammar, and he decided to practise the language by going out with the Arab fishermen on their dhows. 'Oh! never, never shall I forget the delicate effluvia of the Arab boats in Aden, but I got accustomed to it in time.' Fishing enabled him not only to bribe the gluttonous Paymaster, but also to gain a rough working knowledge of the language that was to prove so felicitous.

While the 25th Regiment languished in Aden, the prestige of the Army, already a dominant force in English society, was reaching an apotheosis. General Sir Garnet Wolseley had emerged victorious from the Red River and Ashanti campaigns and, at barely forty years old, became a national hero. His *modus operandi* was to surround himself with a 'ring' of Staff College officers, which compensated for the lack of a General Staff in the British Army. The Regimental system, so successful in breeding loyalty and esprit among both English and native troops, also made it possible for officers to perform eccentric feats of exploration and travel from which emerged some of the great names of the nineteenth century – William Butler and Charles Gordon among them.

Wolseley expected – hoped – to leave for India but, in 1875, the new Disraeli government sent him to South Africa to reform the administration of Natal. The Colonial Secretary, Lord Carnarvon, was keen to unify the South African colonies for a simpler and stronger administration. Wolseley's task as Governor of Natal was to enquire into every aspect of the administration and to persuade the Natal Legislature to reduce its own authority. Wolseley only consented to this unaccustomed political role if it were limited to six months and he could take his own chosen staff.

His selection was determined by his idea of presenting 'a sort of grandeur' to the colonists, and inevitably it comprised comrades in arms: Colonel George Pomeroy Colley – age forty, a veteran of the Kaffir War and the China Campaign; Major William Butler – age thirty-seven, had been with Wolseley during the Red River and Ashanti campaigns; Major Henry Brackenbury – age thirty-eight, an artilleryman who had served in the Indian Mutiny Campaign; Captain Lord Gifford, VC – age twenty-six, 57th Regiment, whose single-handed exploits in West Africa had made his name synonymous with bravery; and, as Secretary of State, the conceited Mr Napier Broome, former staff writer of *The Times*.

This illustrious retinue arrived in South Africa at the end of March 1875 and quickly established itself at the capital, Pietermaritzburg, where Wolseley embarked on a 'champagne and sherry' campaign to soften up the colonials, whom privately he despised. To this end he built a new ballroom at Government House where, by his orders, the waltz sensationally replaced the quadrille. By taking over the leader columns of the *Natal Times* – at a cost of fifty pounds a month out of his own pocket – and instructing his staff in writing them, Wolseley promoted his policy to the general populace while taking a tough offensive in the Legislature to push through the necessary New Constitution Bill; the passage was stormy, difficult, and not without compromise on the Government's part, but nevertheless it was accomplished.

Wolseley's staff, the laurels of war still fresh on their brows, had been cutting a swathe through the hearts of the Maritzburg wives and daughters. Sir Garnet's social tactics had produced unforeseen complications: not only flirtation and casual lust but, for a soldier, the useless inconvenience of *romance*. Brackenbury (unenthusiastically married) was reportedly carrying on half a dozen affairs at once; Lord Gifford (single) was actually proposing to marry a designing young woman whose mother

was a Jewess. Butler was more circumspect in his involvements, but even
Wolseley himself, a married man of impeccable judgement, found the
opportunities for dalliance disturbing. He was glad to drag his love-sick
men away from the capital to explore and report on the state of Natal,
taking with him the inevitable wagon-load of second-rate champagne,
but on their return he still wrote to his wife that 'I seem to be living
on a female powder keg'. He was relieved to hand over the Governorship
to a man whom he had recommended for the post, Sir Henry Bulwer.

Bulwer had expected to be greeted in Cape Town, but Sir Garnet
was still up in Natal and, to make matters worse, the Governor of the
Cape was away at the newly discovered diamond mines at Kimberley,
where Cecil Rhodes was already at work on his grandiose schemes.
Young Rider Haggard, never any good at managing luggage, and in
clothes that were too heavy for the climate, was struggling with all the
arrangements which must be made for the next step of the journey, the
voyage up the coast to Durban, and all the time dreading the entertainment he would have to organize once they reached Natal.

Wolseley left Pietermaritzburg on 28 August, in the manner that he
had arrived − at full gallop, changing horses every eight miles. He had
come to South Africa vaunting the glitter of military Imperial style, and
he had maintained that display in full swagger throughout his six months
of Governorship. His staff had brought executive competence and personal glamour to Natal. It was a triumph of tactics, diplomacy and
showmanship.

When he called upon the incoming Governor, he was frankly appalled
to find that Bulwer's entire staff 'consisted of a leggy-looking youth, not
long I should say from school, who seems the picture of weakness and
dullness'. Rider Haggard, age nineteen, had arrived in Africa. When he
came to write his memoirs, he could not remember whether, at that
time, he had met Wolseley at all.

Rider was still wondering whether he would have to carry on with
what Alfred patronisingly called 'flunkeying', or whether there was a
chance of his being made a Secretary and being paid. On 1 September,
Bulwer's party, which now included the Secretary of Natal Affairs,
Theophilus Shepstone, Napier Broome, who was staying on as the Colonial Secretary, and Rider, left Durban by a four-horse wagonette.

Typically it was William Butler, a fellow romantic, who spared time
to converse with the 'leggy youth' − a kindness which was not forgotten
by Rider. Always sympathetic with the native point of view, Butler did

not concur with Wolseley's recommendation for the swift annexation of Zululand, where he foresaw the gathering thunder of a 30,000-strong *impi* on the border. Butler's natural empathy with indigenous populations had been reinforced by conversations with one outstanding individual of colonial Africa, Theophilus Shepstone. Indeed, Butler's memories of Natal and his appreciation of Shepstone match very closely those of Rider, and underline the singularity of Shepstone's character.

The dichotomy of the English attitude to the colonial dilemma accounts for the fact that Rider Haggard's Empire novels are both appealing and appalling to the late-twentieth-century reader. One part of that attitude is an evangelical Imperialism, which has largely been rejected as morally insupportable, but there is still in Rider's novels a genuine ethic and a rare and sympathetic history of the Zulus.

Shepstone had been brought up in Africa, and his knowledge of the Zulus was intuitive as well as cognitive. Butler said that he even had the 'native habit of long silences', which he would break to tell a Zulu anecdote in a quaint, simplified style – the style that Rider used for his African characters and which has been copied ever since. Butler, with his Irish blarney, called it the 'language which the wild men fashion so easily out of the winds, the waters and the wilderness in which they live'.

The important element which influenced Rider's writing, and which eventually filtered through to generations of schoolboys, was a respect for African cultures. What Butler recognized, and what Shepstone had divined, was that a moral sense was not confined to the so-called civilized nations. Shepstone not only respected the tribal customs but perceived a natural morality inherent in the universe. Butler said of him, 'I think that a day's ride in the company of that old white Zulu chief and statesman was worth a whole term in a University.'[2] It was Shepstone who provided a University for Rider, but what must be remembered is that the course he read was anthropology and theology, not Imperial politics.

Shepstone as a political animal was another matter. He had been a colonial administrator in Natal for thirty years and guided the numerous Governors through their temporary offices. An authority on African law, his personal influence was second to none and he kept the reins firmly in his own hands. He was advocate and administrator of a system which kept the natives separate – a system which, though it protected them to some degree from the abuse of colonists, held within it the seeds of future strife. With little formal education, sixty years old, cunning, isolated and autocratic like the African chiefs he held at bay, Shepstone was a father figure of a most conservative type. Wolseley called him 'indolent', but Wolseley's energy was legendary. To a youth like Rider, still waking from his cocoon, Shepstone's prescient silences and succinct utterances, based not only on the native style but also on his Wesleyan missionary background, proved irresistible.

Initially, however, the dreariness and expense of Pietermaritzburg had a discouraging effect on Rider. At that time Maritzburg was

> little more than a village of thatched houses surrounded by flowers. The buildings were low, single-storeyed, and uniformly ugly. The government offices were housed in a structure described by one contemporary as 'a dilapidated barn on a bankrupt farm'. Wolseley found it in a state of 'unmitigated barbarism' when contrasted with the civilization he found at the Cape. Its sleepy, grass-grown streets were illuminated only on particularly dark nights when there was a moderate starlight.[3]

The climate was debilitating, giving rise to fevers which were usually fatal to children and often so to their mothers.

Bulwer was not a natural successor to Wolseley in areas requiring éclat. And there seemed to be no possibility of Rider becoming Bulwer's secretary; missing his friends and family, he felt himself to be out on a limb in the tawdry little town where emotions and conflicts were magnified. He wrote, 'This is a dreadful place for tragedies, accidents, sudden deaths, murder and suicides.' The life of the native population was even more violent. Mr Fynney, the official interpreter, filled his head with tales of Zulu witches who could keep 5,000 armed warriors in a state of terror as they waited to see who the dancing hags would condemn to death by a touch of their sticks.[4]

While Rider responded so readily to the old Africa hands, his relationship with Bulwer did not develop into that of protégé and benefactor. Bulwer was a cautious man, unable to delegate the heavy workload he carried and, by Rider's account, a jealous one, who resented Shepstone's experience and influence. In Shepstone, Rider had found the intuitive mentor that he needed to begin his journey of self-discovery. Shepstone's acceptance of 'primitive' cultures having a validity of their own provided Rider with the first stepping stone towards self-knowledge. He began to accept his own non-intellectual imaginative sensibilities as valuable in themselves.

Like Henry Graves, the hero of *Joan Haste*, Rider 'was a somewhat plain and silent boy, with a habit of courting his own society, and almost aggressive ideas of honour and duty'. Left to his own devices while his parents' love went out to the brighter brothers, Henry Graves 'said nothing, and he was too proud to be jealous, but nobody except the lad himself ever knew what he suffered under this daily, if unintentional neglect'. In Africa, for the first time, the failures of Rider's schooldays and the poor opinion of his parents could begin to be replaced by self-respect.

In contrast, Alfred, who had begun from a position of ambitious self-assurance, was beginning to find the going rough. A strong linguist, he had applied himself to the learning of Hindustani and in less than a year he had been promoted to the sub-division of Buxar. In Tirhoot, throughout the famine of 1874, he had been much concerned with establishing a new hospital, and then he returned to Buxar for a further eighteen months where his father-in-law had influenced his appointment as Officer-in-charge of the sub-division. From Buxar he had been transferred to Serampore, just thirteen miles from Calcutta, on the west bank of the Hooghly. He was soon to take up both a special appointment and a promotion to the position of Joint Magistrate, which would bring his nominal salary up to 850 rupees a month, or £1050 per annum.

Alfred's progress in the ICS was promising and, when the Bohemian Lord Lytton, a kinsman of Sir Henry Bulwer, replaced Lord Northbrook as Governor-General in 1876, Alfred achieved some distinction with his *Report on Civil Service Training*; Lytton thought Alfred a man of good mental ability and potential. The following year Queen Victoria was declared Empress of India, and the administration of India was bathed in increasingly glamorous light. Privately, Alfred confided to his father that he hoped eventually to become a Political Officer.

But Alfred had already met his *bête noire*, debt. Like many men in India, living up to his own view of his status meant living beyond his means. While he and Alice enjoyed a private performance of Nautch dancers at their bungalow, shopkeepers from Calcutta to Edinburgh dunned him for their bills. The fall in the value of the rupee was 'a terrible trial and the necessary expenses of living . . . enormous'. Although his prospects were good, he would only be 'making up a lea way in storm chase'.

Whether through stress or emotional disturbance, Alfred was finding it less and less easy to control his temper. And once it was unleashed he did not know how the situation would end. Sometimes it might be the stupidity of the chattering washerman which triggered an explosion, and mostly he could handle that – or Alice would handle it for him. The real problem was with his work, the witnesses who came before him and lied without a second thought. His blood would boil, and he did not know how to restrain himself. He tried to fight it intellectually, by reasoning with himself, but the anger was so great that sometimes he was afraid to go into court. His headaches got worse.

On 10 December 1875, Alfred rose long before sunrise – Alice and the boy were away with her family in Calcutta[5] – and began to read *Supernatural Religion*. He was frightened of the violent anger which welled up inside him, frightened of his inability to control it. There was no one to help him and he did not know where to turn. His sister Ella was the one person to whom he could unburden himself. He would write to Ella.

The news from home was increasingly interesting. Will had become engaged, a most desirable situation for the future head of the family; but apparently there was a hitch of some sort. Cissy, too, had at long last received a proposal – from Maximilian Western, a mechanical engineer in partnership with his brothers in a firm in Lambeth. That was not so bad in itself – his family lived in Harley Street.[6] However they were of a narrow religious sect, so the engagement could not be considered ideal. The Westerns themselves were not happy about the match. Still, the important thing was that Cissy would be a wife and mother, which must surely improve her little peculiarities.What Alfred could not quite grasp was why such an enormous rift had developed between the Bazetts and his parents. Judy, of course, was neither tactful nor considerate of his mother. Was it simply Bazett's extravagance which had caught the parental disapproval, or was there something more? Bazett, if he were now undutiful or disrespectful, must surely be acting under Julia's influence. Next year Alfred and Alice would be going home on leave, and he could find out for himself. He finished his letter, sent his love, and got ready to begin the day's work. Already he could sense dark patches round the edges of his mind.

For Will Haggard, far away in Washington, the workings of the mind never provided any problem. Outgoing, energetic and self-centred, he was entirely a man of the world, and if he spent any time imagining at all he certainly could not have imagined the outcome of his marriage to Carrie Carroll. Caroline Mary Carroll, the third daughter of the late William Thomas Carroll Esq. of Washington, was of Irish descent, and well connected.[7] It was not Will's mind but his libido and ambition that she had ensnared and, despite the various 'hitches', the wedding took

Elizabeth Cecilia Haggard was always called Cissy.
This thoughtful portrait was taken in 1875, at the
time of her betrothal to Max Western.

place on 11 December 1875 – when Alfred was only just hearing of its proposal. It was the kind of private wedding that Society loves – private for relatives and friends of the bride, the entire Diplomatic Corps, and various members of the government including President and Mrs Grant, and Secretary and Mrs Fish.

None of Will's family attended the American-style ceremony, which took place at the house of Mr Henry Randall at the corner of Eighteenth and Seventh Streets. According to a Washington newspaper, the bride wore 'a French toilette of celeste silk, made entraine, with poufs and shirrings, corsage high and covered with priceless lace. In her "fair golden hair" were flowers. Her ornaments were diamonds. She had long six-buttoned gloves, white, and carried a bouquet of Boston buds.'

Years later, Andrew Haggard was to say that she wore a yellow wig right from the beginning (as the newspaper's quotation marks would seem to indicate). Certainly Carrie was no blushing maiden, having already been married and divorced. She admitted to being twenty-six years old, but later her age came into doubt.

The winter wedding was an extravagant affair. The reception rooms were decorated with vines, and perfumed 'by the nectar of a thousand flowers'. The wedding breakfast included every 'luxury from sea and land including fresh strawberries'. The President himself signed the marriage certificate, together with the Secretary of State and the English Ambassador. A reporter noted that 'The President's presence was an extraordinary honour as he has never before attended the marriage of any Diplomat. He kissed the bride before taking his leave, and drank the health of the newly married pair again and again in goblet after goblet of Old Carroll Madeira bottled in the year 1801.'[8]

Mr and Mrs Will Haggard left on the afternoon train for New York and sailed for Europe, where Will hoped for an appointment to one of the prestigious European embassies – perhaps Vienna, the centre of the Habsburg empire. Rider wrote to his mother that he hoped the new Mrs Haggard did not have an awful American twang to her voice, and that her previous history would not give 'ill-natured people' a handle. When she arrived, Will's wife was horrified to find that Bradenham Hall, of which she had doubtless heard so much, still drew all its water from an outside well. The Wills settled in London where Will started to work at the Foreign Office.

It was a bustling, prosperous time in the capital, the economy still fuelled by gold which had come in from the Franco–Prussian War. The Tory party was back in power, the Government was buying shares in the Suez Canal and, as a maturing diplomat, the interests of the Empire were Will's interests. The anomalies of Imperial rule were such that various territories came directly under the control of the Foreign Office; moreover, the whole expanding thrust of the Empire was reflected in its relations with the European alliances and competing colonial powers.

Maximilian Richard Western in 1876. He left his family
firm in 1882 to become a Government Inspector in
Rangoon, and later an Inspecting Engineer in Egypt.

It was unfortunate, both for his domestic life and his career, that Carrie's temper was so uncontrolled; it made life awkward, especially as she accused him of infidelities. But he could always retreat to his club. It was a good time to be a gentleman in London, and it was good to be back with his family.

The family was in a state of much relief that Cissy had been unloaded on to Maximilian Western, with whom she was now living in genteel accommodation in a villa in Richmond.[9] Cissy became pregnant almost

immediately – rapid pregnancies were the Haggard norm, as Bazett and
Judy were finding with three sons already. Bazett, who had settled at
No. 2 Paper Buildings at the Temple, was on the Norfolk Circuit, but
he often aired his fancy for doing better in the Colonies. He had recently
aspired to a rather attractive property in south Norfolk, Kirby Cane Hall,
just outside Bungay. Its Georgian frontage belied a seventeenth-century
house with a galleried hall and a Caroline oak staircase of lordly pro-
portions. It was, of course, a ludicrous extravagance for a young barrister,
but its location was convenient – though not too close – to Bradenham
and young Mary was boarding nearby at Lowlands School on the edge
of Bungay. Among Mary's schoolfriends were the robust and forthright
Louisa Margitson of nearby Ditchingham House, and a skinny girl with
dark penetrating eyes and a sharp mind which would eventually help
strike the tinderbox of *She*: Agnes Barber.

In Africa, Rider was already amassing a storehouse of sights and experiences – his own Kimberley of the mind. The Transvaal Dutch were in
an increasingly untenable position. Landlocked and nearly bankrupt, they
were pushing the natives into smaller and smaller areas. The war-dances
of the Zulu warriors roused Rider from his boyhood and spurred Lord
Carnarvon into action. In August 1876, Carnarvon sent the newly
knighted Shepstone back to Africa with an ambiguous and unsigned
Royal Commission and instructions to annex the Transvaal with the
consent of the population. A transport bringing reinforcing battalions
followed Shepstone's ship.

In December, even though there was no evidence that King Cetywayo
would make an attack on the Transvaal, Shepstone made up his mind
to embark on what was called a special diplomatic mission to Pretoria.
He offered to take Rider with him. Bulwer objected, and would only
consider letting Rider go in a private capacity, and therefore unpaid.
Rider wanted to go on any terms. 'If I can go I shall go with the
expedition and then return to England in about three months time.' His
father replied, on 20 December, 'you must yourself be the best judge of
what is best, and that you had better come home as soon as you like.'
Mr Haggard suggested that Rider should consider studying at Cambridge
with a view to the Diplomatic or Colonial Service.

With the matter of his return settled, and Bulwer compliant at last,
Rider joined the 'diplomatic' mission. Shepstone paced out the journey
for thirty-five days, taking every opportunity to stop and talk to the
Boer settlers. With their fundamentalist religion and crude backwoods

manners, they were hardly likely to appeal to Rider – and they did not. It was many a long year before he had any sympathy for the Boers. But in another way, for Rider at the age of twenty, this trek was of the greatest significance: he benefited from the continual companionship of older, seasoned men. 'Indeed we were a band of brothers,' he wrote, 'as brothers ought to be.' And like Butler before him, Rider was deeply impressed by the splendour and drama of the landscape through which they travelled.

The mission, nominally one of support for the Boers, was not welcome. The British would use hospitality as a diversion, but the real business of Imperialism would be done in the usual way, with money and force of arms. Two months later, 13 March 1877, Rider wrote to his father that 'matters had been rapidly advancing, and drawing to a close'. Little opposition to annexation was expected from the Boers, since their ringleader 'had been bought . . . Gold has salved the hurt that honour feels'. Upon application from Rider, who wanted to get back to England to marry Lilly Jackson, Shepstone had agreed to send him home to deliver a verbal report to Lord Carnarvon about all that had transpired. Rider planned to travel overland down to the Cape to ensure that he arrived in London at the same time as the official despatches. The troops and guns were already on their way, in readiness for the 'ceremony' of Annexation.

The timing of the mail was never more critical than when Rider received a devastating letter from his father, forbidding his return to England and upbraiding him for his actions and attitudes. The Squire could not yet have received the news that Shepstone had arranged for Rider to be a personal messenger to Lord Carnarvon. He may have been unaware of Rider's intentions towards Lilly Jackson, or he may have suspected and been against the liaison.

The rationale is of little importance. Squire Haggard fed his need for dramatically charged scenes by prodding his children into reaction. He had acted in a similar manner with Alfred, but, being older, Alfred had fought back. It is quite possible that some of the siblings, including Alfred, may long ago have been irrevocably disturbed by the Squire's bullying. Rider, just beginning to gain confidence in himself, crumpled at his father's displeasure, and immediately changed his plans.

A few days later, on 12 April 1877, Rider joined the assembly in Pretoria's Market Square for the delivery of the proclamation, and on the Queen's birthday, 24 May, he assisted in running the Union Jack up the flagpole as the band played *God Save the Queen*, and at midday precisely the artillery of the 1st Battalion of the 13th Regiment boomed a salute. Having associated with great men of the Empire since his arrival in Africa, this was the moment in which Rider felt that he himself was entering the historical framework.

It was not long before Shepstone was heavily criticized for the Annexation, and everyone associated with it fell into disfavour. A hundred years later, it has been seen to be the critical moment when the balance between the British, the Dutch and the Zulus was tipped. Cetywayo, who hated the Boers but had been loyal to Shepstone and unwilling to attack the British, now saw Shepstone apparently allying with the Zulus' enemies. Suddenly the British were no longer a separate tribe, but at one with the Dutch in the Transvaal. Cetywayo need no longer hold back, and an attack on the British, from this moment, was inevitable. The tri-partite standoff had been transformed into one of Blacks against Whites.

Quietly, and with dignity, Rider obtained a position as English Clerk to the Colonial Office with a salary of £250 per annum. In June, he wrote a rather mournful letter to his mother contemplating spending his life in Africa and, as Christmas approached, his desolation increased. He missed his home and his mother as much as he did his sweetheart. Indeed, his friendship with Lilly was quite slight. But Lilly was an icon of the utmost potency – in the Jungian cosmos Rider had projected on to her his own Anima, the feminine aspect of his soul. He still hoped that he would be able to marry her.

Mary, Ella and Rider's mother were privy to his private hopes and fears, but Ella at least had other things to occupy her, for at long last one of her babies survived. Charles Arthur Maddison Green, to be known as Arthur, was born on 17 June 1877 and, so overjoyed were the proud parents, the Reverend Maddison Green ordered the church bells to be rung loud and long over the village of Lyonshall.

The birth of a child to Carrie was just what Will Haggard feared most. His relationship with his wife had rapidly deteriorated, and she had told him she was pregnant – which had thankfully proved to be false. But the thought of her child being the heir to Bradenham was too dreadful to contemplate. In 1877, after consultations with his solicitor and his parents, and despite the damage it would do to his career, Will determined to leave Carrie. He was already in the undignified position of retreat – even to the extent of hiding under a dining room table to avoid her –

so he asked for a transfer to somewhere as far away from a rail head as possible. The Foreign Office came up with Teheran, which involved an arduous journey on horseback as well as a long tramp by foot.

Alfred Thacker was working in the stables at Bradenham when Will strode in and asked him if he would go with him to Persia. Thacker remembered:

> It came as a great surprise to me. I did not know how to answer him. He said, my notice has been short and yours shorter. 'I must know this evening, Yes or No.' Now these two words will remain in my memory they had such a meaning. Had any other gentleman asked me in this way probably I should have said No. Knowing Mr William as I did, and all the family, I took this advantage in saying Yes, as it might prove to my benefit ... I went and said goodbye to the Esquire and Mrs Haggard. He said 'I am sorry to lose you but as you are going with my son I will not stand in your light and I wish you well.' Mr William came in [and] said why he particularly wanted me. I was used to horses and in that country was all horseback work, no railways.

And so it was settled that Thacker accompanied Will on his journey via Brindisi to catch a P & O steamer for Bombay, where Will was keen to visit Alfred and Alice. After that their route took them up the Persian Gulf to Bushire where the real travelling began. Thacker came into his own, choosing the horses that were strong enough to undertake the 1,000 miles overland trek to Isfahan, Shiraz and Teheran.

These wild eastern places were scarcely what Will had been hoping for, but at least the Great Game which Britain played with Russia over the northern borders of India and Afghanistan gave some significance to the posting. He teamed up with a Norfolk neighbour, Guy Le Strange, and together they wrote *The Vazir of Laukuram* as a language guide for travellers, which was noted for its risqué footnotes.

Rider, too, was pulling himself together and beginning to write articles, and he proposed a visit to Will.[10] In late November Will wrote back, congratulating him on his sketch of Shepstone printed in the *World* and, in his lofty, older-brother tone, he encouraged Rider about his prospects. As far as the journey was concerned, he advised that it would take fourteen weeks and cost £140. The trip never took place.

In the first week of April 1878, Rider was appointed Master and Registrar of the High Court in the Transvaal, at an annual salary of £300 or £400 – a sum which guaranteed his independence. For a few months, his hopes of marrying Lilly gushed to the surface, and he swam in a hot bath of euphoria. The blow, when it came, was all the more deadly. Perhaps she had only been toying with him as she looked for a more mature husband. Perhaps, like Eva in *The Witch's Head*, she was ashamed of loving one so young, and was too weak to stand up for herself in the face of family pressure. Quite probably, she was attracted to Francis Bradley Archer, an affluent stockbroker. Whatever the case, they married on 4 June 1878 in St James's Church, Westminster, and went to live at Somers Place — just around the corner from the Bazetts. For the moment Lilly had escaped the prospect of colonial life in far-off Africa, but she could not halt the influence of the Haggards on the Jacksons, nor could she foresee how that influence would come, full circle, back to her.

Rider pencilled in her wedding day in his pocket diary. After a period of suicidal misery, he did as other young men do; he chummed up with another bachelor, Arthur Cochrane. Free from his bond to Lilly, he and Arthur cheerfully allowed themselves the pleasures of youth. The scales fell from his eyes, and he began to see the world in its true colours: if beautiful women were fickle, it did not make them less beautiful, and there were plenty of women around. The trick was to expect less of life and then, suddenly, one would no longer be disappointed.[11]

Rider and Arthur built a house, which they humorously called the Palatial. Rider wrote confidently and authoritatively to his father about his law cases, as well as commenting on the temptations of life in the colonies and the undesirability of marrying colonial girls. By November 1876, he aired once more the possibility of coming home, and again noted the temptations open to a young man who has no English girl at home to keep him straight. These were warning signals that Rider was getting into hot water.

Although at first he did not feel it, the water into which Lieutenant Jack Haggard plunged when he became engaged to Etta White was icy cold. No marriage settlements were drawn up, so she provided only a distant solace to Jack in his new posting to HMS *Flora*, a naval base on Ascension Island administered by the Colonial Office. His family said he was sent there because he had quarrelled with every commanding officer under whom he had served. If it was, indeed, a kind of ostracism, the garrison was well-suited as a punishment. Indeed, if Napoleon had not been imprisoned on St Helena, it seems unlikely that anyone would ever have thought of living on the godforsaken Ascension.

Somewhere out in the South Atlantic, a little south of the Equator and halfway between Portuguese West Africa (Angola) and Brazil, lay this remote volcanic mound some four miles square. In the Victorian world, Ascension was a coaling station for the West Africa Squadron and for steamships heading for Cape Town. Jack arrived in August 1878.

> From a distance the island looks a rugged mass of volcanic rocks thrown one on top of the other anyhow. When you get nearer you can see several distinct craters (there are 42 altogether) of a brightish red colour with the old lava streams running from them. On the top of the highest peak of all, the Green Mountain as it is called (3000 feet high) between the masses of clinker you can see, here and there, a green patch through a spy glass. Beyond the Green Mountain there is not a patch of green to relieve the eye, not a herb of any kind, nothing but red and black clinkers so palpably burnt stone that you almost imagine them to be hot still . . . and it looks so fresh and new that you can almost fancy the great convulsions of nature that caused it took place yesterday.

The desolate landscape was reflected in the inhabitants, manifesting as an apathetic mental malaise. Jack remarked that 'No one laughs and but seldom speaks,' and the people were devoid of curiosity.

> The settlement is a very small town consisting of barracks for a detachment of Marines, the store houses for containing coal etc . . . and a number of huts used for various purposes. Besides these there are the officers' houses a little further away from the jetty. The jetty is a solid stone pier at which everyone lands and all stores are hoisted on shore. The landing is very bad and often impossible.

There was an unceasing, monotonous, howling south-east trade wind, a water shortage, a food shortage, and none of Jack's messmates were gentlemen. Meals lasted for only twenty minutes, because no one talked. Of the population of 614, there were too few women – or too many, depending upon how you viewed it; the married men kept to their homes but there were inevitable complications.

Jack had been warned by his friend Charlie Fitton about his superior officer, Captain Phillimore.[12] A practice of corruption in the handling of stores had grown up over the years which was now so entrenched it was accepted as the norm. This was an abuse which Jack was determined to uproot. There was also considerable physical work to be done; the island was a turtling station and a limestone quarry, and the Navy was aiming to get several big guns up the mountain by June. For the heaviest work there were labourers from Sierra Leone, but most days included long hours of hard physical labour.

Jack in his late twenties or early thirties, in the full-dress uniform
of a Lieutenant of the Royal Navy. His campaign medal is presumably
from Abyssinia.

At first, Jack thought the place would suit him, 'as I care neither for
good fare nor company', but he soon found that he often went hungry,
and that the solitude, 'like the plague of darkness . . . can be felt'. As a
redhead with fair skin he suffered from excruciating sunburn. He spent
all his evenings alone with his two dogs, Spice and Black, which he had
had the foresight to bring with him. He poured out his observations into
long, diary-like letters to his parents. One of the most haunting impres-

sions of Ascension was of the wind and the sea, which assaulted the rocky shore with 'rollers': 'Imagine the sea to be quite calm and smooth as far as the horizon. Suddenly you see a huge wall of water rolling in (without breaking) until it strikes the shore with a noise like thunder. This wave is probably followed by others of the same sort, after which there may be an interval of unequal lengths of time from a minute to an hour when another set will roll in.' These series of grand rollers occurred every fortnight or so, and made any landing in the harbour quite impossible. Jack was expecting to stay in Ascension for three years but, by January 1880, he was sent home on sick leave. His teeth had rotted from years of poor diet, with the consequence of chronic indigestion. His naval testimonial remarked sparsely on his sobriety and his ability to maintain discipline.

5

Youth Is the Time for Mating

Sir Bartle Frere's ultimatum to Cetywayo in November 1878, demanding the disbanding of his armies and the acceptance of a British Resident, was intended to produce the opportunity for a military offensive. All those who knew anything about the Zulus expected a disaster. Melmoth Osborn in particular warned against Lord Chelmsford's advance into Zululand, in the northern part of Natal. But the 24th Regiment, the Warwickshires, rode out in January 1879, optimistically carrying with them their cricketing outfits. They crossed the Buffalo River into Zululand at a spot called Rorke's Drift, where they left sixty men of the 2nd Battalion under Colonel Bromehead and Lieutenant Chard of the Royal Engineers. They marched by road, and encamped on the evening of 20 January under 'the shadow of a steep-cliffed and lonely mountain called Isandlawhana'.

Isandlawhana was the most spectacular defeat which the British suffered in Africa. The bloodcurdling story of 20,000 Zulu warriors bearing down on 1,700 British soldiers beneath the desolate hill was told and retold – many times by Rider himself – until the whole episode became chillingly glorious.[1]

Rider was in Pretoria when the news arrived, and he wrote at once to his father 'in great haste to tell you of the terrible disaster that has befallen our troops in Zululand . . . Osborn's son-in-law died, and his family wandering about in the Veld. We are sending to their assistance. I have just sent all the money I have in gold to help people.' He ends his letter, unconvincingly, 'Don't be alarmed however,' and with the caution, 'and *don't* publish this.'

Several days later, Rider confirmed the news, commenting that it was the 'old story of underrating your enemy'. He asked his parents not to be alarmed 'when I tell you that I shall very likely go down to the Border with a Volunteer's Troop shortly. The emergency is too grave, and mounted men are too urgently needed, for us to hang back now, especially when one's example may bring others.'

The Dutch and the civilians were not, however, so keen to face the plumed and chanting 'Children of Heaven', and it seemed unlikely that the colonial officials would be allowed to go. Soon the full horror of what had happened became apparent: the British dead had been stripped of their uniforms and disembowelled.

Rider was struck by the fact that his Hottentot washerwoman had received a telepathic message which brought her news of Isandlawhana twenty hours before the official messenger rode in exhausted. How was such a thing possible? White men in South Africa came up against mystical and magical powers which, in Europe, had been eroded by civilization. African witch doctors could find things which had been lost, or animals which had strayed: Rider used such an incident in *Nada the Lily*. Such powers were unsettling and, for Rider, it was impossible to ignore the fact that it was not the intellect but another kind of consciousness – a far more powerful consciousness – at work. He began to wonder about the hidden depths of the human spirit and its relationship to the eternal.

By the end of April or early May 1879, Rider had finally made up his mind to leave the Colonial Service to which, without proper legal training, he was ill-suited, and to join with his friend Arthur Cochrane in a farming venture. They had arranged to buy a property at Rooi Point near Newcastle from Melmoth Osborn, for £1,400 – £1000 down and £400 in eight months. They would also rent the house known as Hill Drop with its 250 surrounding acres, with the right to purchase in five years at £1,500. Rather than selling the Palatial in Pretoria they decided to rent it out and mortgage it in England. The plan was to stock up the farm with ostriches, and then for Rider to come home. His mother had been ill, and Rider could not bear to stay away any longer. Just as pressing, however, was the need to raise some capital at a reasonable rate of interest.

It was also in the interests of discretion that Rider should take leave of absence. Both Rider and Cochrane had had affairs with white settlers in Pretoria: Cochrane with Josephine, a young unmarried woman, and Rider with an accommodating Mrs Ford, referred to as 'the Gay Missus', who was pregnant with his child.

Knowing that his father would disapprove of his leaving the Colonial

Service, Rider wrote ahead to smooth the way for his homecoming. To this end he also enlisted Andrew's help, and suggested that he might like to invest £1000 in the Newcastle farm. Andrew consulted his father confidentially about this proposal and requested that, on his return, Rider come to him at Plymouth before travelling to Bradenham. The Squire had already consulted Shepstone (who had been summarily recalled) over Rider's plans, and had not been encouraged by Shepstone's opinion.

Face to face with Andrew in Plymouth, Rider was evidently very persuasive about the farm, because Andrew wrote to his father with new enthusiasm for the enterprise and urged him not to press Rider to return to 'Pretoria in an official capacity'. Their cousin Amyand Haggard joined them at Devonport for a reunion, and he later recalled meeting Andrew's mistress, or common-law wife, Mary Dixon. Mary was from Beverley, and she had probably met Andrew there or at York.

When Rider and Amyand departed, Andrew brooded on his future. He wrote again to his father on 26 August, in a letter which reveals the family attitude to Rider: 'I hope you will agree with me that he is not such a fool as we thought him . . . the mill they are going to establish I think an excellent thing and I should like very much to put £500 or £600 into it with them . . . When you consider that people must have corn that there is no other mill within 200 miles . . . and that there are coals on the spot . . . it must pay very well.' Andrew was very short of cash, living in a state 'of genteel poverty Devilish genteel but deucedly poor so poor that I often have not a single shilling in my pocket just now notably for expenses have been very heavy lately'. No doubt Mary was one of those expenses, and possibly there was also a child. Still conspiratorial, Andrew ended his letter with the request that it was not to be discussed with Charles and Ella – Ella had a reputation for forthright opinion.

Winter was coming to an end in South Africa, and Arthur Cochrane soon found it a lonely life at the new farm without his partner. The Firm, as they called their enterprise, was heavily in debt to a bank; without Rider, Arthur's youthful optimism waned, his anxiety about the future magnified, and he wrote copious letters to his friend.[2] The ostriches were more than a handful – vicious-natured beasts which could kill or maim a man. Rider had already sent out some pine trees to plant, and Cochrane had established a fence of roses; but without the expected manure from Newcastle, he had to wait to plant fruit and vegetables. He had bought six oxen for £56, and sold 400 oranges for 12 shillings per hundred, but their total income from July to August was £16. He hoped Rider's first letter would end the money worries – surely someone back home would come up with the cash. It would be such a nuisance to have to renew their loan from the Standard Bank, rates being so high. Cochrane also needed Rider's advice on personal matters. He was anxious to keep Josephine at arm's length, but his resolve often melted in the heat of her charms.

For Rider, no advice would alter the fact that at the end of the summer Mrs Ford had a baby. Cochrane wrote, 'the event has come off – a girl – we are to be Godfathers – at least I am – Mr Ford said he felt highly honoured at the compliment we paid him and his family – what a rum world this is . . .'

A letter from Rider telling him that he was proposing to return to the Colonial Service put Cochrane into a state of alarm and indignation. The battle with Squire Haggard had evidently taken a new turn, on top of which, he wrote to Rider, 'your letter gives me to understand that £1000 is all we can raise. If that's the case bang goes the mill – £1000 will not enable us to carry out that scheme and allow at the same time money enough to pay off the Standard Bank (which bill by the way will shortly fall due, shall we be able to pay it or must I renew)', and 'we shall have to begin on altogether a different scale to which I thought'. Arrangements had already been made for a family friend, young George Blomefield, to join the Firm with £550;[3] now Cochrane proposed taking on another partner to invest in the farm.

Amidst all these troubles, Cochrane had been savaged by an ox:

> . . . he came full tilt at the pit of my stomach I jumped away and prevented him ripping me by catching hold of one of his horns with both my hands he all the time digging away at me – by exerting all my strength I kept him off but unfortunately he swung round and jammed me against the trek tow – and gradually bent me backwards goring at me the whole time at last I fell and in falling let go my hold he ripped my trousers and gave me a slight wound on the thigh he then trampled me, putting one hind foot on my groin just missing the old gentleman and appendages – thank God – I then got clear but was very much shaken and bruised . . . the Kafirs caught the ox again we tied him up and knocked him silly with a yoke skey we then inspanned him and I had the satisfaction of lamming him until I could hit no longer . . . No news from Pretoria nothing since the birth of the youthful young one . . . once hit twice shy remember – I'm all right so far.

By October the loyal Cochrane was downright disappointed at Rider's lack of success, and the outlook was bleak. Tactfully, Cochrane sent news that 'Mrs F's baby is a dear little thing, a big child not one of those puny little things', which he anticipated 'will be as alike as two peas'. He was beginning to become seriously fond of his 'jay' and, when Josephine attempted suicide with laudanum, Cochrane agreed to an engagement. To his much needed friend, he wrote, 'I am afraid there will be a heavy reckoning for us two when we go to Pretoria – together – Yes, as you say when she finds that you are determined she will arrive, or some infernal thing, it would be utterly impossible for either of us to think of going back to live in Pretoria – and you, more than I, may think yourself devilish lucky if you get out of the whole business all clear. As for me if the worst comes to the worst I could marry the girl – but you have not even the resource.'

Isandlawhana had now settled into the public perception as something of a novelty. Cochrane answered Rider's request for some Zulu spears with the hugely ironic information, 'I am sorry to say they are awfully scarce here, everybody is buying them and getting them to take home . . .'

Whether to placate his father, or because he was in actual fact getting cold feet – and Cochrane's letters might certainly have produced that effect – Rider attempted unsuccessfully to withdraw his resignation from the Colonial Service and to enlist the help of Melmoth Osborn.

On 8 November 1879, Cochrane, in urgent need of funds and facing a drought, wrote a letter which is unlikely to have arrived before the end of the month at the earliest. In it he enclosed a telegram 'telling of the sudden death of my young God child and of your –? Yes, the poor little thing is dead and perhaps it is a good thing for all concerned.' He added 'I hope to goodness there will be no ravings etc, or any unhappy sentences which may be spoken while under the influence of the great grief she will look upon it as a punishment and I think that it is for the best.'

Two weeks later he followed up with some good news. 'Osborn has agreed to take a bond on the Palatial for his £420.' And they were getting good prices for ostrich feathers. On the black side, Rider's horse Moresco had escaped and was lost, there still had been no rain, and on the whole Cochrane was 'afraid that we are doing or trying to do more than we can manage'.

In Pretoria, 'Mrs F seemed awfully cut up at the loss of the baby poor little thing perhaps it were best after all, for all concerned. Phinny [Josephine] seems to have had a great affection for it and mentions casually that it was not like any of *Mr Ford's* children. The Gay [Mrs Ford – the Gay Missus] is quiet, but I expect biding her time – we must be very careful for you . . .'

Rider apparently wrote back in a state of excitement about the possibility of Cochrane marrying Josephine, because Arthur's next letter, dated 27 November 1879, attempts to reassure him: 'knowing what I do it is scarcely probable that I should risk being put in Ford's position in years to come – No old fellow I fear much more for you than I do for myself. I can only thank God, though sorry for your sake that the child was taken it would surely have led to trouble –'.

The news of the death of his daughter may not have reached Rider until December but he must already have realized that he would do well to marry. To Andrew, also staying at Bradenham, the advantage of a good marriage was equally obvious. Their sister Mary began inviting suitable friends to stay. Round about 25 November, Louisa Margitson visited for three or four days. She was a soldier's daughter; a keen horse-woman, strong, and solid-gold in terms of integrity and strength of character. Her mother had just recently died, leaving her, at twenty, under the guardianship of three uncles. She lived with her companion Miss Hildyard at Ditchingham House in south Norfolk, on the estate that her great-grandfather John Margitson had purchased in 1817. She was an heiress.

Within those few days at the end of November 1879 both Andrew and Rider fell in love with Louie Margitson. They were both affectionate, amusing and full of go, but Louie's heart went to Rider. Seizing his moment Rider proposed and was accepted at once. Louie informed her Uncle Hartcup and, when he laughed, she assumed it was his form of approval.

Andrew was unaware that Rider had already spoken and been accepted and, when he found out, he was devastated and confessed to Louie his feelings for her. Equally smitten, Rider wrote to Louie:

My past life has been so very lonesome and unhappy, that the prospect of your sweet companionship, of your true love, seems almost too good to be true. It is like coming out of the darkness with light . . . Dearest and best you shall never regret this step if I can help it; if it is in the power of man to make you happy, you shall be happy – My past may have been reckless enough, but my future shall atone for it.

Immediate enquiries were made to Mr Hartcup about Louie's income, and the reply delighted Rider's parents. 'Rider is indeed a fortunate young man,' wrote Mrs Haggard to her husband on 7 December 1879. '. . . it is a great satisfaction to us to know Rider is likely to be so well settled, and no further anxiety there – and it is a happy consequence of his coming home, which appeared to you at first a doubtful move.'

Between visits to Bungay (or Bung-g-g-ay, as his brothers and sisters teased him) Rider wrote to Louie almost daily – they were rather mundane letters lightened only by the occasional schoolboy joke, but they established the habit of a lifetime. The lack of romance may be accounted for by the fact that they expected to marry at once. Indeed, by 10 December, Rider was distinctly impatient that the necessary papers were not forthcoming. He was anxious to settle up and get back to Africa. He had already written to Will in Teheran suggesting that he and Louie travel out via Persia in April or May. Little did Rider know how long he would have to wait for his 'own sweet Louie'.

It soon became clear that the Hartcups were not going to approve the match. William Hartcup wrote in the strongest terms to Louie about her behaviour in receiving Rider at Ditchingham on her own, and in allowing him to stay there.[4] Louie's defiant manner gave Uncle Hartcup plenty of scope for complaint. Hartcup was a well-to-do solicitor in Bungay with the advantage of having the insurance company of Norwich Union as a client. It was scarcely likely that ostrich farming in Africa would recommend Rider to him as a suitor for his ward. He did not care to lose control of the Ditchingham estate so easily. John Margitson's complicated will had a codicil which, at first sight, appeared to provide that Louisa would only be a life tenant of Ditchingham. But, as Hartcup and the Haggards soon ascertained, the codicil would not stand, and the Will itself provided for Louie to inherit the estate without any reservation.

Hartcup swiftly made Louie a ward in Chancery. But if Hartcup was quick to invoke the law, Rider was keen to protect Louie from her guardians, of whom he thought one a drunkard, another a fool, and Hartcup he suspected of being a villain. Seeing the advantage of the match, Squire Haggard was wholeheartedly and financially behind Rider. And while Hartcup must have known that the Haggards would not be deterred by litigation, he may not have realized that they actually relished a fight: their letters leave no doubt that their blood was up.

In late January and early February 1880 there was much coming and going between Ditchingham, Kirby Cane, Sussex Gardens, Richmond

An informal picture of Louisa Margitson and Rider Haggard, with
his sister Mary standing behind. The picture was taken at a
photographer's in Queen Street, Norwich, at the time of their
romance in 1879/80.

and Bradenham, as Louisa was enveloped into the Haggard family. In London, she stayed with her aunt in lodgings at Cambridge Street while Rider stayed close by at the Bazetts'. Andrew came to take tea with her, Jack came to call. At Ditchingham Mary and Arthur stayed with her. Judy whisked her off to see her new court dress in the making, and then on to Mayfair to view the pictures in the Grosvenor Galleries. Judy also took her to see Cissy, now a mother of three girls and pregnant with a fourth. Louie was running the gauntlet, but she put Rider through his paces with her many maternal relatives in Clapton.

At a hearing before the Vice-Chancellor in mid-February, a letter from the influential Theophilus Shepstone helped tip the scales in the couple's favour. The marriage was deemed 'suitable', and the proposals for marriage settlements were to go ahead. Uncle Hartcup continued to delay the wedding, but he could not stop it. Rider went forth merrily enough to the Colonial Office, where he submitted a fresh application for employment, and to visit the Western brothers' engineering works in Belvedere Road, Lambeth, to order a mill from Max.[5]

Louie and her aunt removed to the respectable seaside resort of East-bourne, for Louie to keep out of the way of the Hartcups. She was beginning to feel the strain of her situation, and Rider advised her to 'take just as much quinine as will go on a [silver] threepenny bit, and you will be right as ninepence'. In his daily letters, Rider instructed her on restrained behaviour towards her guardians and against any 'bursts of confidence' to her cousin Jessie.

But Rider himself, knowing that the Firm's loan was due for repayment, was on a merry-go-round of nervous indecision. Capriciously he thought he might inspect George Blomefield's fiancée in Scotland. He knew he must visit the Maddison Greens in Herefordshire, who were expecting him to tell them all about Louie. He sent Louie word that he had decided to go to Cumberland for a week, Scotland for a week and then to Herefordshire. Then he got into a complete muddle with his arrangements for Herefordshire, since he must also organize a visit to his Aunt and Uncle Fowle at Brinsop. At the last minute he abandoned his plans to go to Scotland, instead taking a jaunt to Cambridge to visit his youngest brother Arthur at Pembroke College. The 'festive Arthur', as Rider called him, did him the honours, and Rider spent his time eating heroically and watching rowing races on the river. More than likely he renewed his acquaintance with Frederick Jackson.

Louie, meanwhile, had spotted from the newspaper that Melmoth

Osborn was to appoint a secretary, and Rider, jumpy as a cat, immediately decided to apply. The ostrich farm must have looked like a poor bet and the news from Africa was frightening: Cochrane's engagement to Josephine was on again!

In a melodramatic sub-plot, Hartcup took advantage of Louie's absence in Eastbourne to take a high hand. He strode into Ditchingham House like a stage villain, declaring that he was 'the master here', and dismissed the groom for walking out with the parlour maid. Louie, perfectly satisfied with both servants, realized that she must have a spy in the camp; it transpired that her cook, who had her own designs on the groom, had been telling all kinds of tales to the Hartcups about Louie and Rider. To top it all, her cousin Jessie was turning against her, while writing to Louie, 'I agree with you that the talk of the neighbourhood is very unpleasant, especially when there is much in it.'

Unknown to Rider, Louie had another burden to bear. Andrew had made her promise not to tell Rider that he was in love with her, which promise she made, 'not thinking of the consequences'. But by mid-March, Louie felt things were beginning to get out of hand, and she wrote to Rider: 'I had a letter from Andrew today, which has not improved my spirits, there is such an undertone of bitterness running through all he says. He has also I fear been getting into fresh scrapes, making love to 4 young women at once! Remember this is *strictly private* don't lead him to suppose I have made these remarks if you write to him.'

Rider, having settled his visiting schedule for Herefordshire, exasperated Louie with his plan to travel on Good Friday, the worst possible day for trains. She, in the meantime, had returned to Bungay via London, where she began to put her trousseau together. While in London, Andrew had come to visit her, and a very painful interview had taken place which she attributed to his 'unnatural excitement'. She begged him to release her from her promise, but he would not, 'saying it would only make an everlasting breach between [Rider] and him.' On her return to Ditchingham she received a letter from Andrew which was so disturbing that she decided to break her silence.

Andrew was tremendously fond of Rider, but there was a jealousy, too, which did not resolve itself for many years. Andrew's 'unnatural excitement' may have indicated that he was neurotic, or that his restless libido was frustrated by his unhappy relationship with Mary Dixon. Andrew accused Rider and Louie of writing anonymous letters to 'an unoffending person' – presumably Mary Dixon. These letters apparently disclosed Haggard family affairs, setting her against 'the only man in the world she had to cling to and making her hate him'. The whole episode was both obscured and intensified by Andrew telling Louie that he had found out about the letters through a revelation from God, after a period of supplication and prayer. It seems that someone had taken it upon themselves to inform Mary Dixon that Andrew was looking for a wife elsewhere. Having been found out, he was in an awkward and, no doubt, extremely uncomfortable position; whether he had had a religious experience, a medicinally induced hallucination, or was suffering from paranoia is not clear.

His letter continues in the tone of a blackmailer. 'Now then to write plainly what reparation ought do you think be made? For poisoning the mind of one to whom ignorance was happiness; but to whom to be written to as she was to instil hatred and despair into her mind?' He finishes in an irate flurry: 'I said I was unhappy and I am; but do you mean to say that you and he have not both thoroughly been understanding each other about me? and that you do not both desire to see me out of the country as soon as possible?' One imagines that he might well have liked to escape abroad, but did he want Rider and Louie to foot the bill? Ludicrously, he signed the letter: 'Believe me to remain Yrs affectly, Andrew CP Haggard'.

Louie, while immediately sending Andrew's letter on to Rider in Lyonshall, also replied on 31 March 1880 in her clear, bell tones: 'I cannot even guess at the name of the young lady and certainly do *not* know the person to whom you allude. I thought you knew me better than to imagine I could lend myself to anything so unladylike as clandestine correspondence. You must be under some extraordinary delusion. I will forward your letter to Rider and he will doubtless write to you about it.'

Rider requested Andrew not to communicate with Louisa 'on any pretext whatsoever' in future. To Louie he wrote cheerfully, 'I think Andrew must have been off his head when he wrote to you that wonderful epistle. He is behaving like an unmitigated ass . . .' Meanwhile, Arthur Cochrane had admitted to Rider that he had been 'infernally jealous' of Louie, and had 'hated' her, until he got a letter from her the tone of which made him think that she would not come between himself and Rider. Fraternal relationships between young men were often extraordinarily strong – the band of brothers – because of the exclusion of women from their working lives. Rider's engagement was certainly causing a remarkable number of ripples. But, as Rider so often reminded Louie, nothing worthwhile ever came easily.

Back at Bradenham, Cissy had come home for a visit, and her antics caused Rider to comment facetiously that she and Andrew 'had better set up a private Bedlam'. Cissy was teetering on the brink of mental breakdown and it is even possible that she was the author of the anonymous letters to Mary Dixon. But, as spring warmed the bleak Norfolk landscape, Rider and Louie, far from being undermined by their situation, grew more affectionate. Jack, home from Ascension Island, would go rook shooting with Rider, and together they would plan imaginary voyages around the world ending up in Jack's idea of paradise, Vancouver Island. When Rider went to stay at Bungay (at the King's Head) Jack accompanied him and put up with the Bazetts at Kirby. A quarrel brewed up between Jack and Bazett over the care of some geological specimens which Jack had entrusted to him. Louie already knew enough to be careful of Judy and her fragile relationship with Mr and Mrs Haggard. Considering that Louie was an only child, the intricate Haggard jealousies and rivalries seem to have made very little impression on her. Even when she visited Ella and Charles in May, she remarked that she found little to frighten her in the Haggards. It was just as well.

Charles and Ella had a new baby – little Ella – who had arrived the year before. Their small society in Lyonshall was also expanding in prestige: Charles's cousin Richard Green, a wealthy railway financier, had bought The Whittern, a house on the other side of the church. Richard Green began to invest in cattle breeding, a suitable background to public life as a staunch conservative and eventually High Sheriff of the County. Charles himself had been appointed Rural Dean of Weobley and was increasingly involved in diocesan affairs.

Temporarily, Alfred and Alice had also made a home close by. Alfred had suffered a nervous breakdown, nominally from overwork, and they had come home from India on sick leave. But underlying this illness was a serious ideological crisis: Alfred either would not or could not concur with British policy in India. One of his granddaughters believes that he was asked to retire from the ICS and, although there is no written record of this, it is quite likely – and it would probably have been done verbally to avoid scandal. This would be a devastating blow both morally and financially, and Alfred's health was a matter of grave concern.

The same was now true of Cissy. At Bradenham she had taken to prophesying 'the most awful evil to all and every member of her family', to whose sins she declared she was privy. Rider called her a 'modern Cassandra'. As the young Haggards, in blazers and straw hats, enlivened the summer tennis parties and croquet matches of Norfolk, the pregnant Cissy lurked like a Gothic horror up at the Hall.

The letters from Africa flowed in, as Cochrane manfully continued the struggle with the ostriches and the bank. Resourcefully, he embarked on a new project – brickmaking! And, by the way, he was *definitely* engaged to Josephine but he assured Rider that he would not allow her family to be familiar with them. Mrs Ford was getting into a state about Rider's wedding; 'I suppose it will be a case of "prussic" when the morning arrives for the celebration of your nuptials but joking apart, she really seems to be entirely crushed and she is very anxious to know the day of your marriage and begs me let her know when it will be.'

Cochrane could not help but mention, with a touch of sarcasm, that 'your matrimonial arrangements seem to be of the most expensive sort possible – but of course you do not care so long as the wish of your heart be gratified, and I've no doubt that with your powerful friends at home that with their help you will pull through all right. I don't think Osborn's secretaryship would suit you as you do not know the language . . .' Cochrane had raised a loan and hoped that Blomefield would be arriving soon – which he did, Rider having packed him off at the beginning of June.

By the end of July Rider had decided not to rejoin the Colonial Service, of which Cochrane was mightily glad, although he was forced to sell the Palatial. After eight months of wrangling, Rider and Louie finally stood before the altar at Ditchingham Church on 11 August 1880. The final skirmish with Hartcup was over the ceremony itself, since the parson at Ditchingham, Mr Scudamore, was under Hartcup's thumb. Rider had asked an old friend, D. L. Davies, the vicar of Benfleet near Chelmsford, to marry them. Davies replied good-naturedly: 'You will of course send me particulars as soon as they are known – for dear boy you are more or less in the hands of the ladies already. If they do you the honour to consult you in such matters you ought to be thankful.'

Rider was indeed thankful to be marrying a girl whose uncomplicated love was expressed in these lines:

> Oh where oh where is your daring Rider gone?
> He's gone to fight old Hartcup for the settlements aren't done.
> And its oh in my heart that I wish him safe at home.

Oh how and oh how is your Norfolk laddie clad?
His breeches they are baggy and his coat fits awful bad.
And its oh in my heart that I think its very sad.

Oh when and oh when will your Norfolk Lad come home,
When lawyers are defeated then straight back he will come,
And I'll crown him with laurels my bonnie Norfolk man.

Unknown to the family, Andrew and Mary Dixon were married by special licence on 18 October 1880, at the Minster church of Saints John and Martin in Beverley. Andrew and Mary gave their address as Well Lane, but they soon moved round the corner to Cross Street. Mary Dixon was already ill with tuberculosis. Her married life lasted little more than three months; she died on 22 January 1881, leaving behind a child, probably a daughter, of whom there is now no trace. When the marriage was discovered, the news travelled like wildfire around the Haggard family, reaching their cousin Captain Amyand Haggard at sea on HMS *Eclipse*. He replied to his mother's letter on 5 March, saying:

> what an ass Andrew seems to have made of himself, I don't understand his getting married to that girl. I met her when I was at Plymouth in the *Hercules* and also when I was there in this ship. She was a farmer's daughter I think, and seemed quiet enough but certainly not a lady. I thought he was tired of her, but I suppose he thought that as the poor thing would not live long it was best to marry her. What do my Uncle and Aunt say about it? and is the child his?

Amyand then referred to another tragedy which was besetting his cousins: 'What a miserable thing about Cissy? Is she likely ever to get right again?'

At the beginning of 1881, Cissy had been admitted to St Andrew's Hospital in Northamptonshire, a private mental asylum 'For the Upper and Middle Classes only'. An innovative and enlightened institution, it was built like a great country house with its own billiard room, recreation room and theatre, and provided for country sports and activities. The cost was two or three guineas per week (exclusive of washing, clothing, wines, spirits and tobacco) but there were additional charges for private rooms and for accommodating personal attendants, horses and carriages.

Her father had the unpleasant duty of committing Cissy, who had 'still sense enough to understand her condition to a certain extent'. The family could no longer pretend that Cissy was just a little eccentric.

The hospital doctors assumed that the cause was too rapid child-bearing, but the Haggards knew that she had been teetering on the edge of madness for many years.[6]

Her last pregnancy had pushed her over the brink. She ceased to 'continue with her household duties', and Maximilian Western had taken her back to Bradenham, nominally for a 'change of scene'. While there, she had threatened to cut her own throat, and had also accused her father of committing improprieties with two female servants. Of course, no one believed her. She left behind her four little daughters – one just born – to the care of her husband's rigidly pious family.

In the end it was not Andrew but Jack who went out to join Rider and Louie on the farm in Africa. By the time Jack arrived in the Cape on 26 April 1881, Rider and Louie were extremely thankful for a little family support. Circumstances had radically changed over the last twelve months. Wolseley had been brought in to clear up the South Africa problem, and he had so successfully crushed the Zulus that the Boers sought to regain their lost sovereignty in the Transvaal. The Riders had reached Newcastle, to find themselves in the midst of the first Boer War.

By the end of February Colley was dead at Laing's Nek – as were so many of Rider's old friends. In her diary for 7 March, Louie wrote: 'The 58th Regiment have come down from the "Nek" as the men are so panic stricken that they are useless.' The British in their pride had once again underestimated the enemy. Despising the Boers as people, the British officers had overlooked their superb shooting skills. Rider and Louie had many misgivings about staying on when the political situation was so volatile; with a party of friends, they were thinking of starting afresh in British Columbia.

As soon as he arrived, Jack picked up the prevailing opinions against the British Government's policies in the Transvaal, shared by both Boers and English in Cape Colony: 'Mr Gladstone is daily burnt in effigy all over the country.' Jack also noted the widespread unpopularity of the British soldiers, who had been enjoying the favours of the 'proverbially "easy" women of the Cape'. Jack, who took to the country at once, had arrived with letters of introduction in the hope of obtaining an administrative position through Sir Bartle Frere. However, there were many men ahead of him who until recently had been employed in the Transvaal. Sir Evelyn Wood, anticipating that he would not be Governor of Natal for very long, could do nothing for Jack, but Sir Hercules Robinson promised to try and help. Meanwhile, Jack made his way up to Durban and thence to Newcastle. He found Hilldrop two miles outside the town, in a 'pretty situation under a cliff'. How delighted Rider must have been to see Jack's familiar face when he rode up in early May, as Louie was expecting her first baby.

Arthur John Rider Haggard was born at 5.45 a.m. on 23 May. Named after Cochrane and Jack, who were his godfathers, he was always called Jock. Louie wrote to her friend Aggie Barber that she was 'the happy mother of the dearest little boy in the world'. Weighing nine pounds, he was a healthy baby, and Rider developed 'quite a talent for nursing'. Despite the hardships, Louie told her friend that colonial life was one 'which thoroughly suits me'.

With their king, Cetywayo, crushed the Zulu tribal chiefs turned on each other. Melmoth Osborn asked Jack to go with him to Zululand to try to prevent civil war. While he was away, Rider and Louie did some careful accounting and discovered that the last six months on the farm had cost them £450. Despite his previous enthusiasm for Vancouver Island, Jack had inexplicably discouraged them from setting up home there. Louie was fit again, the baby was drinking from a bottle, and Rider's father was urging them to come home. By 1 August it was all decided. They would return to England, and Cochrane, still unmarried, would return with them, leaving George Blomefield in charge of the farm. Jack rode back on 5 August to hear their news. On the 23rd they auctioned off their furniture and, by the 30th, they were all in Durban, where Jack, with a sailor's aptitude for a girl in every port, went to call upon his 'limp lank long Lily love', a Miss Noffman whom he had met soon after arriving in South Africa.

They steamed northward, stopping for two weeks in Madeira, and were back in lodgings in London's Cork Street by mid-October. Will, now posted to Stuttgart, was also in London, intent on getting a divorce from the dreadful Carrie. Suddenly they were all back in English upper-class life, as if nothing had happened and the farm in Africa was no longer really a part of their lives. They went down to Bradenham, where Rider, Jack and Will went shooting. In November they all prepared for the Sandringham Ball. 'The Princess looked lovely in pearl grey satin and was the prettiest woman in the room with the exception of Lady Longsdale who is the finest woman I ever saw,' wrote Louisa in one of the last entries in her diary.

$$\sim 6 \sim$$

The Ungirt Hour

As the New Year opened in 1882 a whisper of mortality slipped into Bradenham Hall on the winter chill. Squire Haggard was warmly protected by his tweed coat as he sat snug in his favourite winged armchair, his grey-knickerbockered legs toasting on the rail in front of the mahogany fireplace. The death at Christmas of his brother-in-law, the Reverend Fowle of Brinsop, had set him thinking: it was time to choose the words for his tombstone. The Squire was sixty-five, and the Haggard stock was not known for its longevity; a distinct lack of tin made him feel older than his years. These were lean times for the gentry, and his children usually had empty pockets.

Alfred, so long in poor health, had found himself a position as Secretary of the London Hospital. The salary barely covered the expenses of a gentleman, but he could not undertake anything more arduous even if he could secure it. Alice's family had money, and they were all living modestly at Wantage. Harry was coming up to eight years old, followed by Gerald, six, and Beatrice, three.

Jack was surviving on half pay. His engagement to the ageing and pious Etta White was still just that, for he had no prospects. Arthur was about to go to Sandhurst, and Mary, now aged twenty-four, *should* have been finding a husband but was proving difficult to match. Cissy remained at St Andrew's Hospital, her state of mind ranging from the restless to the deranged. Her health had deteriorated and she had lost weight. She could be physically violent or vulgarly sexual in her behaviour. Sometimes she asked for her children, but sometimes she just thought they were dead. Often she sank into complete inactivity and emptiness.

The Squire's relations with the Bazetts had so deteriorated that they did not meet and, when Mr Haggard had by chance seen his son on the street in Swaffham, Bazett had been suffering from pleurisy. He was now completely under the thumb of his father-in-law, Mr Barker, who, through his solicitor, had expressed to Mr Haggard his disappointment at Bazett's financial expectations. Mr Barker had understood that the Squire would be providing an allowance of £200 per annum for life.[1] Mr Haggard denied any such intention, remonstrating that Mr Barker 'has himself alone to blame if he supposed that, what was intended from my fatherly interest in him to help my son to a start in his profession, he could possibly have thought to have been a life long allowance'. The problem, as Mr Haggard saw it, was Bazett's way of life, which included a town house for the cultivation of the arts as well as a country house for 'sport and rural hospitality'. Mr Haggard recommended to Bazett 'sedulous attention to his profession' in order to meet his expenses, reminding him that he was not a 'country gentleman but a practising junior barrister', and he suggested the Bazetts move to a small town or to the colonies. All further communications should be sent via his solicitor.

As if this unpleasantness was not enough, the matter of Will's divorce loomed over them; both of Will's parents would have to testify before the court about Carrie's intolerable behaviour, and the worry of it all was making Mrs Haggard ill. It was essential for Will to disentangle himself, since Carrie had borne a child which they feared might be foisted on him.

The case was an unusual one, and the press were quick to point out its ironies. Will had applied for a dissolution of the marriage on the grounds of adultery but, when he had bolted for Teheran in 1880, Carrie had been willing to join him despite his repugnance. Instead, he had sent her £100 and suggested she use it for her fare back to the United States. This she had done, and had obtained an American divorce, subsequently marrying Lieutenant T. Dix Bolles of the United States Navy. Adultery was clearly established and uncontested, but on the other hand Will was guilty of desertion.

As the *Daily Telegraph* reported spitefully, 'He says that his wife was "violent and jealous", and, as the case is pending we will not pronounce on the plea; but there can be no doubt of the great advantage possessed by a diplomatist under such circumstances. It is not everybody who can go to Persia when a wife proves unkind; if it were so, Mr Haggard might not be the only English husband resident in that distant city of refuge, the capital of the Shah.'

Rider and his parents appeared in court to back up Will's plea. Will stayed with Rider and Louie, who were living sensibly in suburban Norwood. The hearing was held towards the end of March in Westminster Hall, before the President of the Probate, Divorce and Admiralty Division.

Squire Haggard wrote to Ella, 'I have very little hope for the result in his favour.' If the case went against him, the *Telegraph* pointed out that it would leave the much-married Carrie as three people: 'The Catholic Church would call her Mrs Kinney; American Law would pronounce her to be Mrs Bolles; while in England she would have a legal right to the name and style of Mrs Haggard. To disentangle her would require a new treaty, and Mr Haggard might be despatched to Washington to negotiate it on the spot. If on his arrival he found her divorced, he might re-marry the lady and thus end the dispute.'

The press enjoyed their witticisms at Will's expense and, although he put on a light-hearted mien to the Riders, to his parents he showed another face: 'Poor Will, he keeps his pluck up pretty well but before he left us last evening, though he did not give way, he put his head between his hands in grief and silent distress.'

The press described Will as 'the precipitate diplomatist – who seems to make treaties and break them with Muscovite facility.' At the hearing, the President could find no grounds on which to justify Will's desertion of Carrie, and decided to defer his decision. The Haggards withdrew and 'all went into the Aquarium . . . and had a cup of tea'. Mr Haggard was in a high state of nerves, but Mrs Haggard was, after all, none the worse for 'her ordeal'.

Will returned to Stuttgart almost immediately and, in the event, the President of the Court favoured him and found a way out of the dilemma. On 6 April *The Times* reported that the President 'was of the opinion that though not legally justifiable, the desertion in this case was not such as ought to induce the Court, in the exercise of its discretionary power, to deprive the petitioner of his remedy; and he [the President], therefore, pronounced a decree nisi.'

Will was free at last, although the divorce was socially detrimental and financially debilitating. The details of the alimony settlement are unknown, but Will had to send two agents to the States to reclaim some family jewellery from Carrie. Nevertheless, Will remained convinced of the advantages of marriage and, when he wrote to Rider in high spirits thanking him for his help, he offered some introductions for Arthur

Cochrane, who was mooning around in London hoping to find a suitable wife.

With another baby on the way, and Louie uncompromisingly behind him, Rider had decided to read for the Bar. Quietly he was nursing hopes of becoming a writer, especially when he saw Andrew busily embarking on a novel. Rider aimed at a more lofty target. In anticipation of the Zulu Cetywayo's visit to England and possible reinstatement, Rider published, largely at his own expense, *Cetywayo and his White Neighbours*. One review said that Rider argued the 'ultra-Colonial view', promoting only his own race and political bias which had 'already been pretty fully set forth – so fully, in fact, that the necessity for further exposition of them at this time does not seem very obvious.' It was an inauspicious beginning.

That summer Jack and Rider went out walking at Bradenham talking of Africa and the farm which George was still running for the Firm.[2] Cochrane planned to go back to supervise Hilldrop in the autumn, and Jack would follow him to try his luck in Africa. Before the Bradenham hedgerows had mellowed, Jack set sail for the Cape but, like some obligatory handicap, he took with him a mentally ill travelling companion, Charles Torkington. Perhaps the Torkington family put up the fares.

On his arrival at Cape Town, and being well entertained by the Attorney General, Jack's spirits and expectations soared. However, the immediate problem was how to get to Durban. Smallpox was raging in the district and the quarantine measures forbade any access from the Cape. Jack and the depressed and dejected Torkington trekked the 600 miles to Kimberley to visit friends, and approached Newcastle from that direction. From this excursion to the diamond mines Jack would certainly have been able to describe the vast treasure horde which inspired Rider when he wrote *King Solomon's Mines*.

By October, Jack, Torkington and Cochrane had met up at Rooi Point. Torkington was so unbalanced that he and his servant lived in a separate canvas hut, while Jack and Cochrane set to work on the farm which Blomefield had badly neglected. Blomefield, 'stupid . . . careless and indifferent', was also deeply racist, displaying open brutality towards the kaffirs. As a result they would not work for him. Meanwhile Torkington, who looked 'sane enough to the ordinary observer', was really 'as mad as he can be', and threatened suicide on a regular basis.

Although the natives in the Transvaal were rising against the Boers, who treated them with increasing cruelty, Jack recommended that Rider and Cochrane hold on to Hilldrop if they could, since it was bound to increase in value.[3] Throughout November, Jack and Cochrane tried to bring the farm round. Meanwhile Jack looked for employment, but he reflected, 'I never remember having a stroke of luck in my life so its hardly likely I shall get one now.' Cochrane was worried about succumbing to dysentery, as he had done before, and Charlie Torkington wafted in and out of melancholia. One of the kaffir's babies was born with six fingers and six toes – Jack 'advised him to knock it on the head and bury it in the Cattle Kraal . . .'

It was true that Jack never did have a stroke of luck, nor did he have the knack of making his own. In the South Africa of 1882 one man alone was seizing all the good fortune for himself: Cecil Rhodes. He had already realized huge wealth, and was working towards the attainment of political power. His dreams, larger than everyone else's, were of Imperial expansion into Bechuanaland, the key to the Zambezi and all the northern lands where Germany was already establishing her influence. Rhodes dared to imagine an Africa – English, Boer and Black – that was united under Britain from the Cape to Cairo.

In 1882 the place for soldiers and consuls to make their reputations was Cairo itself. The action had moved north to Egypt and the Sudan, where Arabi Pasha, the Minister for War, had raised a successful rebellion against the Turkish Khedival overlords. But, bearing in mind her interests in the Suez canal, Britain was not inclined to recognize the Pasha, and sent a force out to support the Khedive.

Wolseley was there, Redvers Buller was there, Wood, Butler, Lanyon, McCalmont, Herbert Stewart were all there – the scarred and heroic veterans of Ashanti and the Transvaal. Only Brackenbury, temporarily on half-pay but soon to rejoin his messmates, and Colley, cold in his grave, missed the fun.

Captain Andrew Haggard, released from domestic troubles, was on his way east in September of 1882 with recruits for Cyprus when they were diverted to Ismailia on the Red Sea. He hoped to see action at last, but a ship coming from Port Said signalled that a victory had already been won at Tel-el-Kebir. Deeply disappointed, Andrew wrote that 'if we were too late for the fighting, we very soon found out that we were not too late for the fatigue duties, a business for which our men in their state of temper were not particularly inclined.'

Andrew had the task of rousing his reluctant men to work in the crushing heat, unloading stores and animals from the eighty-odd ships lying in the canal opposite Ismailia. The canal was full of rotting bodies, the flies and the stench were overpowering, and the water from the 'Sweet Water Canal' was poisonous, quickly causing widespread diarrhoea and dysentery. The local Bedouin tribes marauded at will. Andrew soon decided that he couldn't punish *all* the men for insubordination, so he dealt toughly with the worst offenders and resorted to bribery for the rest. Tots of rum were liberally supplied.

Amid this sordid, stinking mayhem, Andrew remembered one jolly young officer who always looked on the bright side. 'Never mind,' the young man said, 'we shall all get our medals yet. There's a false prophet, a jolly old false prophet, who's kicking up a row somewhere up there in Soudan. We will all go for the false Prophet. Good old false prophet!'

But none of them had heard of the Mahdi – yet.

Once their work in Ismailia was done, Andrew made his way up to Cairo and was immediately enchanted. With his working knowledge of Arabic he was able to enjoy both the old city and its bazaars and the new cosmopolitan city – and, of course, the Pyramids, of which he had heard so much from his mother and from visits to the family's Norfolk neighbours at Didlington Hall.[4]

It was towards the end of October 1882 that Andrew set off for the recently bombarded Alexandria, 'a sink of iniquity', from where he embarked on a hired troopship which arrived in Portsmouth early in November. The Riders were moving from London back down to Ditchingham, which they thought would be more economical, and more comfortable for Louie's confinement. Rider had begun to write his first novel, a romance which would eventually be called *Dawn*, in which one of the characters owns a private museum of Egyptian antiquities.

If Andrew had missed the most famous military victory for years, he had not missed his opportunity. Tel-el-Kebir spelled the death knell of the Egyptian army. It was dispersed and broken up, its officers put on half pay and the regular soldiers converted into a gendarmerie whom Andrew called 'all worthless troops, as they proved afterwards at the first battle of El Teb.' Colonel Valentine Baker was induced to command them, after his appointment as creator of the replacement Egyptian army was vetoed by Queen Victoria.[5] Thus Sir Evelyn Wood was the fortunate recipient of the post of Sirdar of the new army, at a grand salary of £5,000 a year.

Wood took over Baker's aide-de-camp, Lieutenant Stuart-Wortley (nicknamed 'Wortles') of the 60th Rifles, and put together a staff of twenty-three officers, including the Arabic-speaking Andrew Haggard, so that 'the end of January 1883 found me on my way back to Cairo'. The Egyptian army was considered a 'distinct step on the road to Fortune', and Andrew found himself among a group of up-and-coming men which included Reginald Wingate, Hector Macdonald, Leslie Rundle, Horatio Kitchener, and Andrew's particular chum Lieutenant Chamley Turner of the 53rd Shropshire Regiment. All subalterns and captains were made field officers at once, and the prestige which they gained among brother officers in the British Army 'gave rise to a considerable amount of jealousy'.

In Cairo, things were much changed, 'for the visitors from England and elsewhere had begun to regain confidence, and were coming to finish the winter in Egypt, many being relations of fellows who had fought in the recent war. What a jolly and merry crowd they all were! Ah, indeed! Those were cheery days in Cairo, cheery enough at times almost to make the Sphinx laugh.'

There can have been few places and few times in which it was so particularly pleasant to be an Officer and a Gentleman as Cairo in the 1880s. It had the mystery of the East and the comforts of the West, it was both international and reassuringly British. It was smart, glamorous and full of diversions, including sporting and gambling establishments and women of many races and degrees of availability. Above all – or rather as emblematic of all of this – was what Andrew called that 'jolly old caravanserai', Shepheard's Hotel.

Of all the great Imperial hotels, Shepheard's was the most legendary and most beloved, since it had been founded for the overland route to India. The huge, cool rooms had stone floors, high sash windows, and whitewashed walls with frescoes in rough tints of slate, dark reddish-brown and flaming scarlet. Raised stone dadoes deep in cushions, or divans of blue printed calico, beckoned the tired traveller. The hotel sat comfortably on the wide street and eight carpeted steps led up to its most famous feature, the open terrace.[6] From here the jostling, noisy, exotic panorama of Cairo could be surveyed in comfort.

Andrew recalled an episode on their first evening which encapsulates the boyish military style. After dinner at Shepheard's he and a friend strolled out into the moonlit Esbikiyeh Gardens making their way towards Stuart-Wortley's apartment in a quiet side street. Their admiration for the silvery Eastern night was interrupted by 'the sharp sound

Cairo, 1880. Major Andrew Haggard in the uniform of the Egyptian
Army, with his manservant.

of a hunting-horn several times repeated, then, in true Jorrocks fashion, other sounds – namely, cries as of the huntsman encouraging his hounds to cover. "Yoicks! over there, my beauties! Hoick him out there! Hi away in there, little beauties!"'

As Andrew and his friend wandered deeper into the Arab quarter they heard 'the eldritch screech of a view-holloa, then another and another "Whooi! Whooi! Whooi! Gone away! gone away! – away!" Twang! twang! twang! went the hunting horn, then with a burst of melody from twenty throats, representing the hounds in full cry, out bounded a lot of merry fellows through a French window on to a balcony, along the front of it, and in at another window.'

Andrew happily recalled joining the chase, 'gaily giving tongue with the rest of the fellows', and explained the extraordinary performance in the Cairo night: 'Stuart-Wortley was entertaining the officers of Hicks Pasha's force, who were leaving the next day. And Captain Candy, late of the 9th Lancers, the well-known "Sugar", who always was and always will be a boy, was only just giving one of his famous representations of a fox-hunt to cheer them up before their departure.'

Andrew's road to fortune began with a rise in pay: starting as a supplementary officer he soon made second-in-command at £600 per annum. His gorgeous uniform included patent-leather boots, a white frogged tunic with a crescent and star on the buttons, topped by a tarboosh or fez and, to complete the picture, he sported a fine, waxed moustache. There were to be eight Infantry battalions, of which four would have English superior officers, and four Egyptians. The eight battalions would form two brigades, the first under Grenfell and the second under 'a charming old Circassian general, by name Yousouf Pasha Shuhdi', with whom Andrew was to become close friends.[7]

Andrew's first regiment was the Dortingini Orta, or the 4th Battalion EA, the commandant of which was Major Wynne. The first task in hand was to 'form an army out of a wretched lot of fellaheen', made up entirely of new recruits or conscripts. The soldiers, who wore white uniforms with red fezes, were quartered in the Cairo suburb of Abbasiyeh and, initially, language and cultural problems hindered the process of military discipline.

It was the beginning of one of the happiest periods of Andrew's life, and the novels which he based on his experiences emphasize the many social pleasures of life in Cairo.

Half the officers in Cairo in those days lived at Shepheard's Hotel, and
the jingle of the spur and clash of the sword could be heard on the wide
staircases or echoing along the corridors at any hour of the day or night
from four in the morning, when some of the earliest warriors commenced
to get up, until two or later the following morning, when the latest of
the warriors went to bed . . . even those officers who did not actually
live in Shepheard's Hotel used frequently to take their meals there, and
pass their spare time smoking, chatting and lounging about on the divans
in the cool corridors, or on the long cane chairs on the wide verandah
. . . It was like one huge club; consisting of all the British officers of the
English Army, the Egyptian Army, the Egyptian Gendarmerie and the
Police as permanent members, including all the wives and the sisters-in-
law; while outsiders, such as ladies and gentlemen travelling, and other
people in civilian life, might have been looked upon as honorary
members of the institution. And fun and flirtation was the first rule of
the club.

He added discreetly: 'if only the walls of the old part of Shepheard's
Hotel could speak, many a tale of love and flirtation would be related
and many a history of never suspected amourette, or romantic intrigue,
would now stand revealed.'

The officers were feted with magnificent dinners, some of which were
too long and elaborate to be really enjoyable. At one such affair Andrew
and Horatio Kitchener passed the time by competing to see who could
eat the most. 'Alas, for the credit of the infantry, that I should have to
record it, the gallant sapper had far more staying powers than I had, and
I was defeated hollow, for the Royal Engineer could have easily given
me 7lb in a half-mile handicap over the food course. Over the liquor
course I was luckily more successful . . .'

Andrew was fond of a practical joke, and his friend Chamley Turner
('a regular slap-dash hero') was sometimes the intended victim. On one
occasion Andrew hid five asps in a box of 'superfine writing-paper'
and presented it to Chamley Turner on the crowded verandah of Shepheard's. Chamley merely exclaimed 'Snakes! oh ripping!', as he 'plunged
his hand into the box, seized all five snakes at once, and with them
curling round his hand and wrist in every direction, and biting him,
started around to clear everyone off that verandah; which he did in about
a minute and a half or less.' It was only later that he asked if they were
poisonous.

Chamley Turner was fond of jokes himself and, during a cholera
epidemic, would 'writhe on the ground with upturned eyes'. Ironically

he did eventually contract the disease, but it was not to be the end of him. If ever there was a *Boy's Own* hero, Chamley Turner fitted the bill, and Andrew immortalized him as 'Dodo' in his novel of the Sudan campaign, *Dodo and I*.

Between diversions, the officers took their work seriously enough, and it was becoming evident that the system of recruitment was riddled with corruption. Andrew was sent off to investigate the native methods in the larger towns to the south, thereby enlarging his knowledge of Arab life. Discreetly describing the seductive approaches of Syrian and Coptic women, he hails the young man seeking experience: 'Oh my boy! if you be a lover of romance, as you should be . . . you will thank your stars that you spent so many weary hours in acquiring Persian, Turkish or Arabic language. Make, then, the best of your time!'

Andrew was certainly in the mood for romance. In May he married Miss Emily Isabella Chirnside at the British Consulate. He was twenty-nine years old, she a spinster of thirty with money of her own and, at the time, a resident of Cairo. Towards the end of the year, Andrew took his bride home to England. It must have been an odd introduction for her. Bazett was suing his father for the non-payment of his allowance. The affair had simmered throughout the spring, becoming public in the summer when the writ had been served on Mr Haggard. The whole family was up in arms and it was left to the long-suffering Maddison Green to try to mediate.

Charles had made a thorough investigation into the Squire's troubled affairs and discovered that, after all his obligations were paid, he was reduced to an income of eight hundred pounds a year – this figure relying on rents being paid. It was obvious to Charles that Mr Haggard could not pay Bazett an allowance, and he believed that the Squire had never intended to pay him one, but only to help him get started. Charles was forthright in his opinion that Mr Haggard had educated his sons above their real expectations and, instead of putting them into banks or offices, had tried to provide for them to enter the highest professions. Far from cheating his sons, Mr Haggard had indulged them: they were not deprived but spoiled. Nevertheless, Charles wrote to Will, now at the Foreign Office, to set the record straight. Will knew that £5,000 had been raised for him when he left school, but the £100 allowance which he had been promised had never materialized, and indeed he had himself lent his father £2,500 ten years ago. Suavely, Will deplored the trouble to which Charles was being put by Mr Haggard's energetic

Bazett's wife Judy, née Julia Barker. In a rare interior domestic
photograph, she is seen toying with a lute in the drawing room
of Kirby Cane Hall.

correspondence, and joked: 'dear Charlie − I fear and tremble − he has
been given a copying machine [a typewriter]!'

Not all the family could approach the matter with Will's jocularity.
The estrangement between Bazett and his parents was all the more
poignant because they had made him a 'special mark' of their affection
and, 'in their hearts', loved him still. Charles, believing that Judy and the
Barkers were behind the litigation, continued to hope for a reconciliation,
especially since Mrs Haggard's health was noticeably affected by the rift.

Bazett felt that his father had resources which he was keeping from
him, notably a substantial inheritance from Miss Mason of Necton (which
in fact had been spent on debts and Arthur's school fees). Bazett was
keen to talk the matter out with Charles, and invited him to Kirby Cane,
blithely assuming that Charles would drop everything to trail across
England. Charles, of course, was a busy man and suggested a meeting
in London. He continued to remonstrate with Bazett about both the
inadvisability and the hurtfulness of taking his father to court − and the

uselessness of it, since Mr Haggard had no more money to give him. This sorry state of affairs was partially due to Mr Haggard's nature: 'The fact is he is always too sanguine, too easy going in money matters, and does not calculate correctly expenses ahead.'

As suspected, Judy's father was behind the law-suit and was simply pushing Bazett into pursuing the claim because Bazett had a letter which might stand up in court. Nevertheless, it was difficult to understand what they hoped to gain, until Jack casually mentioned to Will that Mr Haggard was thinking of selling the family plate. Will's *savoir-faire* was stretched very thin by this revelation and he wrote at once to Charles:

> when all is said and done I am my Father's eldest son . . . the family plate would have been mine . . . I daresay it is foolish and absurd of me . . . and though of course, my father has a perfect right to dispose of it . . . I do not want the Doveton plate. When my Father dies I become naturally the head of the family, and I do not care to have the plate with any other crest on than my own.

It transpired that Mr Haggard had already consulted Charles on the matter of selling the plate to pay debts, and Charles had suggested that, if it must be sold, it might be offered to his sons first. This had come back to Will in a roundabout sort of way with the implication that Charles was advising Mr Haggard on the sale – which was far from the truth. Mr Haggard either foresaw having to pay off Bazett, or the Barkers already had their eyes on the heirlooms.

By the end of November 1883, Bazett and Judy had the whole family lined up against them. All except Cissy and Jack signed a printed letter of protest against Bazett's proposed action. The document underlined the family belief that Bazett had benefited 'exceptionally from our Father's favor [sic]' having had two or three times the amount given to the other children. The expenses of the legal action would in themselves be a further claim upon the Squire's dwindling resources, and they feared for the stain upon the family name.

Even Charles finally was too disgusted to continue pouring oil on troubled waters. During an interview in December, Bazett had asked for the family plate and jewellery in lieu of money. Charles said it savoured of Shylock, and he would have nothing to do with it – he would be ashamed to do so. Bazett was bartering the friendly esteem of his family for the price of some silver. He reminded Bazett that, though he might have grievances, so had his father and mother, but 'of a nature I don't like to speak of, of very long standing'.[8]

The court action was pending when the Andrews returned to Cairo, taking Alfred Thacker with them.[9] All this time the military authorities had regarded the new Egyptian Army 'with the very gravest suspicion', a suspicion not lessened by the news which filtered through at the end of 1883 that Hicks Pasha and his troops had been slaughtered. Hicks had led 10,000 men across the wastes of Kordofan, marching for weeks in the heat and dust, before they were ambushed by Dervishes in a dense forest at Kashgil. William Hicks and his vast army were annihilated, never more to hear the view halloo.

Stirred from their insular preoccupations, people in England sat up and wondered about these fanatical followers of the Mahdi and this inhospitable land of the Sudan. When it was learned that, in the wake of his victory, the Mahdi was collecting an army to march on Khartoum, Andrew observed: 'The British Government commenced to be vacillating in the extreme ... to the loss of the prestige of Great Britain, of blood, and of money.' Having tried unsuccessfully to hand over the government of the Sudan to the Turks, the British liberal policy lacked the determination necessary to subdue and hold that troubled land.

Andrew was wholeheartedly behind Sir Samuel Baker (brother of Valentine), 'who knew more about Egypt and the Soudan than anyone living', rating his judgement above Gordon's because of the latter's strong religious bias. Baker urged the construction of a railway from Suakin to the Nile, and was unorthodox enough to suggest paying one of the great Korosko desert sheiks to secure the wells from Berber to Suakin, thus opening a route to ensure the safety of Khartoum.

Baker was ignored by the Consul-General, Lord Cromer, and by the British Government. Instead, early in 1884, General Gordon, the former Governor of the Sudan, set off up the Nile with the specific instruction to secure the withdrawal of troops, civilians and their families. Despite his respect for Gordon's reputation, Andrew, like many other soldiers, never could understand why he didn't stick to his orders to evacuate Khartoum when he could.

In the eastern Sudan, an Arab leader named Osman Digna raised an army of tribesmen in response to the Mahdi's call and laid siege to two Egyptian garrisons. Valentine Baker was sent down to protect the essential sea port of Suakin. With him went Andrew's friend, Colonel Sartorius, and the flamboyant traveller and writer Captain Burnaby (of the Tissot portrait) who had turned up unofficially for the action. Overloaded with unwilling Egyptian troops, and having too few of the warlike Massowahs, Baker's Gendarmerie was routed by the Dervishes at El Teb.

Unfortunately the cowardice of the Gendarmerie reflected on the new Egyptian Army, so that the authorities were not inclined to let them see any action. But Andrew was one of three officers detailed to help reorganize the remnants of Baker's force in Suakin. He took his two horses, the Squire and the Parson, with him on HMS *Carysfoot*. By some administrative anomaly, Andrew and two fellow officers, Pigott and Hallam Parr, were 'borne on the books' of HMS *Euryalus* under Admiral Hewett. Even Alfred Thacker, a civilian servant, was enrolled as a sailor and, when he wasn't looking after the horses, would go back and forth to the ship to draw all their rations.

Suakin was at once a dreadful outpost and a rather magical place, with elaborately decorated Arab houses, many of whose walls incorporated broken shells which shimmered with a ghostly glow at night. Andrew described it as a 'flat-roofed Arab town on an island enclosed by two creeks, which themselves ran out of a very narrow but deep inlet of the sea, which widening opposite the town, made an excellent harbour. On one side it was connected to the mainland by a causeway, and the houses and huts beyond this causeway formed the suburb of El Keff.' El Keff was protected by earthworks, outside which were two wells again protected by earthworks and joined by a high bank. Forming part of the line of entrenchment were two stone buildings 'fit for Europeans' which were turned into forts and called Fort Euryalus and Fort Carysfoot.

Baker and Burnaby were still in Suakin when Andrew arrived, and the limited defences were being bombarded under cover of dark by the Dervishes. Valentine Baker, Frederick Burnaby and Andrew Haggard were at El Keff one night, three soldiers walking in a starlit dusty street, when a bullet struck the wall close by Baker's head, 'the pieces of brick sprinkling all over his face'; as close as that to death.

7

Imperial Fire

The news of the Mahdi's successes spread rapidly through the many British colonies and territories which had Muslim populations. Many of the more fanatical were ready to rise up and follow the heaven-sent leader. It was commonly believed that the armies which Hicks Pasha and Baker Pasha had led against the triumphant Dervishes were composed of British soldiers, and this had a most unfortunate and unsettling effect throughout the rest of Africa. The Mahdi's followers had already appeared in Zanzibar, where they went 'howling all night in the mosques', and had 'gained sufficient converts to beat off the Sultan's soldiers who attempted to turn them out'.

With Will's help, Jack had secured one of four new Vice-Consular appointments on the coast of East Africa. Will wrote to his father about the prospects: '£500 a year and travelling allowance amounting to another £300 or £400, the consul to be an active enterprising man, on which account they particularly wish for Naval Officers.' Britain was extending her sphere of influence out from Zanzibar where Sir John Kirk, who had explored Central Africa with Livingstone, had been the Agent since 1873.[1] Grateful for the opportunity, Jack left England in November of 1883, arriving in Zanzibar about five weeks later.

Zanzibar and the coastal regions of what is now Kenya were ruled by a Sultan and a series of Arab governors. The four new British consular stations were Kilwa and Sindi to the south, and Mombasa and Lamu to the north. Naval officers had been recruited for their ability to spot Arab slave boats getting ready to weigh anchor, and to negotiate the complex coastal waterways. Of the four consuls and a doctor who were sent out, two of them soon died of fever and one retired because of its effects. Initially, however, the climate at Lamu seemed quite favourable to Jack, and he was far more concerned that the Mahdi's influence would cause a general rising of Muslims against Christians, which could extend to India.

In Zanzibar, Jack began to learn the language and to study the form in the local court. There were many thousands of British subjects, native Indians, living along the coast: 'all the wealth of this country is in their hands and they are terribly litigious'. Jack would be expected to act as magistrate which, without any legal training, he found a daunting proposition, but one which he took very seriously. He was assembling his household of nine men – an interpreter, five Askari or soldiers, a valet, a cook, and a boy. Negotiations on the rental of an Arab house were under way, and he organized the repair of the three boats he would need for travel, exploration and sport – two dinghies for the creeks and a ten-oared cutter for the harbours.

Lamu was situated on one of a series of islands opposite numerous bays and inlets. It was a part-African, part-Arab town with an Arab Governor; there was not a single white man within 200 miles, and the African population of Somalis and Gallas were known to be fairly savage and fanatical. While maintaining good relations with the Governor, it would be Jack's objective to secure trade routes into East Africa, to curb and suppress the slave trade, and to increase the British income from Customs. For his own part he looked forward to good game shooting, and collecting specimens – for, like so many Victorian travellers, he had his eye on a little modest immortality. The game was to discover new species and get them home intact to the Natural History Museum before some German got his collection back to the Berlin Museum.[2]

Towards the end of January Sir John Kirk, himself a sportsman and naturalist, accompanied Jack to Lamu, staying with him for his first month before the steamer returned to Zanzibar. By March, Jack had moved into his new home on the seafront, from where he could view any maritime activity. The two-storey square Arab house, built round a courtyard, had been used for live animals, and extensive replastering and whitewashing were necessary before it was fit for habitation. There were no glass windows but only wooden shutters which, if they were closed, excluded all the healthy sea breezes. Having little or no furniture, Jack suffered many discomforts.

After Kirk left, Jack found Lamu 'rather a solitary shop', but the mood suited him. He had just heard from Etta White that she was formally breaking off their engagement, and he was mightily relieved. He was sick to death of her religiosity and preaching and prayers, and sent back

Lieutenant John George Haggard RN retired, Her Britannic
Majesty's Vice-Consul, stationed in Lamu. The photograph was
taken by Sir John Kirk in 1884/5 outside the Vice-Consulate and
includes the consular and household staff.

all her letters with alacrity in case she should change her mind. What annoyed him most was her lack of honesty: 'She won't say her reasons for giving up the engagement *in toto* are her health and dread of the Sultan of Zanzibar's dominions', pretending instead it was because Jack 'was low enough to take her at her word when she broke off our engagement first of all and to go away from England disengaged'.

Jack railed to Will, 'Women are an infernal nuisance, and are more trouble than they're worth, it wouldn't matter so much if they didn't cost such a lot; if I had never met Etta White I should have been £150 richer than I am now.' To his sister Ella he discoursed on the drawbacks of matrimony, suggesting instead a 'three yearly system'. As it was, he was relieved to be free from Etta, having 'almost no cares or anxieties and my only source of irritation are the fleas'.

As the only white man in the district, Jack was particularly careful of his dress and his behaviour, 'as I am naturally the observed of all observers'. He found the urban Arab habits of suspicion and underlying aggression repulsive. He kept an armed man with him at all times, which he thought better 'than having the appearance of wearing arms myself, which they know is not the custom of Englishmen'. In a similar vein, although he made sure to have a flagstaff on his house (made of an old man-of-war's torpedo pole), he only hoisted the Union Jack on Fridays when the Governor hoisted his own flag, and on days when a steamer came in. 'There is no need to jam the flag down his throat when his own is not hoisted.'

Keeping up a dignified presence was no easy matter. He had only to walk down the street and the women would often run away shrieking from him. Yet at other times, in camp, they would invade his tent and examine all his possessions – and even his person if he did not fend them off. Gradually, over the months, he reduced the oppression of slaves so that they were no longer kept in chains, and he introduced a new note of honesty into the trading practices. But all this hard, careful work could be undermined overnight – and most outrageously – by the British. On one occasion when a mail steamer came in, three male first-class passengers disembarked, drunk, and raped a slave girl. There was uproar in the town and the natives surrounded the three men in a house where they had sought refuge. The Governor sent for Jack, who was obliged to take his own soldiers to give the men safe escort back to the steamer. He was appalled at having to secure their escape, especially since because of the tides he had no time to send a letter with the steamer to Sir John Kirk.

Jack immediately decided to build a lock-up on the ground floor of his house, so that if any such incident should occur again, he could keep the culprits safe from the mob until justice could be done. He was not 'sure if it would be quite legal to shut a white man up, but like old Alfred I should "damn legality" in a case like this one.' The incident made him 'more sorry than I can say', since it gave the 'White Man such a bad name'.

Coming to terms with the rudimentary conditions of African towns was no easy matter either. The prevalence of slops and offal in the streets disgusted him and made him very wary of blood poisoning. The shrieking and yelling of horseplay between the slaves, the roaring of a stud donkey and the reply of a she-ass, the bleating of goats and the crowing of cockerels were the common noises of the town from which he withdrew in his new house. On one occasion, he told his father, his civility was taxed to the limits when an Arab gentleman came to call and complained of having caught the itch (a skin disease). When he left, the Arab offered Jack his hand. Although it almost made him sick, Jack took the proffered hand at once and 'held it slightly longer than usual to show I did not shrink from him'. As he pointed out, 'He had no business to offer his hand, but having done so I was bound to take it.' He told his father that on the west coast of Africa a 'palaver-stick' was the common method of avoiding the dilemma. The stick was white at one end and black at the other and only ever touched by men of corresponding skin colour. By the use of this baton, the 'craw-craw' disease was avoided.

Jack's letters from this period are more cheerful than previously, and he was most interested to detect remnants of the Persian occupation of the area 700 years earlier. Extraordinary, thick china plates adorned many of the walls, but he could not get the local people to part with any of them. He felt certain that the china had been handed down from the Persians and, when he visited the Watiku tribe, he discovered that they had Eurasian rather than Negroid features, and their skins were almost white. This may well be the origin of the mysterious white tribe which features in Rider's book *Allan Quatermain*.

Jack wrote home a little scathingly of Andrew's appointment to the new Egyptian Army, a hint of the old rivalry between sailors and soldiers. Ironically, of course, Andrew was temporarily on the Navy's books, having been applied for by Admiral Sir William Hewitt, Governor-General of the Red Sea Littoral. Andrew and Hallam Parr were labouring away in Suakin, organizing defences against the marauding Dervishes and quelling the mutinous black Gendarmerie. The Egyptian soldier was now so distrusted that the Queen backed up Wolseley's plan to send in British regular soldiers. Under Brigadier General Gerald Graham, an Expeditionary Force of 3,000 men and a naval detachment arrived at Suakin. Among the officers were Major General Sir Redvers Buller, Colonel Herbert Stewart, Colonel Clery, and Chamley Turner – who had bullied his way into the action by bringing down some men with the Camel Corps.

Graham led his force to rout out Osman Digna, which he did at the second battle of El Teb at the end of February 1884. Andrew commented that Stewart was 'very active in charging the enemy whenever possible', which was rather ineffective against the Dervishes, who 'stepped behind bushes as they approached, or, lying down behind mounds, jumped up suddenly and slashed and cut at the horses' hocks'. The enemy also threw curved sticks at the horses' legs to bring them down and there were huge cavalry losses. Colonel Burnaby did rather better with his double-barrelled shotgun: 'Loaded with slugs, he bowled them over right and left like snipe.' The Dervishes themselves had plenty of Remington rifles and ammunition, 'two Krupps, a brass mountain howitzer and some rocket tubes'. Nevertheless, they were defeated, 2,000 of them being killed.

Throughout his time in Egypt, Andrew wrote copious notes and diaries, and eventually published several books and articles in magazines. But his letters home were often for Will's information. Will, in the Foreign Office, was very keen to have first-hand accounts of what was going on in the world, and he in turn tried to help his brothers with their careers.

When Andrew heard that there was going to be a second expedition against Osman Digna he was determined not to be left out, but there were so many staff officers ahead of them that he and Hallam Parr had to be content with a billet in the transport department. It was on this attachment, looking after the native camel drivers, that Andrew joined the march to Tamai. Andrew and Alfred Thacker, both on horseback, escorted a convoy of camels carrying water to the troops. In the still desert night the camels trudged silently across the sand, while Thacker, armed with a revolver and hunting crop, aided his master in keeping the unruly camel-drivers to their task. They halted at Baker's zariba and slept against their saddles under the stars. Early next morning they set off to find the army.

Andrew remembered that it was a most glorious morning and that the desert grass grew green after the rains, while gazelles, hares, partridges and sand-grouse scuttled about in all directions. It was the sort of day when you are glad to be alive, and yet, 'although it was, as far as I remember a Sabbath morn, it was a day devoted to killing and slaughter, and to nothing else'.

When they reached the cavalry Andrew soon found his friends Chamley Turner, Hallam Parr and Pigott. 'They all wore, as I did myself, a bright red puggaree around their white helmets ... very pretty, too, I thought it looked as I saw Pigott sitting grimly on his horse in front of a cavalry regiment, his one spot of colour relieving the whole tedium of a regiment in sand-coloured kharkee.'

There were two squares – one under Redvers Buller on the right and one under Davis on the left, with Parr, Chamley Turner and Haggard at the zariba where they were attacked from all sides. At one stage in the battle there was a serious reversal when the enemy got inside the second square. Cameron, the war correspondent of the *Standard*, rushed off to telegraph the news back to London.[3] But a subsequent cavalry charge frightened the enemy and, to avoid the problems of El Teb, this was followed by an infantry advance which recaptured the Gatling guns. The British took Osman Digna's camp in the village of Tamai and razed it to the ground. Andrew remembered that General Graham was very brave and cool: 'He rode about everywhere where the fires were hottest, with a red flag accompanying him to denote his presence, as calmly as if he were walking his horse up Rotten Row.' In the heat of the action, Andrew heard echoes from his boyhood of Macaulay's stirring lines:

> And in they burst, and on they rushed,
> While like a guiding star
> Amid the thickest carnage blazed
> The helmet of Navarre.

Even wounded Dervishes would attack their captors, so the British took no prisoners at the battle of Tamai. Thacker discovered he had an aptitude for despatching the heathen, and wrote to Jack of his bloody exploits:

> I went round the battle field soon after the second fight, and never did I, or ever wish to see such a horrible sight again. I amused myself by shooting the wounded, and some there were laying sculked [*sic*] under the bushes with a sheet of some kind over them. I believe they never were tutched [*sic*] but they could not see there [*sic*] road clear to escape.

The splendid effect of my shots showed me that they were as lively as I was myself. All I saw in this position got no mercy from me. I shot one who had been wounded badly. He had a nice spear and how he did cling to it and also a knife. I captured them and a shield, there was any amount laying about . . . I know what battle is like now but before had people told me it was like such I could not believe it . . . It was a very interesting day to me but a most cruil [*sic*] days work, and I was sorry to leave so many brave men behind never to see there [*sic*] dear old country again. What brave men the Enemy was, see them rush up to the point of the bayonet as if they did not fear death in the least.

After Tamai, Admiral Hewitt asked Andrew to undertake a special mission to Massowah in Eritrea, to negotiate with an Abyssinian brigand Prince who was blocking the egress of an Egyptian regiment. Rather grandly, if temporarily, Andrew was to be the new Governor of Massowah, to which he sailed on the Khedival steamship *Mansurah* in late March, in the company of Captain Speedy, who had been one of King Theodore's prisoners at Magdala, and Fred Villiers of the *Graphic*. The journey took him down to the south of the Red Sea, close to where Jack had been on the Abyssinian expedition and not so very far from where he was at that time in Lamu. Thacker was 'surprised to think that we should work our way up so close to your [Jack's] quarters but truly sorry to think we shall not be able to see you . . .'

Jack was amused by Thacker's letter – 'the open manner in which he tells how much he enjoyed disposing of the wounded is delightful' – and sent it back to Bradenham for his father to read. He himself was waiting to read Rider's first novel, *Dawn*, and asked his mother to remind Rider to send him a copy. He added, 'I've got a first rate plot for a novel myself and if I could see old Riderius I'd submit to him to manipulate, it's too much trouble to attempt it myself.' Jack had already invited Rider, Louie and Frederick Jackson to come out to Lamu for a year, to 'have the time of their lives'. Jack suggested that Rider and Jackson should finance the trip through elephant hunting, and Rider should write his books in between, while Jackson collected smaller species. Perhaps at that time Jack had in mind some kind of collaboration with Rider on stories.[4]

During April and May, Jack made his first exploration of Pate Island and the towns of Faza and Sizu. His object was to visit British nationals and, through local contacts, to try to establish trade with a dangerous tribe called the Waboni. His adventures on the tidal creeks are the stuff of which Allan Quatermain was made:

> The roar of the water was now so great you could hardly make yourself heard, but we slid into an oily whirlpool kind of water where to make things more pleasant some hippos rose round the boat, grunting and snuffling to a pretty tune . . . then my conscience smote me for shooting at the poor brutes in the afternoon. I have scattered them, I thought, and sent them down here, and now they'll split the boat . . . I had not much time for thinking for at that moment we violently took the ground (I thought that's a hippo) and were thrown up on our bilge on a sandbank in the middle of a roaring, seething, foaming and contending flood . . . in an old worn out and leaky boat . . . However, there was nothing for it but to let her sweat where she was. I had the anchor carried out, and loaded as the boat was, let the crew lie in her. I thought if she is bilged she is bilged and there's an end of it, their extra weight won't hurt, and exhausted as the men are, my refusal will only cause mutinous conduct. Then as I lay down myself in the bottom of the boat I thought to myself, as sure as eggs is eggs the boat is bilged, these bloody minded Waboni will cut all our throats in the morning, and I determined to make a good fight for it before they succeeded with mine.

Jack's progress in opening up the interior was obstructed by the Arab Governor who, while superficially charming and amenable, found devious ways of undermining Jack's plans. He was fearful lest the expansion of trade with the tribes should reduce his tithe of elephant tusks. Nevertheless, Sir John Kirk was pleased with Jack's work and planned to come up and see him. Unfortunately, Kirk was a law unto himself. He worried about no one's convenience but his own, and time and again he delayed or changed his plans so that he could follow some good hunting. Jack was left kicking his heels for months in Lamu when he could have been getting on with the job. It was only travel and outdoor life which kept him healthy and sane. In Lamu he was almost a prisoner in his own home. He had no distraction from his increasing loneliness, and he began to fall prey to fevers and depressions.

Dawn was originally published in three volumes in April 1884 and told of an ill-fated romance. Agnes Barber, who now lived with Rider and Louie from time to time, had acted as editor and sometime muse to Rider. The volumes arrived in Lamu in July, and Jack read the book in two days but argued with the plot: 'his theory of the immortality of the affections is very nice, but what's to become of those forlorn souls

Five of the Haggard brothers, around 1885/6. From left to right:
Alfred, Andrew, Rider, William and Jack.

who fetch up in Heaven without a "Polly", are they to stand off and
watch the rest spooning? If so it will be very slow for them.' In an
amusing critique, Jack disproved the possibility of Rider's heroine going
to Heaven at all. Rider can hardly have found Jack's comments encouraging – any more so than the public's response to the jolly but rather
wandering novel, which earned him a meagre £10.

Perhaps because he was piqued, Rider wrote Jack a rather patronizing
letter, essentially telling his 'dear old Jacky' to buck up out of his Haggard
morbidity and count his blessings. Discussing at length the nature of
life, Rider responded to Jack's cynicism with his own brand of cosmic
optimism.

A visit to Zanzibar towards the end of July lifted Jack's spirits, although
Kirk curtailed the stay and sent him back to Lamu before he was ready
to leave. He found time to purchase thirty Java sparrows[5] which he
intended to turn loose at his house, and three mongooses to keep down

the rats. Jack's plans to explore Galla country with a black missionary friend were once again threatened by Kirk, who proposed a visit to Lamu in August and insisted on Jack's being there. But this time, Jack took no notice and undertook his journey to Witu (west of Lamu) to see a rebel chief called Simba, who promptly held him prisoner and threatened his life unless he undertook to run guns and ammunition for him through Lamu. Jack refused point blank, and was eventually permitted to leave uninjured.

In view of the increased danger, Kirk instructed Jack to deter white people from coming out to the coast, and Rider and Louie, mindful of their young family, never did visit Lamu. They spent August holidaying in Morvin House at Criccieth with Fred Jackson and his sisters. Having no real reason to work, Fred had failed to take his degree at Cambridge and had been out shooting in Kashmir. Jack thought that if he kept to his naturalistic pursuits (shooting and taxidermy) and stayed reasonably close to Lamu, a visit to Zanzibar would be fairly safe. The expedition was to settle the course of Fred's life.

Fred Jackson's young chum Arthur Haggard had no such easy billet, and had joined Chamley Turner's regiment, the King's Shropshire Light Infantry. Money was so tight that the Squire had passed round the hat between the other brothers to provide Arthur with an allowance of £100 a year, to get him on his feet. Before long the Shropshires made their way to Egypt so that, by the end of 1884, there were three Haggard brothers in Africa. The P & O steamer which brought Andrew up from Aden in the spring had the Australian cricket team on board, and Andrew shared a cabin with 'the demon bowler', Spofforth. Amidst the jollities and carousing, he lost any number of his trophies to the Australians and, in a flirtatious incident, nearly lost his sword to a delightful young lady, 'a bride of nineteen summers' who found it lying on a deck lounger. Thus 'commenced a friendship which . . . lasted for many years'.

After sending his wife off to Italy, Andrew returned to Suakin for a month or two, where the repair and extension of the defences was his daily care. Gordon had reached Khartoum in May but, when Berber fell to the Dervishes, he was cut off. The political wrangling that followed in London is notorious. It was not until mid-September that Wolseley received the go-ahead to send a relief expedition. His plans to use whalers and Canadian *voyageurs* to portage through the cataracts of the Nile drew on his Red River experience (and presumably inspired Fred Jackson to take a similar boat out to Lamu). Butler was in charge of commissioning the boat-building and miraculously the first batch was ready for him at Aswan at the beginning of October. But he was still 600 miles from Khartoum.

During the summer, Andrew had been assigned to Intelligence in Cairo, and he drew up an itinerary for a route to Khartoum via Kassala (due east of Khartoum), which was adopted by the War Office. In the autumn he returned to Suakin as commander of the 1st Battalion of the Egyptian Army, under General Sir Frederick Stephenson. Andrew was very proud of his efforts in fort and defence building, and there is an evocative collection of photographs of Suakin taken by the Royal Engineers, now in the Royal Commonwealth Library. In *Under Crescent and Star*, Andrew himself recorded 'To this day the Foula Fort bears a superscription cut in beautiful Arabic letters on a stone tablet over the door by one of my men, a cunning mason and stone-cutter, which inscription states that the fort was erected by Andrew Haggard Bey, with the date in both the Mohamedan and Christian eras.'[6]

The vicissitudes of the Sudan Relief Force are well documented and, like everyone else, Andrew waited and watched. Wolseley's was not the only career that hung in the balance. The reputation of the Egyptian Army came under fire – particularly from Butler, who was impatient of their movements at the cataracts, which he thought impeded his progress. Horatio Kitchener was heavily criticized by both Gordon himself and Andrew. In one letter to his mother, Andrew called him 'this claptrap catching sapper' who was stealing the glory from Leslie Rundle, one of the original officers of the Egyptian Army. Andrew said that Kitchener's report of being stopped at Dongola by 3,000 Arabs was all 'bunkum' and that 'the line to Dongola was as open as the Thames embankment but he [Kitchener] has hoodwinked the B.P. Well we know his Arab Sheikhs were all a do and that they would never go anywhere unsafe we also know he was cracking himself up and never mentioning . . . old Rundle.'

Rundle had written to one of the officers at Suakin, and Andrew quoted him as saying:

> Kitchener has ratted and left me in the lurch, I am furious. Our Sheikhs have just refused to go to Merawi [close to the fourth cataract]; an impossible order he has sent from Dongola [just south of the third cataract] . . . Kitchener is so greedy he has kept me here the whole time . . . because he is afraid if I got away from him I may do something which will clash with his own notoriety with the public.

The letter exists only as a fragment, presumably because Andrew had asked for some of the pages to be sent on to Will at the Foreign Office. He added a note that Kitchener had chummed up with Sir Samuel Baker, and was 'spooney on his daughter' (this, by the way, is the only heterosexual attachment that Kitchener, a rather lonely character, is known to have made).

Andrew himself was feeling rather lonely, since so many of his chums were on the Relief Force while he laboured away in the eastern Sudan. Many of them died during the campaign, and Andrew was later to record:

> As I write these lines and think of all my brother officers with whom in those days I was hail-fellow-well-met – think, too, how we fought together, drank together, had together good times in Cairo, and rough yet cheery times in the Soudan – it does indeed make me sad. There was not one of them much above thirty when he died, and most were between twenty-five and thirty.

He remembered Lamb's lines,

> I have been laughing, I have been carousing,
> Drinking late, sitting late, with my bosom cronies –
> All, all are gone, the old familiar faces.

Loneliness was now the least of Jack's worries in Lamu. He had been taken severely ill with an inflammation of the bladder, caused by a spasmodic stricture.[7] It was an old complaint which he thought had been cured but, when it recurred, he had no access to medicine or doctors and was forced to lie quiet for nearly six weeks. There was no hope of escape to Zanzibar as the South-West Monsoon blew up the autumn seas outside his house into a six-knot current running northward. His condition became so severe that he thought he was about to be 'promoted upstairs' and, when he finally recovered enough to write to Will, he enquired about being promoted instead to Madagascar, where a vacancy was coming up. He felt he could do little more to further himself in Lamu, and the dangers were increasing. He complained to Will that the Government didn't care sixpence for its subjects, and he didn't care to risk his life any longer. The gunboats which would make so much difference to his safety had not appeared at Lamu, even though Admiral Hewitt was known to be cruising in the area.

In November, Jack managed to get down to Zanzibar for treatment, and he celebrated his recovery on his return with a bottle of champagne which, after three months of abstinence, made him royally drunk and lustful. His enthusiasm returned and, with the assent of the Governor, he planned a road into the interior. By constructing a fort at the head of Mongoni Creek he hoped to protect the route from the Somalis, and the Sultan gave permission for the establishment of a garrison. In Lamu, Jack proposed building a summer house on an island opposite his home, for both his own use and that of Frederick Jackson, who was due to arrive at Christmas.

The great thing was that Will, in true Palmerstonian style, had arranged for a gunboat to be seen off the coast. It had the desired effect of subduing the natives. The Haggard network was beginning to work.

— 8 —

Honour All Over the Earth

Agnes Marion Barber was no beauty. Although her mouth was pretty, it was dominated by a strong nose and a tall brow, and the overall effect was softened only by waves of dark hair. Uncomfortably thin, at best she might have been called petite. But, looks aside, at twenty-four, Agnes had a remarkable personality and a strong literary bias. Rider was the first Haggard brother to fall under her spell.

Aggie came from a family of three sisters brought up at Castle Hill, Rastrick, in Yorkshire. After their father's death in 1881, Mrs Barber moved the family to Bungay, perhaps because of Aggie's long friendship with Louie. One daughter married, and another, Marjorie, considerably younger than the others, had a spinal weakness. Aggie spent long periods with Louie and Rider, helping to look after their children. Privately, she rather thought that Louie was more interested in her own sporting pursuits than in raising her family. Certainly Louie was not a maternal woman, but Aggie could be a possessive one.

The Barbers were a well-educated family, devoted to antiquarian pursuits, but Aggie's mother had a talent for mesmerism, and both Aggie and Marjorie had inherited her psychic disposition to a marked degree. Rider was already fascinated by the idea of telepathy and second sight and, when Aggie began helping him with his writing as 'muse' and editor, he could not but warm to her attractions. Later, in his novel *Jess*, he developed Aggie into the heroine of a love triangle: 'He was not himself aware how large a proportion of his daily thoughts were occupied by this dark-eyed girl or how completely her personality was overshadowing him. He only knew that she had the knack of making him feel thoroughly happy in her society.'

While continuing with his law studies, Rider had begun to work on a new romance. Called *The Witch's Head*, it is the most overtly autobiographical of his works, telling of a young man's blighted love and subsequent adventures in Africa. For the first time he included historical characters, like Shepstone, alongside his fictional ones; it was a device he was to use successfully many times in the future. Hurst and Blackett published a cautious 500 copies in December 1884, so that the book's success was scarcely measurable. Favourable reviews caused the book to go out of print almost immediately, but the publishers would not reprint it in a cheaper form, and it was soon pirated to America.

At the end of 1884, in a mood of pique and disappointment, he decided to concentrate his energies on his legal career. Louie found a house for them in London, in Fairholme Road, and back they all trailed, with three children now, to try once again to make a living. London may have been the hub of the world, but in the mid-eighties it was in the economic doldrums. Rider wrote: 'things are dreadfully bad in every way here and the whole country seems depressed, indeed almost paralyzed. Nobody knows what the government will do next.'

However, once back in the metropolis, the critical success of *The Witch's Head* encouraged him to think about writing once more. Aggie had come with them, and he began to show her Jack's letters from Lamu. The idea for a new novel emerged; it was to be entirely about Africa and entirely an adventure. The only novelist who had written about life on that continent was Olive Schreiner, whose book *An African Farm* had been a runaway success. Olive Schreiner had arrived as something of a celebrity in England in 1881, and Rider had written to her and met her. Unknown to him, Jack had also been enchanted with her book, and he too had written to her from Lamu. She was flattered by their charming, gentlemanly attentions. Jack was so taken with her reply that he asked Rider to interview her for him. His thoughts were turning once again to matrimony.

Rider wrote back that he had already met Miss Schreiner, and praised her good looks and superior intellect. The drawback was that 'Miss Schreiner is as complete an atheist as ever walked this earth.' Rider added, 'I doubt if she would marry you, my boy, or anyone else. I daresay that if she was fond of you she would have no objection to living with you, but marriage to her would be the emptiest ceremony and one not unattended with inconvenience. Very likely she has already lived with somebody.' Rider's final observation, that Miss Schreiner had 'little in common with her sex except its physical attributes', is an acute one. She was the only woman in whom the misogynist Cecil Rhodes showed any serious interest.

Jack temporarily had the company of Fred Jackson and his entourage, but when Fred left for his hunting expedition on the mainland Jack embarked on a trip of his own. He was once again incapacitated by stricture of the bladder and, on his return, he was struck down with what he called a form of local mumps, which produced glandular swellings all over his body.

In March, the refreshing annual change in the weather renewed his strength, and he hoped to go elephant hunting but was perturbed by the presence of some German explorers, the Denhardts, whom he suspected harboured ambitions to annex parts of East Africa. A German man-of-war had already anchored off Lamu, and the German officers had begun to make trouble with the Sultan and, indirectly, with Jack. Frederick Jackson was already planning a three-month cruise up the Tana river to collect specimens, although Jack wrote to Will that 'he is a good sportsman and a good stuffer of birds and animals *for specimens*, but about the scientific part of a naturalist's work he knows nothing, and is naturally too indolent to do anything in that line, which is a pity as he has a grand field here . . .'

By May of 1885, Jack was writing seriously to Will about the bogus treaties the Germans were making with village headmen in Zanzibar; about how they had no intention of colonizing in the British sense but only wanted to make money out of trade and slavery, 'which will flourish with renewed vigour under the Germans' better management'. In Lamu the Germans were stirring up trouble with the rebel chief, Simba, at Witu and, having made treaties for the cession of various lands, one night they attempted to seize the coastal town of Kipini. Fortunately the Arab officer in charge successfully challenged them, although he had the weaker force, and the Denhardts escaped to Lamu hoping for Jack's protection. Although they told him a pack of lies about their situation, Jack hustled them off back to Zanzibar. Jack himself advocated swift action to secure British interests and ensure the suppression of the slave trade, but such simple decisiveness was seldom part of British policy. Jack reported to Kirk, wrote to Will, and waited, spending some of his time packing cases of souvenirs, which included:

A Muscat turban for my mother.
A small Hippo Head and a Lion's Head for yourself [Charles].

Two Somali shields and two Somali knives for Rider.
Two slave irons and poles for yourself.
Three Lamu mats for Ella

and one of the Lamu chairs which he had already sent to other members of the family.

News of a Russian attack on Afghanistan had reached East Africa and, once again, rumours of a British defeat unsettled the population. Jack despaired of the British Government which so undermined its colonial officers by giving in at every challenge:

> . . . we have been living for years upon our prestige, and now we have forfeited it an enemy will appear in every bush; to my mind there is nothing more demoralizing to a Government, a Nation or an Individual than making a practice of surrender of rights, for each concession to dishonour makes the next one look less serious; it has the same deteriorating influence on character as when a man makes a custom of accepting charity.

Barely a month after writing this, Jack's condition became so severe that he went down to Zanzibar to consult a Russian doctor. Unfortunately the cure made him worse and, ill as he was, he had no choice but to return to England for hospital treatment, leaving Frederick Jackson to his ornithology and his hunting. As he had seen at first hand, the 'Scramble for Africa' was underway. At the Berlin Conference the great powers were carving up the map, and at home Sir William MacKinnon was founding the British East Africa Association with the aim of establishing trade routes between the Lakes and the coast. If British prestige was indeed sinking, one event hastened its decline that year – the death of Gordon at Khartoum.

At the beginning of 1885 the Desert Relief force had been disastrously attacked at Abu Klea, with the mortal wounding of Herbert Stewart and the death of the legendary Colonel Burnaby. The British victory was of no consolation to Wolseley for the loss of Stewart's experience and judgement. Sir Charles Wilson, who took over command, waited three days in the desert before marching on Khartoum and arriving an unforgiving forty-eight hours too late. Despite Sir Redvers Buller's pithy comment about Gordon that 'the man was not worth the camels', the epic quality of the expedition to save him, culminating in such a narrow disaster, appalled the British public in just the way that it most liked to be appalled. Distinguished and hard-won careers crashed into the desert sands.

The news did not reach Andrew in Suakin until 13 February, when he wrote in his scribbling diary that a wire had been received from Wolseley to say that Khartoum had fallen at the end of January and that Gordon had been killed. In the wake of the disaster, the British planned the reconquest of the Sudan by General Graham, but with British and Indian troops and, for the first time, an Australian contingent. Andrew's Egyptian regiment was ordered back to Cairo and, although he had volunteered to remain during the expedition, he went with them. 'It is hard lines after having been here during the last campaign and the whole of the succeeding year to have to go away now,' but leave he did on board the *Queen*, on 8 March.

As the ship steamed out of Suakin harbour, a delightful coincidence occurred:

Sightseeing at the pyramids, *c.* 1886. Major Arthur Haggard (front row, third from right), with his wife, Emily Haggard, née Calvert, on his right. Granny Calvert sits third from the left in the front.

... on passing a transport, the *Deccan*, coming in crowded with troops, I heard my Christian name loudly shouted by an officer in a red coat standing in one of the ship's boats swinging at the davits. It was my own brother, Lieutenant Arthur Haggard of the Shropshire Regiment, the 53rd, my chum Turner's old corps. He was going on active service just as I was leaving it. We only had time to exchange a hurried greeting when the two ships passed clear of each other, and for all we brothers knew, it might have been our last meeting on earth.

However, the *Queen* ran aground at the entrance to the harbour, and Commodore Molyneaux took Andrew off on his steam launch and put him on board the *Deccan*, where he spent a jolly night with Arthur and his brother officers. 'And thus ended my year's fighting at Suakin, to which I look back as one of the happiest periods of a not wholly uneventful life.'

Andrew's wife, Emily, had returned to Egypt to meet him, and once again they took up the social life of the city. Andrew was received by the Khedive, who expressed his appreciation of British discipline and training of the Egyptian troops and awarded him the 4th Class Osmanieh, which he was allowed to accept by Royal Warrant. Soon after this he had to undergo a serious operation, and so found himself back in England for the summer where Jack too was recuperating. Whether or not they saw Bazett, also ailing from a heart complaint, is doubtful. At the last minute, and to everyone's relief, Bazett had withdrawn from the case of Haggard *v.* Haggard, largely through the reluctance of his own counsel and Rider's intervention. It was a sad end to a distasteful, and potentially sensational, business, and it left Bazett routed and isolated. It is a fair indication of his circumstances that he was appointed a Revising barrister in 1885 – a position no successful barrister would have undertaken.

The slings and arrows were falling fast on Alfred, too, as he clung to his appointment at the London Hospital. Under the influence of Positivism, Alfred's views were growing more and more unorthodox. Not only did he question the whole premise of Imperial rule, he also rejected the idea of a personal God in favour of the idea of the Deity as a principal. His restless intellect was unchannelled in his work; he wrote pamphlets and gave lectures expressing his views on India.[1] In his frustration, he applied for the position of Assistant Commissioner of Police – which was not forthcoming – and schemed and dreamed of huge colonial concessions. He now had four children with a fifth on the way, and longed to regain some prestige and wealth.

Will was progressing rather better financially, but his promotion in July 1885 to Secretary of the Legation at Rio de Janeiro, took him out of the mainstream of European Diplomacy. After several thwarted attempts at matrimony, he became engaged to the recently widowed Emma, Lady Tenterden. Prior to marrying the elderly Lord Tenterden (a permanent undersecretary at the Foreign Office) Emma had been the wife of Henry Howcliff QC.[2] Her history was reminiscent of Will's first wife's, but the Haggards did not disapprove of the connection and, after the engagement, Will departed for South America.

'Sunrise in far Brazil!' wrote Mary Haggard as the opening line to her novel *His Chief's Wife*. Mary either accompanied Will or soon followed him. She can have had little idea of what was in store for her halfway across the world but, at twenty-seven and unmarried, she had little reason to stay in England. According to Andrew, he lent her fifty pounds for her passage, and off she went in search of a husband. She had grown into a formidable young woman, forthright and fond of hunting. Like Rider, she was unable to pronounce her 'r's, which came out like 'w's, but she was well-educated and spoke at least French, and probably German and Italian too. If she was unworldly before she left, she soon observed and accepted the sophisticated *mores* of consular society, where sexual liaisons were by no means uncommon as long as strict conventions were observed. These conventions were flouted at one's peril, and Mary's novels often set up the conflict between the passions of the heart and the requirements of Society; Society generally wins, and the heart triumphs only when death is imminent.

Although it was soon to be challenged, Britain was still enjoying a position of trading and social pre-eminence in Brazil. At Rio, the Diplomatic Corps withdrew for the hot season to the hill resort of Petropolis. From the creeper-entwined verandas of their houses, the diplomats could refresh themselves with views of forested, rugged mountains, and in the cool of the morning they could ride out on their splendid South American ponies. While servants catered for their domestic needs, the consular élite were free to enjoy their social pursuits and the variety and richness of the unspoiled natural landscape. The dense vegetation of palms and dark mango trees was woven with trailing, knotted vines, made vivid by magenta and scarlet blossoms and alive with the noise of parrots, humming-birds and monkeys.

Despite the steamy, alluring setting, the milieu was one of a superficially rigid propriety. Mary looked around for a suitable beau. None

Eleanora Mary Haggard, usually known in the family as Mollie, at about the time of her engagement to Baron d'Anethan in 1885.

of her letters from this period survive, but in *His Chief's Wife*, her romance of Brazilian diplomatic life, the desirable hero is the 'younger son of a Cambridgeshire squire . . . A good-looking young Englishman of the Saxon type, with fair curly hair, fresh complexion, and bright blue eyes shining with intelligence' who, although not rich, had his small pay supplemented by 'an allowance of five hundred a year, from his father'. In addition, her hero was well read, charming, popular and full of laughter.

In reality, what Mary found in Rio was a balding, short, Belgian diplomat. Albert was thirty-six years old, with a career developing on satisfactory lines. When the Japanese Iwakura mission had visited Belgium in 1873, Albert had been assigned to accompany them, and he had subsequently spent three years in Japan when that country was first opening up to foreigners. Many of his postings had been in Europe, and he appears to have had enough money to sustain himself in prestigious embassies.

Andrew, who disliked him, said that Albert smoked like a chimney and drank like a fish. Even when she became engaged to him, Mary wrote home that he looked like a toad. But a young woman can grow fond of a toad – and this particular toad had a title. Baron Albert Jean Louis Marie d'Anethan came from a highly distinguished family, very close to the Belgian throne; Albert's father had been secretary to King Leopold I.

The position of a Belgian in Brazil was not as detached from Imperial concerns as one might think. The Portuguese had a long history of importing African slaves into South America in order to develop the jungle. Leopold II of Belgium was creating a personal empire in 900,000 square miles of Africa's Congo basin where, with the help of Stanley, he was opening up the interior, building railways, exploring mineral deposits and farming cocoa, coffee and – what was to become notorious through Roger Casement's exposé – rubber. At the Berlin Conference the Congo was recognized as a sovereign state where, apparently, Leopold was gradually eliminating the Arab slave trade. But, as had happened in East Africa, other countries were at last beginning to wake up to the huge wealth waiting to be developed, and the French, Germans and Portuguese were soon making their own claims in central Africa.

The collective mind of the Great British Public had now been exposed to the savage power of Africa. It had cheered the defeat of the Ashanti

Baron Albert d'Anethan. His diplomatic posts included Rio,
Washington, Constantinople, Vienna and London. In 1906 he was
made a Commander of the Order of Leopold.

tribes, reeled at the onslaught of Zulu warriors, watched a be-suited
Cetywayo being received at court, read about Dutch farmers, followed
the Sudan campaign against the 'fuzzie-wuzzies', and drooled over the
glittering wealth of Kimberley. When Rider submitted his much-touted
manuscript of *King Solomon's Mines* to the publishing house of Cassell,
they recognized a winner.

Rider had produced a lean, sharp, active story of three Englishmen
looking for hidden treasure in the interior of Africa. The characters were
based on the men he knew – Jack was the basis for Captain Good, Allan

Quatermain was an idealized version of Rider himself along with liberal dashes of Fred Jackson and the white hunter Frederick Selous, and Sir Henry Curtis was a stereotypical Viking hero – the racial ideal. Umbopa was based entirely on Umslopogaas, Shepstone's aide de campe. The landscape, conditions and tribes were all familiar to Rider. How much of the irresistible yarn was his and how much Jack's we may never know. In later years, Jack said that he had provided most of the incidents for both *King Solomon's Mines* and *She*. Jack was certainly home that summer, and he had, in any case, been writing extensive and descriptive letters for years. But it was Rider's work and imagination which created the whole.

Cassells intended to make the book a success. They had developed new production processes which made assembly and printing in bulk much easier, and they were going to avail themselves of the new strategy of an advertising campaign. One morning in September, London woke up to see the billboards and omnibuses plastered with posters declaring: KING SOLOMON'S MINES – THE GREATEST STORY EVER TOLD. The public bought the book in droves. Reprint followed reprint followed reprint.

At last Rider had his feet firmly placed on the literary ladder, and he did everything he could to foster that prospect. Already under the wing of Andrew Lang, he soon joined the Savile Club and cultivated the contemporary men of letters. But, at the same time, he carried on writing in a sustained burst of creativity that was to form the bedrock of his future. He realized that what enchanted the public, apart from the thrill of a treasure hunt and the exotic settings, was the character of his hero, Allan Quatermain. This was the kind of honourable man of action whom the English wanted to believe was representative of their colonials.

Allan Quatermain was a trader and hunter, a gentleman by accident of birth but, more importantly, a man who had committed himself to an honourable code of behaviour in the face of vicissitudes, wars, and many temptations. He is described early in the book as a timid man – a literary device to establish the reader's empathy – but any timidity is soon eclipsed by the action. The definitive Quatermain was a hardy, outdoors man, knowledgeable about Africa and its peoples; a man who was economic with his words and his philosophy but knew how to act when the time came. With Quatermain as the narrator, Rider gave *King Solomon's Mines* a no-nonsense, contemporary style, with numerous touches of humour and irony.

★

Overnight the Haggard name had become famous – an attribute which
some of Rider's brothers used freely while others found it very tiresome.
Andrew, returning to his regiment in Egypt, had his own considerable
reputation on which to lean. The Government had been delighted to
use the excuse of trouble in Afghanistan to withdraw most of the British
troops from the Sudan. So it was that, late in 1885, the Egyptian Army
had a chance to prove itself; Andrew and the 1st Battalion headed south
once more to subdue the Dervishes. Alfred Thacker was with him and
so were his two horses, the Squire and the Parson. 'Never,' Andrew
advised, 'if it can be avoided, leave a horse behind anywhere . . .'

Christmas was spent in a tent in the desert, but turkey had been sent
from Beni Soueff, 'and Thacker had brought a tinned pudding from
Cairo, champagne [was] found amongst the Greeks who always accompanied the armies in the Soudan . . .' The journey continued by rail
through desolate mountain country to Akashe, above the second cataract
of the Nile, after which each man marched under the weight of a
Martini-Henry rifle, eighty rounds of ammunition and his greatcoat.

General Sir Frederick Stephenson, commander of the troops in Egypt,
and Major Grenfell, now Sirdar of the Egyptian Army, were in command.
On the morning of 30 December, Andrew woke early:

> In spite of all attempts at silence, a sort of continued murmur seems to
> rise into the cold night air; vague forms are seen moving along, which
> prove perhaps to be camels; a dull tramping is heard – it is a regiment
> moving off; a rattling and clanging of chains next attracts your attention
> – the guns are passing! And no one says a word, no matches are struck,
> no pipes are lighted; orders are given in a low tone, and passed on
> quietly from company to company. The dust rises heavily and fills the
> air while through that dust is somehow felt to be moving a grim resistless
> force of men, going on to death or glory, controlled solely by the love
> of honour and the iron hand of discipline.

Andrew remembered the grim sensation of subdued excitement which
he knew would disperse as soon as the first shot was fired; but he thought,
too, that it was 'a sensation well worth having lived to experience,
because it is like nothing else in existence'. The first shot, when it was
fired, unleashed what was to be called the Battle of Giness.

Stuart-Wortley, who should have been in Cairo attending to his duties
as military attaché, had found a way to join in the fighting. It is the
figure of 'Wortles', gallant and arrogant, which Andrew used to set the
scene for the battle in *Under Crescent and Star*. At the start of the day,

Stuart-Wortley 'looked superb, as, faultlessly attired with white kid gloves, and with rather more than his usual delightful swagger, he sat on his horse, and, with the utmost nonchalance, lighted his cigarette under a hail of bullets, while calmly discussing with me the prospects of our "having a good bag".' And then, beside this epitome, Andrew gives us a view of the soldiers lined up on the ridge above Osman Digna's village, waiting and anticipating the battle ahead. Suddenly the tension is broken when a hare runs in front of the Yorkshire Regiment, 'amidst the roars of Tommy Atkins'.

At Giness, Andrew had the opportunity to vindicate the belief he had maintained in his Egyptian soldiers and the training he had given them. An anonymous friend wrote of him: 'Over and over again they followed him without shrinking in his frequent successful sorties against the dreaded Dervishes . . . His regiment finally proved to the hilt the truth of his opinions of them at the crowning battle of Giness, where with the greatest dash of gallantry, they cleared out the houses of a village full of Dervishes.'

After the battle, General Butler insisted that the English have some of the trophies, although Wodehouse wanted them all for the Egyptian soldiers. That night the army bivouacked, cold and exhausted, near burnt-out Giness, but Thacker had had the foresight and initiative to return to their previous camp and had brought up the regimental camels with everybody's (officers' and men's) greatcoats. 'I never knew a soldier who could beat him at *finding* useful things,' Andrew wrote. But then Thacker, as his letters so vividly testify, was no common batman.

Instead of using their advantage and pushing on to Dongola, the Government ordered the retreat of the field force to a dreadful advance post called Mograkkeh. Andrew and Thacker now spent a miserable three months in mud huts full of flies, with their only occupations being drill, reconnaissance and a bit of hunting. In April of 1886 they withdrew to Wadi Halfa to build field forts. It was the hottest time of the year and the water was bad. Andrew's health gave way and, with little action likely in the foreseeable future, he decided to retire from the Egyptian Army. When he embarked, he was overcome by the effusive farewells, 'the hand-kissing, and the exuberant blessings in Arabic which were showered upon my head by these swarthy sons of the Nile'. Andrew had taught them to play British tunes, but by the time the boat finally left he wished they hadn't learned *Auld Lang Syne*.

Andrew was awarded with the Order of the Medjidieh (3rd Class) by

Khedive Mahomed Tewfik, and he travelled home by way of Turkey. After recuperating, he rejoined the King's Own Scottish Borderers and went out to India. Late in 1886 he was awarded the Companionship of the Distinguished Service Order for action at Giness, in the first Gazette of that distinction.

Back in England, of course, he must have enjoyed something of a hero's prestige and, with Rider's name now widely known, the Haggards may have felt they were at last coming into their own. Mr Haggard continued, as he had always done, to lobby his political associates such as Lord Walsingham for favours for his boys, and Will had helped Jack secure the position he wanted in Madagascar. But Jack had no intention of enduring another tropical posting as a single man. While in London with the Riders he naturally came much into the society of Aggie Barber. She was a competent, practical, resilient woman much used to looking after herself and her relatives, and she had had plenty of time to observe the Haggards; she and Jack saw that they could make a match, and they decided to marry in January.

News travelled fast amongst the Haggards. Only three days after Jack had informed his father of their plans, Aggie replied to criticism from Ella Maddison Green in a letter which established at once her tough, occasionally disdainful character: 'I am very pleased to find that you do not object to *me* personally, as although of course it could have made no difference to my marrying Jack, still one prefers to be, to a certain extent welcome to the relative's of one's future husband . . .'

Ella must have raised the matter of income, since Aggie defends herself on this count: 'upon the death of my mother . . . I shall come into the small fortune of £3000 which will be settled upon me on my marriage, so you see I am not *quite* penniless.' To Ella's attack about supporting a family, Aggie lunged with a riposte which managed to include an attack on religion: 'I *quite* agree with you that it is exceedingly wrong for people to have children for whom they are quite unable to provide, and yet, if I had not had the prospect of a farthing I think I should still have gone the way I am going: not, believe me, from any fool-hardiness, or superfluity of faith in a Providence which according to some provides for everyone who can't help himself, – but because I know I should never have sunk under my burdens or lost heart and hope.' Aggie finishes her letter triumphantly: 'Jack had an exceedingly nice letter from Mr Haggard to day and I had one from Mrs Haggard as sweet as any prospective daughter-in-law could desire, so I trust Jack's marriage will not be unwelcome in his family.'

It was cousin Fanny Haggard who wrote to Ella to describe Jack's wedding, which took place on 28 January 1886 at the brand-new church of St Mary's in Fulham. Aggie's uncle, Mr Barber of Chalfont, performed the ceremony, and it seems that Alfred was the best man. Mr Haggard, Rider and Louie were present, along with a number of Aggie's relatives. Aggie wore dark blue with a white veil, and white flowers on a muff. Louisa wore a ruby-coloured costume, but many of the others wore mourning black, enlivened by shawls, flowers or waistcoats. Mr Haggard wore 'a resplendent pair of white kid gloves, a new pair of trousers and a nearly new hat.' Jack, who was thinner since his illness, looked well but pale. 'He clapped the ring down on the book with an air, and when the clergyman took it up and gave it to him again said, "What do I do with it?"'

Jack had already received his commission to be Her Britannic Majesty's Consul for Madagascar, and in May he was also commissioned to represent Norway and Sweden. He travelled ahead of Aggie to Madagascar, arriving in November, but he was in England long enough at the beginning of the year to contribute ideas to Rider's new novels. Aggie, who followed in September, did much more. She and Rider concocted a lovely piece of fiction, the story of the Sherd of Amenartas, which was to provide the proof of the novel *She*.[3]

Early in 1886, Rider plunged into a period of exceptional creativity and hard work. In eighteen months he wrote *Jess*, *She* and *Allan Quatermain*. Just why this should have happened at this time is subject to interpretation. His success with *King Solomon's Mines* opened the floodgates of his imagination, and *Jess* and *She* are full of autobiographical signposts. The strength of the symbolism in *She* would indicate that Rider himself was probably not aware of what forces motivated him. It does seem that he experienced an almost violent awakening of the ceative spirit.

She was, and is, a most striking and powerful story. Drawing deeply from the well of his passion for Lilly Jackson, he produced the theme of a love which transcends death itself. In the character Ayesha (pronounced Ass-ha) Rider created a new archetype for the modern world – the surging, amoral forces of femininity personified in an immortal, all-powerful queen. From a man whose ideals were honour and respectability, it is an extraordinarily odd creation which bears witness to Freud's ideas about the subconscious. Freud himself dreamed about *She* and the symbolism of the perilous journey into an undiscovered region with a woman as a guide. In Freud's dream his own fears of death combine with some of the events in *She*, and he reflected on the strangeness of a novel in which a person's identity is retained through a series of generations for over two thousand years. The fact that Ayesha greets Leo Vincey as the descendant of her former lover does indeed point to a hereditary principle of personality, which is in keeping with the Haggards' cultivation of family history. It is also seminal to Rider's belief in the immortality of the soul and his preoccupation with death.

However, it was Carl Jung, the psychologist of the twentieth century, rather than Freud, the psychoanalyst of the nineteenth, who eventually offered a key to the mystery of *She*. Jung proposed the idea of the anima as soul-image and suggested to his pupil, Cornelia Brunner, that she study Rider's book. Because Rider wrote the book in six weeks, at a feverish pace, Brunner in her analysis *Anima as Fate* felt justified in interpreting the novel as if it were a dream, and suggested that he wrote it in response to a personal crisis. By doing so he was able to externalize his long-suppressed conflict and thereby develop spiritually. This spiritual growth in Rider manifested itself in a growing empathy towards other people. Brunner argued that *She* was a success not because it was an adventure story but because it painted a picture of a man's soul – his *anima*. Brunner sees Rider's historical significance, as a man who was able to be 'a mediator for the urgent, yet still unconscious, problems of his time'.[4]

If one accepts this interpretation, the seeming incongruity of an Imperialist from an upper-class English family intuitively representing the dilemmas of his age becomes understandable. Only a person from such a background and such a family could be so immersed in the Imperial ethic and reality to fully understand its complex psychic and sexual effects. To this extent all the Haggard brothers contributed to Rider's success, and everything in their background conspired to this end. The chance element was Rider's highly developed, intuitive and imaginative faculty – yet even this could be traced to a family trait, and inherited characteristics were an essential part of the English aspiration.

She was first serialized in the *Graphic* from October 1886 until January 1887, at which time it was published in its entirety by Longmans. According to his mother, Rider was in a highly excited state as he waited for the reviews. Mrs Haggard had other excitements on her hands. In November 1886 Mary Haggard married Baron d'Anethan, a Roman Catholic, at St James, Spanish Place, in London. Mary wore a dress of rich white satin covered in old Irish lace, with a tulle veil trimmed with orange blossom and pearls. Among the guests were the Bazetts, the Alfreds, the Andrews, the Riders and the Maddison Greens. Mrs Francis Archer sent a white-painted fan, and Alfred Thacker sent an oriental mat and pen wiper. The Baron and Baroness left London the same afternoon for Brussels, en route for Vienna.

Will's romance with Lady Tenterden had not fared so well. He wrote from Brazil that he was now engaged to a Miss Margaret Hancox, but begged his parents not to publish it until the New Year in case Bazett should hear of it. But although Mr and Mrs Haggard remained silent, they were amused to find the news abroad through Lord Walsingham, who was trying to get Will a coveted European appointment at Budapest. However, the best Walsingham could manage was the offer of Athens, where the annual salary of £500 was only half what Will desired.

Mrs Haggard took up her pen to discuss Will's new betrothed with Ella.

> The father is a Contractor, and has works connected with Brazil . . . he is going to give her £1000 for her trousseau, £500 a year for allowance; and talked of furnishing a house for them . . . This is all very well if 'business' goes on well, but Will did not talk of any settlement, such as you allude to . . . There are 5 *children* . . . so Nitie [Margaret] will only have a share of worldly goods . . . Will met her at Rio . . . He seems very fond of her, and I hope she is so of him. She did not like the Lady Tenterden affair, but seems to have got over it . . . I only hope she will not change her mind . . . there is always an element of doubt as to Will's matrimonial prospects.

Mrs Haggard went on to discuss Nitie's looks, education and attitude to religion, concluding: 'At any rate, though full young, she will be far better than those blasé women of the world with whom he has been in contact; *very old* in heart and not young in years!'

Mr and Mrs Haggard had been staying at 20 King Street, near Portman Square in London, and had entertained many members of the family over Christmas – including Cissy's children. Andrew was on his way out to Meerut, north-east of Delhi, soon to be followed by his wife 'Emmie'. Arthur was going to Malta, the Baroness d'Anethan was with her husband

Emily Margaret Hancox, known as 'Nitie', and Will Haggard in
Rio de Janeiro at the time of their marriage in 1887.

in Naples, Alice was bothered by rheumatism, Louie had a bad cold, Alfred Thacker had recently married, and Aggie was high in the mountains of Réunion, a French island in the Indian Ocean about a hundred miles west of Mauritius.

9

Distant From the Seven Hills

In his biography of his grandfather, James Pope-Hennessy remarked that the men appointed to Imperial outposts were often the civilian counterparts of Kipling's Gentlemen Troopers. The climate and conditions were too extreme to attract those men who might make a success back in England. Sir John Pope-Hennessy had been appointed Governor of Mauritius in 1882. He had the same problem as Sir William Butler and Sir Roger Casement: as Irishmen they empathized with subjugated people. From the British point of view, Pope-Hennessy had been a disaster all over the Empire, dedicating himself to reforms which caused huge dissatisfaction amongst the resident British while raising the hopes of the native peoples to a level which he could not sustain. In Mauritius, his attempts to reform the Constitution in favour of French Creole independence had prompted an official inquiry into his actions and, when Aggie and Jack were first in Madagascar, Pope-Hennessy was still in London.

Aggie's letters to her 'darling mother', from the time she left England in the autumn of 1886 until the beginning of January 1888, form an impressive account of how a nineteenth-century woman met the challenges of the Tropics. Aggie was heavily pregnant when Louie accompanied her on the initial leg of the journey to Paris and down to Marseilles, where she boarded the *Salazie* which sailed across the Mediterranean to the Red Sea. In the Suez Canal the temperature in the cabins hovered above the 90 degree mark, and bathing did little to refresh one: 'To have a bath in lukewarm sticky sea water the stickiness whereof remains, and then struggle into stockings and vest in a boiling bathroom with a steam pipe through it is an awful operation.'

Once past Aden, the *Salazie* was in the teeth of the trade winds, and everyone was fearfully sick. Completely overcome with nausea, Aggie was nursed by a kindly missionary and survived on brandy and cold beef tea, cocaine having been found to be ineffective. Unable to stand or wash for several days, she was well aware that she stank of sweat and sickness, which made her retch all the more. Because of her pregnancy, she and Jack had decided that she would stay at Réunion rather than join him immediately in Madagascar, where the heat would be almost intolerable until March. But landing at Réunion was no easy matter. The coast was rock-bound and had no proper breakwater or harbour, and the seas were always rough. To disembark from the ship 'you have to jump down into the boat as it rises on the crest of a huge wave and the same process is gone through at the jetty'. The Consul, Mr St John, and his wife took Aggie in, and she soon began to recover and become acclimatized. Jack was off in the interior of Madagascar, and she was unlikely to see him before the birth of the baby, which at this stage she called Nyleptha.[1]

The St Johns had two cottages up in the mountains at Hell Bourg, and it was here that Aggie set up home. She had heard nothing from Jack since she left Aden and the mails became her chief source of solace. She wrote long, informative letters about the flora and fauna of Réunion, and about the Creole (with their 'terrible taint of . . . black blood') and Indian inhabitants. In November, as the baby became restless in her womb, Jack turned up for a brief twelve-day visit, which delighted her – they were, after all, little more than newlyweds. For the rest, she filled her days with gardening and cooking, in which she took great pride, and soon she found she hardly knew the day of the week.

Their daughter Phoebe was born on Saturday 11 December 1886. Aggie was attended at first by an ignorant Creole girl and then by a French doctor. 'I gave myself an injection [enema] and then superintended all the arrangements of the bed with mackintoshes etc. and made ready the necessary little ligatures (a day or two before I had two bands of that strong webbing I bought at the stores sewed round the bar of my little iron bed at the bottom with a wooden handle at the bottom of each to pull with'. With only a four-hour labour, 'you can tell I had a sharp time of it.'

Not long after the birth, Aggie became seriously ill, and she wrote long, detailed accounts of her condition and the health of her new baby. Her mother's letters have been lost, but from Aggie's replies we know that Mrs Barber was much troubled by the neurotic behaviour of Marjorie, Aggie's precocious younger sister, who looked to be set on a misalliance with the son of a veterinary surgeon. Marjorie was proving to be an obstinate and difficult girl, given to nervous illness when she was thwarted, and at every stage Aggie condemned her behaviour and egotism.

Madagascar, lying east of Africa and south of the Equator, was mountainous and tropical. The French had long-standing interests in the island, and had only recently wrested some aspects of control from the dominant Hovas tribe by force of arms. However, the Hovas still maintained partial rule from the capital of Antananarivo. The situation was still highly volatile when Jack Haggard arrived as Consul and Chief Judge of the Consular Court.

It had long been customary, principally to avoid the drastic punishments of Islamic courts, for British Consuls to undertake the handling of justice in the case of British subjects living and trading abroad, and of others who came under their jurisdiction. It made the workload of the Consuls very heavy, especially if, like Jack, they had no formal legal training. When Jack brought Aggie and Phoebe back from Réunion, he was already feeling hard-pressed. They were to be based in the east coast port of Tamatave, where their house was 'very picturesque but exceedingly rotten'. Jack soon began plans to replace it with a new one on the south side of town, far away from the native smells.

To Aggie, the morals and customs of the Creoles were unbelievably despicable, in addition to which they were ravaged by the effects of cheap, coarse rum.[2] But she enjoyed the open air markets where, although the butchers hacked at the meat with complete disregard for shape or bone, and the locally grown staples of rice and sugar were as expensive as in England, she could buy a great variety and profusion of vegetables and meat cheaply. Her letters give a superb account of household management in the outposts, telling how she maintained standards in spite of drunken or pilfering servants, rotting linen, corroded cutlery and sweltering heat. She and Jack dressed for dinner every night to distinguish themselves from what they saw as the degenerate humanity beyond their gate.[3] The table was set with doileys, finger bowls and silver – she even had more silver sent out from England (to Louie's amazement) – and houseboys were trained to serve the multiple-course dinners she prepared for guests as well as the more simple meals they enjoyed themselves. One astonishing menu comprised: 'Giblet soup, tinned salmon fishcakes, chicken cutlets and fried potatoes, boiled turkey and white sauce with boiled tongue, roast beef and Yorkshire pudding garnished with water-

Agnes Haggard, née Barber, Jack's wife, with baby Phoebe and nurse in
Tamatave, Madagascar, 1887. Jack was a keen amateur photographer.

cress, potatoes and french beans . . . plum pudding, custards and jellies
in glasses, cheese and biscuits, dessert and coffee.'

Catering was not the only challenge in Aggie's married life. Jack, when
he was overtired, would become 'nervous and fidgety about himself'
and would lean on Aggie so completely that 'I sometimes feel the responsibility quite a heavy one . . . I see all his most important dispatches
and often suggest amendments which he almost always adopts.' She made
a substantial contribution to the writing and revising of his first Trade
Report, while bringing up the baby, making clothes and running the
house. Many things were quite unobtainable there, and her letters are
full of requests for items to be sent out: half a dozen toothbrushes, flannel,
Valenciennes lace, a straw hat and trimmings, a wire bustle. She and Jack
had decided to have no more children for the present.

The new house in Tamatave was of two storeys, the lower one being given over to offices and storerooms. All the domestic living areas were upstairs, and access was by two stairways which were raised up at night and the hatches battened down so that there was no access for intruders to their sleeping quarters. All around the second storey was a huge, airy veranda with sea views. They now pulled together Jack's furniture from Lamu – which apparently Fred Jackson had misused and damaged – and Aggie ordered a white dinner service with the Haggard crest.

But in spite of these attempts at civilization, they could not ignore the growing agitation of the Creoles. Sir John Pope-Hennessy, whom Aggie called 'that arch traitor', had returned to Mauritius, and his presence alone was enough to agitate the natives. Jack bewailed his workload which was 'so heavy it is impossible to get through it, and all these extra cares produce actual bewilderment, for they must be attended to . . . In addition to the Consular work and Diplomatic work, which just now is most important, I have the judicial work and it almost drives me wild.' Tamatave was a violent, restless place, and a number of the 200 cases waiting to be heard were murders.

Jack had been afraid of 'something going wrong in my head from the strain'. Although the new house had provided a refreshing and healthy domicile for his family, he himself had few outlets for recreation. There was no riding or shooting, and few people with whom they could mix. His one pastime was photography, and even with that the climate often ruined the chemicals. Jack was homesick for Bradenham: 'I often hear Jack say "How lovely the place must be just now!"'

In September 1887 the Creoles in Tamatave had tried to storm a prison to release a man whom Jack had imprisoned for assault. Jack 'had to load [his] gun and prepare [his] house for attack'. The violence subsided, but the ringleader was himself murdered two Sundays later. 'Sundays are the usual days for murders,' wrote Jack to his father; 'the Creoles having nothing else to do but to indulge the villainous propensities of a bastard and mongrel race.' This outlook, together with his poor relationship with the French officials, put him on a collision course with Pope-Hennessy, whom Jack thought guilty of 'corruption and intrigue'.

Jack, 'through some extraordinary error in the Order in Council for Madagascar', was sued in the High Court of Mauritius for judgements given in the Consular Court. A case brought before the Consular Court concerned some bags of rice which allegedly had not been paid for. As Consul, Jack was privy to information which influenced him as a Judge.

The Plaintiff took the case to the Mauritius High Court on the ground that Jack had both exceeded and abused his authority. When the court in Mauritius gave judgement against Jack – fining him 200 rupees – the Foreign Office swiftly recalled him by telegram. He was not, however, dismissed, but sent as part-Consul, part-spy to the French Naval base at Brest, where his antagonism to France could be harnessed. His salary remained the same.

Before this apparent relegation, Aggie had already expressed her envy: of Rider's successful situation in England; of Arthur, recently married to Emily Calvert,[4] and mixing with royalty at the Curragh; of the d'Ane-thans, swanning around the capitals of Europe; and of Will, who was newly posted to the civilized, if unimportant, post of Athens as the Chargé d'Affaires.

There were as yet no tourists scrambling over Greece's temples and amphitheatres and, when Lord and Lady Jersey arrived in Piraeus, they were delighted that 'Mr Haggard met us with a boat belonging to the Harbour Master's Office, and as soon as we had settled ourselves in the Hotel d'Angleterre at Athens (a very good hotel) he began to make all sorts of arrangements for us – so that instead of three days we stayed for some three weeks in Athens and about a month altogether in Greece.'

Will was a success as a Society Diplomat, but he was no doubt aware that it was Lord Palmerston's high-handed actions towards Greece in 1848 which had established the efficacy of 'gunboat diplomacy'. Palmerston's autocratic demeanour, as well as his unrelenting crusade against slavery and corruption, represented the backbone of Imperial attitudes. Will was wholeheartedly in favour of gunboat diplomacy, and later he was to be placed in circumstances where he could fully manifest it.

If Greece had no tourists, Egypt certainly had its share, and, in the winter of 1887, Rider set off to fulfil one of his greatest ambitions – to see the tombs of the Pharaohs. By the time he came back in late spring, both *She* and *Jess* had been published. *She* was both acclaimed and derided by the critics, and *Punch* published a satirical piece called '*Hee! Hee!*', soon followed by '*Adam Slaughterman* by Walker Weird' which made pointed reference to the source of the story.

Punch's sly hint was nothing compared to the vituperative accusations of plagiarism which flew through the literary press about *She* and *Allan Quatermain*. The literati were out for Rider's blood, since he had been foolish enough to write an article criticizing other novelists when he himself was barely out of the literary egg. Neither did he present a

very sophisticated figure in London Society. The edition of *Punch* of 15
September 1888 reviewed a play based on *She* which Rider himself
attended. The reviewer of '*She-That-Ought-Not-To-Be-Played*' had a field
day at the expense of 'a pale person in a pince-nez' who not only *never*
fell asleep during the interminable performance but at the end appeared
in front of the *loge* and began to praise the piece.

Rider had a critic much closer to home. Alfred simply could not
stomach the gore and violence of Rider's books, and didn't much like
him being successful either. But for the moment he needed Rider's help
and influence. Alfred had recently resigned from the London Hospital
and applied unsuccessfully for the position of Governor to the King of
Siam. He aimed so high that his lack of success was scarcely surprising,
but, impecunious and nearly forty, he turned his attention to Africa. The
formation of the Austral Africa Exploration Company for the purpose
of acquiring mining concessions in Matabeleland gave Rider a chance
not only of profitable investment but also of keeping his hand in the
real world of African politics. Alfred was the Managing Director.

By 1888, Rhodes was Prime Minister of Cape Colony, leading the
push to gain control over Matabeleland and Mashonaland, the kingdoms
which were to become Rhodesia. The British Liberal Government,
which had previously wanted no truck with his plans, had woken up to
the need for action when they saw that the Germans and the Portuguese
were making huge inroads into central Africa. Rhodes himself was
regarded with serious misgivings in many official quarters, some under-
estimating his importance, others simply ignoring him on the grounds
that he wasn't a gentleman.

In order for Rhodes to apply for a Royal Charter for a public company
to develop the lands, he needed a substantial concession from King
Lobengula, the Ndebele ruler. Lobengula was an intelligent but dangerous man who had watched other African kings and their armies fall
inexorably to European guns. His fertile kingdom was already under
pressure from concession hunters, and he knew he must eventually make
some kind of deal with the British. He undertook not to give away his
lands without the sanction of the British High Commissioner.

Rhodes's emissaries, Charles Rudd, F. R. Thompson and Rochfort
Maguire, with the connivance of the Deputy High Commissioner for
Bechuanaland Sir Sidney Shippard, duped the illiterate Lobengula into
signing a concession of mining rights the terms of which would open
the path to monopoly and settlement. It was crucial to Rhodes to keep

Alfred in 1888 with his youngest son Dan, aged two, and Godfrey,
aged four. At this time Alfred bore a distinct likeness to Rhodes,
which did not go unnoticed in South Africa.

the deception quiet as long as possible, to buy off his rivals. With the cooperation of Lobengula he spread rumours that Matabeleland was not safe for white men, and Thompson and Maguire stood guard, as it were, to repulse any concession hunters who might still turn up.

Alfred arrived in Africa in September 1888 with John Fellowes Wallop, second son of Lord Portsmouth. Representing the Austral Africa Exploration Company, they intended to travel to Matabeleland to make their own deal with Lobengula. One of Alfred's first letters to his son Harry[5] from Mafeking illustrates how different were Alfred's perceptions to Rider's: 'Some of the questions here are very interesting, there is the English party, the Dutch party and the natives. The English use the native against the Dutch . . .' Rider, however, was rightly more sceptical about Lobengula, who had murdered two of his friends in the 1870s.

Coincidental with Alfred's arrival, the prospectus of the company was published in Cape Town, unfortunately giving the Rhodes party plenty of warning. Alfred and Wallop prepared for their trek. They travelled in the traditional Boer way in waggons each drawn by fourteen oxen; there were no reins, only a long hippo-hide whip to control the beasts. By 8 November Alfred and Wallop had reached Shoshong in Bamangwato (now Botswana), 'the biggest town in this part of the world, which is a collection of huts'.

They did not expect to reach Matabeleland for at least a fortnight, and had already met a number of chiefs. 'I like the natives very much they are so merry and genial in which I think they have an advantage over English people who seem hardly to know how to laugh.' When they did reach the Tate Settlement in Matebeleland, Alfred found a letter waiting for him from Maguire, ordering him to stop, and on 2 December, when he wrote a letter of protest to the Marquis of Salisbury, he was awaiting a Matabele detachment which had been instructed to enforce the order.

To a friend named Ellis, of Wanstead,[6] he wrote more confidentially:

> I am now awaiting permission to enter Matabeleland, I expect the answer tonight or tomorrow. The country seems much quieter, confidence is reviving here, though all work is stopped. There is a gang of people interested in keeping others out, by fair means or foul . . . I ought to tell you confidentially that arts have been employed *in the highest quarters* to dishearten Mr Wallop with our scheme. And I am not sure that overtures have not actually been made to him by Cecil Rhodes, who dislikes us . . .

At present Rhodes would seem to be successful, but the tables appear to be turned by Maund, the agent of Baring's, being on the point of bringing a Matabele deputation to England. This will bring Matabeleland out of the domain of Cape politics, into the Imperial domain; which is what ought to be the case.

I am so glad to think I determined to go on, not with standing Rudd's apparent success.

A few days later a small, menacing army of Ndebele warriors led by Maguire swooped down on Tate and blocked the road to Matabeleland. To have tried to push their waggons through would have invited violent attack. Alfred was furious, but had no option but to withdraw. Back in Cape Town he did what he could to deprecate the Rudd–Maguire Concession and implied that he himself represented the forward-looking 'spirit of the Foreign as contrasted with the Colonial Office in London', implying that Rudd and Maguire would throw the country into the arms of the Colonial Office.

Maund, who had arrived well ahead of Alfred, was more successful in challenging Rhodes's perfidy. He had raised doubts in Lobengula's mind and persuaded him to send two envoys to Queen Victoria. Threatened with exposure of the fraudulent concession, Rhodes set about paying off the claims of his rivals. In the case of the Austral Africa Exploration Company, Rhodes feared not Alfred's rumour-mongering in the Cape, annoying though it was, but Rider's pen, which might have undermined his plans. But Rider never attacked Rhodes, perhaps being more familiar with Alfred's shortcomings.

Opposition to Rhodes's bid for a Charter for Matabeleland disappeared after Rhodes had spent some time in London and put men like Scott Keltie of the Royal Geographical Society and W. Stead of the *Pall Mall Gazette* on his payroll and offered others the chance to buy shares at par. Many influential men were simply bewitched by his vision, which was able to pick up on 'Harry Johnston's talk of the "all-Red" route from Cape to Cairo'.[7] Cecil Rhodes was the one man with sufficient power and wealth to link his Chartered Empire with Mackinnon's East African Empire in Uganda and the Upper Nile.

Nevertheless, the condition of Colonial Office support was the amalgamation of the major claims. Rhodes set up a new Central Search Association, into which the rival companies were absorbed in exchange for valuable shares. For the Austral Africa Exploration Company he paid £2,400 worth of shares; theoretically it would also receive exclusive

charge of the minerals in a 400-square-mile area to be selected by Austral
Africa. The Haggards were no match for Rhodes and, although the deal
seemed sweet at first, Alfred soon found its hard, bitter centre when he
was quite unable to realize the mineral wealth.

All these negotiations took place in London in 1889. Alice had succumbed to a rheumatic illness, so she and Alfred decided to leave
Wanstead and, after a summer in Norfolk, took up residence at 28
Wellington Square, St Leonard's on Sea. Alice hated the house, but the
milder climate was presumed to be beneficial for her ailments. Her
recurrent illnesses and her growing deafness must surely have played a
part in Alfred's frustrations.

In the summer of 1889 the fruits of Rider's trip to Egypt were published
in the form of a new – and what he then considered to be his best –
novel, *Cleopatra*. Rider dedicated it to his mother, who had so inspired
in him the love of antiquities. Mrs Haggard had suffered a stroke and
was confined to a wheelchair; she was barely able to lift and read the
book when it arrived at Bradenham. The dedication moved her to tears.

Apart from the Alfreds at Sheringham, Mrs Haggard had the distraction
that summer of the Andrews, who came to stay a few days although
Andrew himself was unwell, suffering from perpetual fainting fits and
attended by his personal servant 'Ahmed the Ethiopian'. Later in the
year Mary was also with her mother, but she then rejoined her husband
as the possibility of their being posted to Japan loomed large.

Will in Athens was expecting a visit from Rider who, typically, was
making extensive arrangements and had partially paid for his trip. On 5
November 1889, Elizabeth Hocking, maid, nurse and family friend to
Mr and Mrs Haggard, wrote urgently to Ella Maddison Green asking
her to come and stay before Christmas on account of Mrs Haggard being
so unwell: 'In addition to her feet she have a great many *blind boils* in a
very delicate part, so you see there is quite enough to make her low
spirited.'[8] The Squire had a bad cough and cold and could not read, and
the county was by now so depopulated that there were no neighbours
to visit on any kind of regular basis.

A month later, the end was near. Rider was called to Bradenham,
where Ella was already in attendance. Mrs Haggard was fading fast, and
she died on Monday 9 December 1889. She was buried in the churchyard
at Bradenham.

Four of her sons were at her funeral and initially the devastating loss
bound together their affections. Rider arranged for his friend Charles

Alfred's wife Alice, née Schalch, in mid-life
after ill health and tribulations had undermined
her good looks and vivacity.

Longman to reprint Mrs Haggard's narrative poem *Life*, with a new memorial preface. But it was not long before fraternal affection began to fragment. Rider blamed Will for his having to abandon expensive travel arrangements. The division of Mrs Haggard's jewellery provided another opportunity for squabbling: Ella and Mary were accused of taking everything. The brothers who lived abroad were offended at not receiving items which they felt should have been theirs. The unifying centre of their life had disappeared. Ironically, it was often the very letters which Mrs Haggard had encouraged them all to write, and which have ensured their immortality, that prompted their disagreements. Living so far apart, they wrote constantly to each other, voicing their immediate reactions without due consideration for the delayed effect at the other end.

But writing had turned out to be a lucrative business for Rider, and Andrew was beginning to think he might follow suit. His first novel about Egypt, *Dodo and I*, had been well received. It was followed in late 1890 by *Ada Triscott*; then he undertook a narrative poem of Egypt called *A Strange Tale of a Scarabaeus* which includes these semi-autobiographical lines:

> Married? yes, alas! I married
> When I was a silly fool,
> In a township where I tarried,
> To a virgin fresh from school.

Andrew's dateline is 'December 15 1890 Near Kansas City' – he had already begun to drift around North America and, in February of 1891, Blackwoods published his article 'Yankee Homes and Buffalo Haunts'. The dedications in his books hint at numerous affections: *Dodo and I* to A.L.Y.; *Ada Triscott* to Lilias Eaton (from Paris in January 1890); *Scarabaeus* to Mrs George Augustus Sala (from Plymouth in 1891). When he decided to retire from the Army, a profile was printed in *The London Figaro* of 26 September 1891. 'Captain Haggard proposes ... to exchange the career of a soldier for that of a literary man. As he is on the sunny side of forty, he has every right to suppose that he can gather fresh laurels in a sphere of life which is comparatively new to him.'

Despite producing regular articles for *The Field* and *Blackwoods Magazine* and a respectable output of novels, Andrew never wrote anything outstanding, with the result that he was often reduced to penury. It was a terrible shock to the man who had been Governor of Massowah and had stood shoulder to shoulder with the heroes of the Sudan, and from time to time he bitterly resented Rider's success.

Colonel Andrew Charles Parker Haggard – from the front of
Under Crescent and Star, published in 1895.

With the help of the agent A. P. Watt, and by writing fourteen books in seven years, Rider had assured himself of a steady income from royalties. Rider's two great advantages were that he had Louie behind him and that he wrote quickly. But, as Robert Louis Stevenson pointed out, the prose was rather slipshod. Although *Kidnapped* and *Treasure Island* appeal to the same readership as *King Solomon's Mines*, Stevenson by contrast was a dedicated craftsman.

Stevenson's poor health led him to look for a safe haven, where he could live cheaply and write in peace. He found Samoa, or the Navigator Islands, in the Pacific, and settled in Apia where he built his now-famous house Vailima. He had not been there long when, under the provisions of the Berlin Conference, three Land Commissioners were sent out to Samoa to arbitrate claims, one from Germany, one from the United States and one from England. The English Land Commissioner who arrived in Samoa in July of 1890 was none other than Bazett Haggard. He had probably obtained the post through Will or Lord Walsingham. Bazett and Stevenson became close friends, and it is due to this friendship that we have some record of Bazett's life in the South Seas.

If the Haggard brothers pined for home during their long spells in the outposts, at least they had their day. Cissy's confinement at St Andrew's Hospital had by now lasted for nine years. After a period of poor health she had regained some of the weight she had lost, but still only reached a little over 8 stone. Her behaviour was characterized as noisy, turbulent and destructive. Schizophrenia was not a recognized condition, but her symptoms suggest that diagnosis. She cannot have been completely out of her mind; she cried with disappointment on one occasion when she was told that her husband had called and left again without seeing her.

In Our Very Death

Jock Haggard, Rider's son, was a much-loved and by all accounts delight-ful little boy. Painted from a photograph after his death, he is posed with a golf club which now hangs, child-sized, beneath the portrait – a ghost and his toy. He was presumably being tutored at the time in Louie's latest sporting enthusiasm. One of his remaining letters is an affectionate, dutiful little note to his father, rather wistfully hoping for his return. Rider was to make much of his premonition of a parting from Jock, believing that it was he himself who would die.

Their children were still young – Dorothy was five years old, Angela six and Jock nine – when Rider and Louie decided to go to Mexico together. Rider was to research a new novel, while Louie aimed to be the first white woman to travel in the remote Chiapas district in the south of Mexico, and visit the ruined city of Valenque. For Rider at least there was the added lure of a treasure hunt for the gold which Cortez had reputedly left as he fled from the revenge of the Aztecs. Rider had been inspired by his new friend, the adventurer Gladwyn Jebb, who already had a house and financial interests in Mexico City. Jebb had come up with an extraordinary tale of a man who had located the old mineshaft down which the treasure was said to have been flung, but the man needed Jebb's influence with the owner of the mine to continue his excavations for 'antiquities'. Rider, it seemed, wanted to take part in one of his own novels.

Young Jock had been ill the previous year with symptoms which had never been pinned down, although typhoid was feared.[1] In the autumn of 1890 he had been seriously ill again. Alice wrote later: 'Poor, poor little boy, I wish we had had him at Bradenham.' But Jock did not go to Bradenham with any of his Haggard relatives, although Will's children were staying there while he and Nitie made a trip to Rio to visit the d'Anethans. Instead, Louie made other arrangements: the girls were to stay with the Hartcups in Bungay while Jock, accompanied by his nurse, joined the family of the literary critic Edmund Gosse, after which he was to go to visit some friends of Nitie's, the Barrington Footes, in London.

Rider and Louie were much fêted in America on their arrival early in 1891, but the Wild West was still very much in evidence; the train which followed Rider's through Texas was held up and robbed at gunpoint by a gang of masked men. Reaching Mexico City on 23 January, Rider and Louie were immediately captivated by the ornate Spanish city dominated by two great volcanic hills. They planned to start for Chiapas in about ten days' time.

The element that confused everyone about Jock's illness was that when he arrived at the home of Mr and Mrs Gosse he was already carrying the measles virus, which rapidly developed and spread to the other children in the house. Although Jock's was a severe case, all of them apparently recovered after three weeks. But the measles took the attention away from other symptoms.

On 25 January, at the time the Riders had just arrived in Mexico City, Alice Haggard wrote to her son Harry that Jock was with the Barrington Footes and was ill with typhoid fever. 'It's very sad, typhoid is so serious and dangerous.' This was the first diagnosis of anything more serious than measles.

Alice wrote again on Thursday 12 February 1891:

> I have such sad news for you, that poor dear little Jock is dead . . . I think I must have told you in my last letter he had got measles, he was very ill but they said he was getting better and could get up, but on Friday he was taken worse, in terrible pain, and on Sunday morning at 2.20 he died. They telegraphed for Mr Hildyard and Miss Hartcup but neither arrived in time, and the poor child was with strangers. Mrs Barrington Foote (he was spending the holidays there), was very ill herself with measles and the two boys also.

Lucy Hartcup wrote to Mr Haggard from London. '[Jock] had been going on well, in fact on Thursday afternoon we had a letter from his doctor giving a capital report of him. On Friday he was suddenly attacked with sickness etc this grew worse and though the best advice in London was called in Dr Jee and another whose name I forget, they could do nothing for him, and he died at 2 o'clock on Saturday night.'

Alfred wrote to his son that Jock had been in bed with measles for three weeks and 'in the end had violent pains in his bowels'. Alice discussed the matter further: 'They think this ulcer must have been going on ever since the illness he had in the autumn, and the doctors say he must have suffered pain, and cannot think how it was not discovered sooner.' A post-mortem cleared up some of the mystery, but the death certificate was inaccurate, citing 'peritonitis after measles', as though they were connected. Lucy Hartcup wrote to Ella Maddison Green, on 13 February:

> The peritonitis had nothing to do with the measles of which the child was practically recovered and . . . A curious fact is, that it is now ascertained Jock never did have typhoid, which always leaves traces behind, but that attack was pleurisy, only the doctors in the country never discovered it, but there was adhesion of one lung. The doctors say 'gastric ulcer' is utterly unaccountable as to cause, and is almost unknown in a child. Even up to the Friday morning he was going on well, though not gaining strength so fast, but the deafness [caused by measles] had occasioned his being kept still to one room for fear of a chill. He never could have lived, as this ulcer must have been of old standing, and when it broke death must ensue.

Will wrote along the same lines: 'How extraordinary that the ulcer should never have been discovered – as also the fact . . . that he had had bad pleurisy. It seems inconceivable that these . . . maladies should have passed unnoticed.'

The news was cabled to Rider and Louie and, within twelve hours, a return cable from Rider was received: 'We wish our beloved son to be buried at Ditchingham near the Church Porch.' Alfred could not attend the funeral but, at Mr Haggard's particular request, Jack came from France and Arthur from Ireland, as well as Bazett's eldest son George. Mr Haggard was also emphatic that Jock's sisters, Dollie and Angie, should attend, despite their age. Ditchingham House was being altered and decorated, but the small oak coffin was placed 'in the recessed part of the new hall' and piled up with flowers – thirty and more wreaths, all of which were white except for a few violets.

Unsure of how best to handle the matter, Lucy Hartcup had the coffin and flowers photographed in case Rider and Louie wanted to see it – but they need not see the photograph if they did not care to. The grave was also photographed for the same reason. The men walked to the church from Ditchingham House, but the girls and Lucy Hartcup were driven. Then Angie was taken by Jack to the graveside, and Dolly by Arthur. 'Poor dear little things, they were very good, I doubt if they understood much, but they did not cry. I fancy the only persons who did not.'

Numbed with grief, Rider and Louie stayed on in Mexico and carried on with their trip. No gold was discovered, but Rider did get enough material for his next novel, *Montezuma's Daughter*. When they returned to Ditchingham in April, Louie wrote to Aggie thanking her for her sympathy. 'There is no need for me to dwell upon the awful shock our darling's death was to us coming as it did without the least warning. Rider with his nervous and sensitive nature naturally suffered terribly, and I think this helped me to bear up until the first brunt of it passed away as I saw that one of us must do so. Rider has now I am glad to say nearly quite recovered his usual spirits but of course the next few weeks must be trying ones.'   Alice candidly wrote to her son that Louie 'is not a person who shows her feelings at all and it *must* be a terrible sorrow to her'. But Louie was quite determined to maintain her outward façade, and she wrote to Aggie: 'I have not been to the grave yet I felt I could not face the congregation the first time.'

Will offered Rider what consolation he could: 'The fact that he could not possibly have lived under any circumstances more than a few months more should resign you to the inevitable.' But, to Alfred, Rider appeared inconsolable. Whether or not Louie realized it yet, Rider was already brooding; he wrote to Jack: 'I can never get over his loss and one of the greatest hopes of my life is that its end may be the hour of our meeting. From this world he is gone and for us there is nothing left but his memory which will not die. Somehow death completes and perfects affection and I think that the dead are nearer to us than the living. They never can be estranged.'

Thirty years later, Mary wrote the following lines after a visit to Jock's graveside:

> The weary years have sped away my dear,
> Since thou wast laid within the churchyard green,
> The years have flown, and yet how very near
> Thy boyish form with me today has been.
> Thy bright young voice that callest through the hall,
> Thy pure blue eyes, sparkling with fun and joy;
> Ah! who could dream that thou – replete with youth
> So loving and so loved – so talented – so brave; –

Dream that thy gifts, thy virtues, and thy truth,
All – all should vanish neath this little grave?
And yet thou liest now where boyish pain
Is felt no more – Beyond is lasting joy!
Say! who of us would call thee back again
To fold thee in our arms? Not I – my boy!

Although it was Jock's death that cast a pall over Ditchingham and became the 'significant' death in the Haggard family, they had already been affected by the high incidence of child mortality; Ella and Charles Maddison Green had lost four infants at, or soon after, birth. And there had been one sad little death which had gone by unremarked in those letters which remain: in 1888, nine-year-old Caroline Western, the daughter of Cissy and Maximilian Western, had died at her uncle's house in Maidenhead where she was living. One wonders if her mother was ever told or ever realized that she had died. Unlike Jock, Caroline, if she was mourned at all, was apparently soon forgotten.

Bazett, who had himself suffered from pleurisy at various times, may well have thought the islands of the South Seas would benefit his shaky health. Robert Louis Stevenson always gave the impression that Samoa was a little paradise and at first Bazett seems to have been equally enchanted by his new circumstances. As the British Land Commissioner, 'He had been endowed with a Foreign Office uniform and a Red Box which were sources of infinite gratification and innocent pride.' Bazett's magisterial work involved sorting out claims in court as well as travelling to the other islands to investigate disputes. Foreigners tried to cheat Samoans over the price of property, and Samoans were likely to sell the same piece of land several times, so he had his work cut out. The Chief Justice was a Swede named Cedarcrantz who knew no English when he first arrived in Samoa and had to be sent off on a course. According to the British, he knew little more when he came back.

While the Germans dominated the islands, there were two rival native Chiefs vying for supremacy, one supported by the European governments and one by the Samoans. Stevenson drew a parallel between the rebel king Mataafa and the Jacobite Young Pretender, and naturally he aligned himself with the rebel. Stevenson used his pen and his influence to tell the world about what was going on, as well as embroiling himself in intrigue and preparing to take up arms.

The social life of Samoa was an easy-going affair amongst the Europeans; Stevenson extended his hospitality to half-castes, Samoans, and

Vailima party. Robert Louis Stevenson and Fanny are together at
the top centre. Bazett Haggard, with beard and glasses, stands to
the left of RLS in the back row. (*From the Royal Commonwealth Society
Collection by permission of the Syndics of Cambridge University Library.*)

visiting sailors. At Vailima, their estate above Apia, Louis and Fanny
Stevenson reigned over a peculiar menagerie of sponging relatives and
loyal and/or unreliable servants. While developing the property as an
agricultural concern and building extensions to the house, Louis was
maintaining his prolific written output to secure their living. Louis and
Fanny had an uneven relationship, and his grown-up stepchildren added
a cocktail of jealousy, lust, deceit and intensity to the domestic machina-
tions. Louis drank a great deal of wine and behaved with the dramatic
style of his heroes. Desperately emaciated but hauntingly fiery, he often

dressed like a pirate with white trousers, a red sash and a velvet jacket, while the ample Fanny abandoned her stays for a native frock. Fanny once reflected in her diary, 'They must think that Vailima is a sort of imitation Wuthering Heights.'

Into this half-comic, half-melodramatic, and often uproarious situation stepped Bazett Haggard replete with several pairs of new pyjamas which he had designed himself with feet on them to stop mosquitoes straying up the legs. Bazett's typically Haggard character has been described as 'unreasonable, stentorian, quick-tempered – vain and eccentric, charming and "gaily indiscreet"',[2] but Stevenson thought him the ablest man on the islands and 'though not well-mannered, a king of men in soul'. Indeed Stevenson soon described Bazett warmly as his 'companion in arms' and began to feel that he knew Rider through Bazett and had difficulty in remembering that though he corresponded with Rider he had never met him.

Apia beach bordered a broad picturesque bay dramatically scarred by the wrecks of rigged ships from the storm of 1889. Weatherbeaten wooden houses of two and three storeys with spacious verandas were set wide apart around the bay and jetties reached out to the sea. Behind the settlement the vegetation drew dark and dense, and a mountain loomed above the heady, hot little paradise. Bazett abandoned his first residence after an unfortunate incident of cock shooting and moved into Ruge's Building near the harbour. The long-gone Mr Ruge had made his money in Mexico, and he built the house so that it could be defended. All the living rooms were upstairs and the ground floor was protected by a network of iron bars. Stevenson described the building, which he said was haunted, as like some 'strange monastery' with 'vast empty sheds, the empty store, the airless, hot, long, bare rooms, the claps of the wind that set everything flying'. By the time Bazett arrived the place was rotting, having been eaten away by ants. Bazett actually had a little painted hut at the back of the building which he used as an office-cum-bedroom with his travelling camp bed. The house itself had been considered by the Stevensons for themselves, but they had rejected it because of its location: 'the air close and deathly . . . certainly not a healthy situation'. Unwisely for a man who has had pleurisy, Bazett stayed there and entertained there for long periods, moving out occasionally to lodge at the Tivoli and returning when he fell out with the landlord.

Not long after his arrival Bazett was called back to Sydney where he was entertained by the Governor of New South Wales, Lord Jersey, and his wife, Margaret Villiers. Having been looked after so well by Will in Athens, they were delighted with Bazett, offering him a friendship which he badly needed. In her memoirs, Lady Jersey remembered him with affectionate amusement: 'Previous to a ball at Government House he asked with all the solemnity appropriate to a budding diplomat whether I would dance with him as first representative of the Foreign Office at Sydney. After the dance he laid aside his sword for the rest of the evening, assuring me that this was proper etiquette, to dance the State dance wearing the sword and subsequent ones without it. No doubt he was right.'

Bazett, when he visited Sydney, was soon known as 'Samoa' Haggard because he talked of nothing else. Nothing else, that is, except for Norfolk. Lady Jersey recalled: 'Apart from Samoa the universe for him revolved around his native county, Norfolk, whence sprang all that was finest in the British race, particularly the Haggard brothers. I forget how many there were, but they had, he said, all loud voices, and on some occasion won a contested election by the simple process of shouting.' Sadly, his love of his family was not always reciprocated. Alice wrote to Harry: 'Uncle Bazett you know is at Samoa and it is to be hoped he wont come home yet.'

Bazett was under the apprehension that women found him irresistible and he did indeed get offers of matrimony from native women of the islands when he visited on official business. He was also rather taken, as were others, with a young woman, of English/German parentage, named Bella Decker who crops up in the diaries and memoirs of the Stevenson/ Osborne family. But Bazett's real weakness was for drink; occasional over-indulgence soon escalated into episodes of drunkenness which were officially noted by the British Consul Cusack-Smith.

European intriguing makes the Samoan politics seem now rather ludicrous but, after Mataafa broke with the European powers in May 1891, there was an acute danger of an uprising. Stevenson's labour force was comprised entirely of Mataafa supporters who at best were likely to desert Vailima, at worst to slit the family's throats. Louis laid plans for a defence of the house and Bazett was equally excited by the possibility of hand-to-hand combat – apparently he longed to take a chivalrous role in defence of the European women.

Stevenson was becoming an embarrassment to the governments which administered Samoa, and several ideas were postulated about how to remove him from the scene. Bazett should have remained strictly outside

Stevenson's intriguing, but he threw himself into the imbroglio in a most un-diplomatic way, giving the Consul cause for considerable concern.

The best-documented episode of high jinks was the visit to Apia in August 1892 by Lady Jersey, her daughter, and her brother Captain the Hon. Rupert Leigh as guests of Bazett. At the time, Louis's cousin Graham Balfour was staying with him, and between the Vailima family and the Ruge Building's guests there was plenty of scope for fun. Stevenson recounted that 'the great Haggard' awaited Lady Jersey's arrival in some agitation having expended much time and effort in re-painting rooms and fixing up a bathroom which he insisted on showing Stevenson, 'his chief joy, the new seat of the water-closet I thought he would never be done with.'

Lady Jersey brought with her an assortment of preserved meats and plenty of champagne to supplement her host's stores. Bazett gave a dinner when they arrived: 'I shall never forget the moment when I first saw him [Stevenson] and his wife standing at the door of the long, wood-panelled room in Ruge's Building . . . every word every gesture revealed the man, and he gave one the impression that life was for him a game to be shared with his friends and played nobly to the end.' The Countess went on to record that it was during that first meeting that they had the idea to form an 'Apia Publishing Company' and from it later grew the project of writing a story in which Bazett should be the hero. It was Stevenson himself who suggested the title *An Object of Pity, or the Man Haggard.*

The Countess found Bazett kindness itself, despite his oddities and unpunctuality, and she felt sure that he was an 'excellent and capable Commissioner'. Bazett in turn was enchanted to entertain the Countess' party and called her 'a kind and most brilliant sister so to speak' – but Fanny Stevenson bluntly judged them 'a selfish "Champagne Charley" set', marking the Countess herself as 'tall leggy and awkward, with bold black eyes and sensual mouth; very selfish and greedy of admiration, a touch of vulgarity, courageous as a man, and reckless as a woman'.

The natives called the Countess 'Queen Sydney' and regarded her as a political figure. She was entertained by Laupepa, the official king of Samoa, but Louis and Bazett hatched a plot so that she could meet Mataafa without compromising her husband's position. Stevenson would pretend that she and her brother, Leigh, were his Balfour relatives and take them to Mataafa's hut. The elaborate secret arrangements show just how far Bazett's and Louis's imaginations had run riot. Bazett led the

Jersey party out on a ride to a spot where they were to meet up with Stevenson, Lloyd Osborne and Mrs Strong who were hiding in the undergrowth, like Jacobites in the heather! In Stevenson's words: 'Haggard, insane with secrecy and romance, overtook me, almost bore me down, shouting "Ride, ride!" like a hero in a ballad.' After taking 'infinite, and deliciously infinitesimal, precautions' to cover their tracks by diversions, Bazett returned to Apia with Lady Jersey's daughter while the rest of the party rode up the mountain to Mataafa's quarters. Mataafa, although he was not fooled for a minute, played along with the charade, and gave the conspirators an elaborate Samoan feast and kava ceremony, followed the next day by various audiences.

This excursion became one of the strands in the story which the Stevensons and the Jerseys were writing about Bazett. They compiled it between them, doing a chapter each and giving each other pseudonyms. Bazett's own copy, still in the family, is annotated with explanations of the names and references. Bazett was kept in ignorance of this project until the time of a party at the Stevensons, when RLS gave a reading of the finished work. 'In the end we posed as a group, Mrs Strong lying on the ground and holding up an apple while the rest of us knelt or bent in various attitudes of adoration round the erect form and smiling countenance of Haggard.' Unfortunately the photograph did not come out well but Lady Jersey's mother made a coloured sketch from it. Later Lady Jersey had a number of copies of the manuscript privately printed.

Bazett was flattered beyond measure, but when he sent a copy home to Ella Maddison Green he wrote firmly on the front page: 'This is most "Private" and particular [*sic*] only for perusal by Charles E.M.G. Possibly Father, Mary and D'Anethan and maybe Aunt Fanny – as this is printed for *most* private circulation by my late guest. *My only* copy. To be got back from Bradenham if sent there by you – by *you* or Charles M.G. [signed] Bazett M. Haggard. Apia, Samoa November 9 1892.' In a letter of the same time he wrote to Ella that she might show it to his Father if he was weak with illness and would be amused, but 'I do not intend my friends to be laughed at, or made a fool of, or myself. It is not to be kicked about on the table at Bradenham . . .'

The Object of Pity is a delightful document, not only in the detail it gives about Bazett's character and activities, but in its sense of fun. The authors dedicated it to 'Ouida', the extravagantly romantic novelist, because they felt as if they had somehow strayed into one of her wildly unbelievable tales, and they cribbed her exaggerated style.[3] The Epilogue,

Bazett Haggard in Samoa. The inscription reads 'To Lloyd Osborne from his friend Bazett M. Haggard, Sep. 29 1894'.

written by Graham Balfour, sets Bazett up as an aged lord holding court like a Saxon thane in his banqueting hall in Norfolk and remembering his life in Apia.

Stevenson laughed at Bazett's eccentricities, but he enjoyed him as a friend; he did not judge him as his brothers judged him. In Samoa Bazett had status and could give sumptuous feasts and picnics: one of his dinners consisted of soup, tomato and crayfish salad, Indian curry, a tender joint of beef, a dish of pigeons, plus pudding, cheese, coffee and fine wines.

And if he was discovered drunk no one much minded. Fanny Stevenson might berate him occasionally, and his posturing defence of the ladies (he insisted on locking Lady Jersey into her bedroom) might seem excessive, but he was allowed to be himself.

Lady Jersey recorded that on one occasion when she was presented to Samoan royalty, Bazett donned his diplomatic uniform and brought his interpreter, who was instructed to translate his speech *exactly*.

> He first dilated in flowery language on the importance of my presence in Samoa, on which our guests interjected murmurs of pleased assent. He then went on to foreshadow our imminent departure – mournful 'yahs' came in here – and then wound up with words to this effect: 'Partings must always occur on earth; there is but one place where there will be no more partings, and that is the Kingdom of heaven, where Lady Jersey will be very pleased to see all present.' Imagine the joy of the Stevenson family when this gem of rhetoric was reported to them.

After Lady Jersey's return to Australia Stevenson reported that Bazett was 'absolutely inconsolable and at least partially insane'. Bazett had been reported for neglect of his duties which made him highly indignant. Fortunately he was diverted by the arrival of one of his Haggard cousins. In mid-September 1892, Stevenson wrote to Sydney Colvin: 'A few days ago it was Haggard's birthday, and we had him and his cousin – bless me if I ever told you of his cousin! – he is here anyway, and a fine pleasing specimen, so that we have concluded (after our own happy experience) that the climate of Samoa must be favourable to cousins, in which they join with gusto.' Stevenson's cousin Graham Balfour was still at Vailima and an extended joke developed: 'We have pitted them against each other at milking and at piquet, but neither of these competitions has come off. His cousin can play the guitar and sing; we are honest enough to confess that he scores there; but then *our* cousin doesn't pun.'

Following the birthday dinner Stevenson read out some birthday verses he had written especially for his friend: 'Haggard is verse mad and cannot write an invitation to dinner without rhyming.' After a long-winded reply by Bazett extolling Lady Jersey, 'he went out on the veranda in the lovely moonlight, drinking port, hearing with secret envy the cousin play and sing, and learning with diabolical pleasure that the said cousin was not "a Norfolk man" after all but only a party from Berkshire.'

Interestingly, the Victorian racial romanticism came out in this joke, since 'Haggard tried to rally round his disconsidered relative with some talk of his being a Saxon; but the man's position is shaken beyond repair . . .' since he was only 'a common Berkshire man'. The ribbing continued long into the evening until Stevenson began to think it had become offensive but 'how I did misjudge the Land Commissioner! We heard him suddenly and passionately make an aside to Pelema, "keep it up, Balfour!" and so no doubt he would all night, had not the Saxon been a man of moderation and removed him in the midst of this absurdity.'

The comedy of Samoa was heightened sharply by the all-too-real possibility of death. At the end of 1892, Bazett's health was already suffering from the chills caused by tropical downpours (the natives sensibly wore few clothes). He had suffered a bad fever and cough and his weight had gone down to 10 stone 4 lbs. He felt he was keeping the Commission going single-handedly, since the American Commissioner had returned on leave, and the German, whom Bazett liked, had little initiative and simply followed Bazett's lead. The usual colonial complaint of remoteness was telling on him – he seldom saw the papers unless his wife (now living at Battlecrease Hall, Shepperton) bothered to send them.

A year later in January 1894 Stevenson was writing to his mother that Bazett was eating little or nothing, and drinking perpetually. Louis had come to hope that Bazett would not live to go home, since 'there seems no place possible for him. It is a beastly pity.' By October 1894, Bazett was at a low ebb and on one occasion Stevenson wrote that he was 'as d--k as they make 'em. As he sat and talked to me, he smelt of the charnel house, me thought.' Ever a soft-hearted friend, Stevenson bewailed that 'he looked so old . . . he spoke so silly; his poor leg is again covered with boils, which will spell the death of him.'

Surprisingly it was Bazett who survived to write to Ella in December 1894:

> I have nothing to write about except death and destruction. Mrs Cusack Smith our Consul's wife has 'gone', 14 days back, from malarial fever. She dies at 4.10pm we bury her at 8 am the next day. R.L. Stevenson the great vaunter of this climate dies suddenly (not from any disease save so called apoplexy) but really the climate; a terrible hot day and 'heat' apoplexy. He was the *thinnest* man I ever saw but a *great* friend. He died on Monday the 3rd at 8 p.m. We were nearly distracted that at 6.10 p.m. he was struck and at 8 p.m. dead. He is all to blame for what has been written about this 'glorious climate', but his entourage will go on and

keep up the falsehood as long as they can. In spite of these terrible shocks I am far better than I have been, though I go to a funeral once a week – nowadays. Expect me in England in May, if I am allowed to live so long. When death is so rampant as it has been here, one can only expect one's own 'dimittis'. Yr Loving Brother Bazett M. Haggard.

Bazett did live to return to England, but he never saw his father again. Mr Haggard, lonely after his wife's death, had at first tried to escape the isolation of Bradenham by gadding about staying with relatives, and according to Rider engaging in love affairs which were a strain on his health. But latterly, according to Alfred, he had lived 'the life of a recluse and goes nowhere, and no one hardly comes here . . . the place looks rather neglected . . . my father moons about, in a disconsolate way and sees nothing'. He was suffering from jaundice. 'It is a question whether it is a form of jaundice which yields to treatment or whether it is that form of jaundice known as "senile", which really involves the entire breakdown of his health and will prevent his living very long . . . I fear that he is very dangerously ill. He looks awful and is getting weaker and is losing flesh.' The Squire developed hardening of the liver, and dropsy, but made a remarkable recovery in November and rallied through the winter, only to die in the spring, on 21 April 1893.

Harry Haggard was home on leave from the Navy and attended the funeral in place of Alfred, his father, who was out in Ecuador with Will.[4] Harry stayed at Bradenham, as did Rider, Arthur, Charles and Ella Maddison Green, Mary d'Anethan and Nitie. The following morning James Haggard, George Western, Fred Jackson and George Haggard arrived. 'The coffin was carried on the shoulders of 6 tenants and the procession headed by Uncle Charles and Mr Hetherington went to the church by road. Down by Shearings there were a large number of villagers waiting to join and by the church still more. There must have been between 3 and 400 people present.' Charles conducted the service and the coffin was laid in the grave beside Mrs Haggard. The Local Government Bill had removed the administrative power of the Squirearchy, so that when William Meybohm Rider Haggard died, so did the last of the Squires of Bradenham.

Jack was furious with Rider that Frederick Jackson had been invited to the funeral. Jack had a long-standing wrangle with Fred about money and furniture from the Lamu days, and he accused Rider of disloyalty. Jackson had become something of a celebrity in his own right and, although he spent much of his time in East Africa, he and his unmarried sisters had taken a house in Earsham near Ditchingham, where they entertained in style; Alfred commented on the sumptuous hospitality in 1891. The very next year, the Jackson fortune collapsed when it came to light that Lilly's husband Francis Archer had been gambling on the stock market and lost all the Archer money. The bailiffs moved in and Archer fled to East Africa, where Jackson gave him sanctuary. It would be interesting to know exactly what Archer did out there; it was a long time before he was in a position to send for his wife. Their three sons, who had been destined for a life of comfort, were suddenly thrown upon the world. Francis, who had been at Hawtrey's prep. school, was abruptly taken out of Eton, and Rider arranged for him to be articled to a solicitor. The prospect of a quiet, professional life did not appeal, however, and the boy, who grew to a height of 6' 4", later joined the Norfolk Regiment and subsequently the racy and flamboyant King's African Rifles.[5] Geoffrey, the second son, attended Dr Raven's School in Beccles and, at eighteen and 6' 6", he was sent out to Africa to train for the Colonial Service with his uncle.

Lord Cranworth referred to Fred Jackson as 'The Whitest Gentleman who ever crossed the shores of Africa'. He was a tremendous sportsman, writing nine chapters of the first volume of the Badminton Library edition of *Big Game Shooting* (1897). Over the years he made a collection of 12,000 bird skins, covering 744 species. He was a dapper, neat man, tough and well able to keep his own counsel. When the Imperial East Africa Company was founded in June of 1889, with Sir William Mackinnon as its president, the board asked Fred Jackson to take charge of the Masai Caravan which was to open up East Africa, and make a treaty with M'wanga, the King of Uganda.[6] Not only a tremendous challenge, the expedition was also a race against the Germans; Dr Carl Peters, who was despised by the British, was bent on the same mission. In a notable incident Peters intercepted a letter to Jackson and took advantage of the information, but it was because Jackson had to finance the trip with ivory that he was delayed and Peters won the race. However, Lord Salisbury (Prime Minister and Foreign Secretary) later retrieved Uganda in exchange for Heligoland.

Many in Britain wondered what on earth the Empire was to do with yet another new territory. Rhodes urged the retention of Uganda and offered to carry a telegraph from Salisbury to Uganda at his own expense. Major Arthur Haggard, who left the Army in 1892, tried unsuccessfully to get himself appointed to the Uganda Commission. Arthur was living

at Southsea and working for the Army Service Corps at Portsmouth, but
he, too, had turned his attention to writing sympathetic tales of the
ordinary soldier, and produced *Only a Drummer Boy*.

Alfred, who had failed to secure any concessions in Brazil, and also
failed to build a Suakin–Berber railway, now developed the most extravagant and potentially most exciting project of his life. He proposed the
harnessing of the Victoria Falls to generate electricity. The idea had first
begun to emerge during his visits to South Africa in 1888–90, and he
had pursued it with his Athenaeum smoking-room friend, Professor
George Forbes, who had worked on Niagara.

Alfred had applied for a concession to the Victoria Falls in 1895, only
to find that H. B. Marshall of Johannesburg had already applied and been
refused. Alfred and Forbes were so convinced of the potential of their
plan that they decided to go out to see Rhodes at once and, if necessary,
come to some agreement with Marshall. Rhodes had never visited the
Falls, and the technology required was still in the early stages of development, but Forbes had the experience necessary. However, as Alfred later
wrote to *The Times*: 'It was in no respect Cecil Rhodes's scheme or his
conception, and that he never in my presence showed the faintest interest
in it or belief in the possibility of such great results as I was convinced
of . . . We and our scheme were laughed at and obstructed . . .'

Alfred's son Godfrey added the detail that Africa was so sparsely settled
at this time that few could conceive of the electricity being wanted, even
if it were possible to produce it. Nevertheless, The Africa Trust Company
Limited was formed, and Godfrey wrote:

> There were meetings of hard-bitten Directors at which the man of ideas
> went to the wall. I found this pencilled appeal scribbled on the back of
> one of my own letters to him with the heads of his remarks to the
> Board: 'Advize me! I am being squeezed out, wheras it was *my* scheme!'
> I see him outplayed and indignant, passing this hastily spelled cri du
> coeur to his neighbour at the board. (Forbes no doubt.)

Alfred salvaged a block of shares from the débâcle which shored up
his fortunes for a little longer. At Will's suggestion, he tried again with
a scheme to build a railway in Ecuador, from Quito to the coast at
Guayaquil; and later there was a Nile Dam scheme. Nothing came of
any of them, but he spent large sums of money on travelling which he
could ill afford. He was gradually relying on his wife's money and sinking
into penury while trying to maintain the standards of a gentleman. Having

no capital and unable to evaluate his abilities realistically, he had for years been pursuing ideas which he could not manifest and which Rhodes was only too capable of utilizing. What riches to have had a stake in the minerals of Rhodesia! What fame to have been the man who dammed the Nile! But if failure can kill the inner man, then Alfred undoubtedly began to decline when his inspired ambitions for the harnessing of Victoria Falls were purloined by tougher, sharper men.

~ II ~

Many Roads Thou Hast Fashioned

Baron and Baroness d'Anethan disembarked from the *Empress of China* at Yokohama harbour on 2 October 1893. They were accompanied by Mary's friend and companion Miss Ella Tuck, and by their Belgian household servants. From the Customs House they took jinrickshaws to the Grand Hotel, and then went off with friends to inspect a house for their temporary accommodation until the Belgian Legation in Tokyo had been made ready for them. Joining their party for the afternoon was Mr Thomas Cook of the eponymous Cooks Tours. Japan, which had for so long closed its doors to the outside world, now embraced European and American travellers who, in their turn, marvelled and gasped at the utter exquisiteness of 'Japanese Things': Professor Basil Hall Chamberlain had just finished cataloguing the culture which he knew would die of exposure to the West.[1]

Albert had been appointed Belgian Minister to the Imperial Court of Japan in Tokyo, where they were given their first audience at the Palace. Mary recorded that the petite, oriental Empress 'was dressed in a fabrication straight from Paris, of lovely mauve *broche satin*, with a *gilet* of pale pink, and she wore as ornaments one large diamond brooch, and the star of her country. During the whole time of our interview she never moved a muscle of her face, keeping her small and beautifully shaped mouth partly open, and speaking in a whisper.' Afterwards the Grand Chamberlain showed them the staterooms, built of precious woods and filled with lacquer, china and embroidery. Electric lighting had been installed in the Palace, but the Emperor would not allow its use because of the fire risk. These details are emblematic of the crossroads at which Japan found itself in the late nineteenth century. The Government was urging the country into the modern world but, having been so long isolated, the sudden changes sat uneasily with the country's ancient aesthetic.

Less than thirty years had passed since America forced Japan to open up six Treaty ports to trade. But almost immediately Japanese artefacts, especially Samurai militaria such as those pieces which Alfred put up on his Pimlico walls, had become popular items for importation into Europe. The first sight of Japanese prints at the Paris Exposition of 1855 had decisively changed the vision of French painters, and that influence had continued steadily and irrevocably to affect Western styles of domestic decor and design.

Ironically but predictably, in Tokyo Mary and Albert lived in ornate European opulence. The Belgian Legation had been built on European principles by a forward-looking Samurai, who had been murdered for his foresight and his body laid out on the drawing-room floor – an historical detail which intrigued the 'She-Baron' (as one of the Japanese servants called Mary). The timber house was a suitably spacious, ambassadorial residence, which the d'Anethans cluttered with huge, comfortable armchairs, day beds and stools, draperies, pictures, what-nots, ornaments and photographs. Japan began outside, in the superb chrysanthemum and iris beds of the varied and elaborate gardens.[2]

While Albert's priority was the development of trade, Mary's days revolved around the social aspects of diplomatic life; dinners, receptions, at-homes, excursions and picnics, race meetings and garden parties were the daily currency of diplomacy between the Europeans and the Japanese Court and Government ministers. For the first months she was also sight-seeing as widely as possible; like every other visitor Mary stood in awe of Mount Fuji, marvelled at the scale of the Kamakura Buddha, attended Noh and Kabuki theatres, and hauled herself and her substantial costume up steep hills to struggle with *hashi* in remote tea-houses.

From family tradition and a reference in a letter from Rider, it seems that Mary had lost a baby at, or soon after, birth and was unable to have any more children. Her energies went into amateur dramatics, charity works and writing romances. She also kept a diary upon which she based her book *Fourteen Years of Diplomatic Life in Japan*. In the introduction to the book Takaaki Kato, the Japanese Ambassador to the court of St James in 1912, speaks in the most friendly terms of Baroness d'Anethan, praising her qualities of character which were so apt for her role – she was broad-minded, but discreet. Discretion, however, has little to offer posterity. While Mary's memoirs account for her official activities they give few clues to her personal life. Typical entries illustrate the d'Anethans' exclusive but stuffy milieu:

186 *Children of the Empire*

April 9 1894: We dined with Prince Arsiguawa at his palace. It was a banquet of many Japanese. I was placed between Viscount Hijikata and Count Kuroda, both of whom only spoke Japanese.
April 11 1894: We dined at the British Legation to meet Sir William and Lady Robinson.[3] He is the Governor of Hong Kong, and he and Lady Robinson have come to Japan on a trip, and are staying at the British Legation. A Japanese conjuror performed his wonderful tricks for the edification of the guests.
April 12 1894: We attended the Imperial Cherry-blossom Garden party at the Hama-go-ten Palace . . . It was a picturesque sight, witnessing the cortège of the Court, followed by the Corps Diplomatique and a vast concourse of people, traversing the artistic and beautiful bridges, bordered each side by overhanging cherry trees . . . The party was attended by thousands of globe-trotters, among them a vast crowd of Americans.

One thing their position could not protect them from was earthquakes:

April 13 1894: . . . at three in the morning we were aroused by a very bad earthquake, the worst that Tokyo has experienced for nearly two years. It was certainly most alarming, and all the Japanese ran out of the Legation. E. [Miss Tuck] rushed into our room, and the house shook terribly. A. [Albert] got up, but the ruling passion being strong in death, he promptly, but with the greatest *sang-froid*, filled his pyjama pockets with cigarettes, and quietly lighting a match, he started smoking. I remained in bed until it was over. The whole house rocked and made a terrible noise. Nothing – wonderful to relate! – was broken.

But two months later the seismograph went higher:

June 20 1894: There was a small earthquake in the night, the forerunner to a most terrible one at two in the afternoon. Clocks, vases, photo frames, ornaments of all sorts, were precipitated on to the floor, and nearly all the chimneys were cracked, and we thought they were coming down. The godown was cracked all through. The whole household rushed out of doors in the greatest terror, and it was truly awful watching the building from the garden, rocking backwards and forwards, and feeling the heaving of the earth underneath one . . . My Belgian lady's maid, the only person who seems to have been upstairs at the time, completely losing her head, in a frenzy of terror jumped straight out of the window of the upper storey. Providentially she lodged on the projecting gable of the roof, whence later on we dragged the semi-conscious girl back by ropes, into safety.

Mary's diary of official and charitable functions is littered with the names of friends, acquaintances and guests who recur again and again throughout the Empire, and come largely from the same core of upper-class society. While Sir Ernest Satow, Professor Basil Hall Chamberlain and Mrs Bishop (Isabella Bird) are particularly identified with Japan, there was a whole cast of Chargés d'Affaires, Colonial Secretaries and Naval officers who popped in and out of the social life of the legations. One is hardly surprised that a tiffin party at the Yokohama Races in 1896 included Colonel Sartorius, last seen by us in the Sudan with Andrew Haggard; or that George Ford Barclay, who became Secretary to the British Legation, had recently been dining with Alfred Haggard at Monkham in Norfolk.

George Ford Barclay's brother, Henry, was also a great traveller in Japan, but not for diplomatic reasons. There is a very good explanation why so many European men gravitated to Japan, and it was one that Mary certainly did not mention in her memoirs but which she romanticized in her fiction. Pierre Loti's novel of the 1880s, *Madame Chrysanthemum*, opened up the Western imagination to the possibility of temporary liaisons with Japanese girls, and temporary liaisons were a wonderful antidote to the restrictive sexual *mores* of Europe. Secondly, Japanese women were trained to be subservient and solicitous and, to many Englishmen restrained by the excessive masculinity of Imperial culture, the delicate, submissive young Japanese girl was an ideal mate.

Generally speaking, those Englishmen who lived with Japanese women lived away from the Europeans; by the same token, residence in a Japanese district was a good indication that a man had a Japanese mistress or wife. Some of them became devoted to their companions, and fathered children, as in the case of the new British Minister. When Mr Fraser died in office on 4 June 1894 he was replaced by Sir Ernest Satow, who was no stranger to Japan.[4] Mary described him as a 'tall, slight, rather careworn-looking man, with an intellectual face and the stoop of a student . . . he and A. were old friends, having been colleagues together from 1873 to 1876, at which time Mr Satow was Japanese Secretary to the British Legation, and A., whose first post it was, was Secretary to the Belgian Legation.' It is now known that from that early time Sir Ernest Satow quietly kept a Japanese wife and had a child by her. From Mary's diaries it is clear that Albert and Satow were as friendly as ever, and they all spent a good deal of time together. It seems unlikely that Albert or Mary were ignorant of Satow's domestic arrangements.

In her novel *The Twin-Soul of O'Take San*, Mary writes of an English lord named Owen Garleston who falls out with his bad-tempered wife and, tired of big-game hunting, decides to make a restorative journey to Japan. Garleston takes with him his personal servant, Andrew Shearing, who is transparently based on Alfred Thacker (Shearing was another surname common in West Bradenham). Garleston visits friends at the British Legation in Tokyo and soon takes up with a Japanese girl called O'Take Yoshida, who falls in love with him. Thus the tragedy begins:

> Owen Garleston escorted the Japanese girl and her maid O'Hana to his bungalow by the sea at Ninomea . . . And from the beginning Owen lived in one long dream of happiness and content. Never was he likely to forget the impression of those first days in his Japanese home with his young companion whom from henceforth he looked upon and treated as his bride . . . Owen told himself he was indeed dwelling in the land of the gods . . .

Having surveyed the exhilarating landscape which transforms their love with a natural spirituality, Owen asks O'Take: 'And you regret nothing – nothing O'Take?' He asked again: 'You believe in me? You trust me? And you do not regret that – that – we – are not – married, O'Take? Tell me, my child, I have not then broken your dear little heart?'

To Owen's satisfaction, O'Take then explains how different she is from a European woman and, as he reflects rather hazily on the ancient philosophies of the East, Owen's misgivings and his conscience are quieted.

> Who could desire any better fate than the companionship of this refined, sweet girl, so delicate in her discernments, so quickly able to understand his moods and his feelings, and so careful never to wound them? She seemed to Owen the ideal of perfect unselfishness and sweetness, for never so far in this intercourse of months had he seen her show a moment's impatience or anger. If he had allowed it, she would have asked nothing better than to wait on him morning noon and night, and even as it was she made everything comfortable and dainty for him in their peaceful little home . . . Owen loved to watch the girl flitting about in her pretty kimono, arranging the flowers for the Tokonoma, dusting the shelves, or feeding the tame goldfish in the pond . . .

It was no wonder that the European male was drawn to Japan; a few, like Lafcadio Hearn, did stay with their Japanese families, but many more left when their lives took a different turn. In the case of Henry Ford Barclay, his family insisted he married his Japanese mistress, and the child was brought up in England.

Andrew, who stayed with Albert and Mary at the Legation for three months in the spring of 1899, presented a very much more realistic, if ungrateful, picture of life with the d'Anethans. Despite their lavish hospitality, Andrew fell out with Mary; he said she and d'Anethan had been rude to him, and he sniped at them for their puffed-up pride, calling them 'grandees who are too big for their boots'. Albert he accused of drinking Kirisi and Yebisu beer to excess: 'I used to be asked to pretend to get it for myself, in order that he might drink it on the sly when he had had far too much already.' Andrew also implied that their relationship was far from perfect, writing 'her husband' between quotation marks as though this was not the actual state of affairs, calling Albert a 'twopenny halfpenny husband' who vetted or dictated Mary's 'ramrod' correspondence.

Andrew's letters are the only glimpse behind the veil of decorum which shrouded Mary during her marriage. The circumspection with which she compiled *Fourteen Years of Diplomatic Life in Japan* is uncompromising: 'I hear that poor Mr Boag has shot himself in Yokohama . . . It is a terribly sad case' is all that she will allow. With reference to the sensational Carew arsenic murder the Baroness is downright infuriating: having said that they knew 'the culprit, the counsel for the defence, the Crown prosecutor, the doctors and the greater number of the witnesses in this extraordinary and most painful case', she abandons the subject, adding only a social footnote that the trial became such a *cause célèbre* that it was taboo as polite conversation, and a special card game was invented as a diversion.

Compensation for these omissions lies in Mary's highlighting of well-known political events, and it is these which make the most interesting reading. The Siege of the British Legation at Peking during the Boxer Rebellion of 1900 had everyone in Tokyo on tenterhooks – many of the Legation's diplomats being friends and some, like Satow, having themselves been in China.

July 2 1900: Terrible news has been received. The German Minister, Baron von Ketteler, was killed by Chinese soldiers on the 13th of last month . . . one report says that his body . . . was dragged through the streets of Pekin. His poor young wife! – one's heart bleeds for her, and I ask myself How will she survive the horror and tragedy of her loss?

July 3 1900: News is received through Sir Robert Hart, by the Japanese Consul at Chefoo, that all the Legations in Pekin, except the French,

German and British are destroyed. The Belgian Legation was the first
to be burnt. The British Minister is sheltering within his compound all
the Ministers and the staff of those Legations which are destroyed. A
heavy rifle fire is being kept up by the Chinese. The position is desperate
but up to the 24th of last month they were still alive.

July 5 1900: I sent some verses to the *Japan Times* on Sir Robert Hart's
message, 'The situation is desperate: make haste.' We hear that the
German Emperor is sending 10,000 troops to China.

July 6 1900: My verses appeared in the *Japan Times* with a leading article
upon them. Thank God! they seem to have had some effect and to have
moved people . . .

The six-stanza poem, *An Appeal from Pekin!*, began:

> Make haste! Make haste! Ah! list the frenzied cry
> We fling across the world. Will none reply?
> While Powers pause, while armies vacillate,
> We vainly pray for help. Come not too late.

The verses lingered on the fate of women and children in conditions of
starvation and parching heat. Rumours of fearful mutilations and massacres filtered into Japan from Shanghai, but all information was unreliable
until refugees from Tientsin reached Japan. Mary met the Dettering
family, whose house had been ransacked and razed and who had spent
a week in a cellar, 'feeding only on rice and potatoes, and never taking
off their clothes the whole time'. While they waited for reinforcements,
and with ammunition getting low, it was decided that the men should
shoot the women and children rather than let them fall into the hands
of the Chinese. 'Mrs Dettering saw her husband looked very sad, and
at last succeeded in eliciting from him what was intended. She told her
daughters and they all said they were resigned. At last in the nick of
time, the reinforcements got to them . . . and after a last desperate fight
they were rescued . . .'

It was not until August, after two months' incarceration, that the
Legation at Pekin was relieved, but Mary could be justly proud when
Sir Claude Macdonald, who had been Minister in Pekin and subsequently
replaced Satow in Tokyo, told her that her poem had been instrumental
in persuading the Japanese to send armed forces into China to help raise
the siege. Through her simple but forceful lines she had been able to
sow the seeds of an emotional empathy with the Westerners which had
been entirely lacking before.

One of the survivors of Pekin, Polly Conduit Smith, who had been brought to Tokyo, gave an informal account of the siege to a party of diplomatic wives:

> She slept for two months on the floor, eaten alive by cockroaches and mosquitoes, and poisoned by awful smells. One of the chief horrors endured was a plague of enormous bloated bluebottle flies, which divided their attentions between the besieged within and the corpses without. At one time, for four days, when the Chinese had put fire in three different places in the Legation, and all the wells were dry, they were each allowed only one tumbler of water for washing purposes. This with the thermometer over 100°! ... It was arranged that at the last the husbands should shoot their wives. Polly being a spinster, found that she had to look around for some one to perform this act, so she fixed on M.M. as a likely person ... [and] ... asked him if he would undertake the terrible task. Naturally he declined the honour, but informed her he would show her the best way to shoot herself ... During the siege they were living on one sardine apiece, and an occasional horse rissole. Polly herself fabricated and filled with earth five hundred sacks for the barricades, and of course thousands and thousands of sacks were made. She says, the rage and the cursing in every language, when it was first discovered that Admiral Seymour was prevented from coming to their relief, was truly awful ... Polly had kept a full diary of all that went on during those two months. I hear it is most vivid, and I am to read it when it is typed ...

Polly Conduit Smith had come away from China with a vast quantity of 'lovely embroideries and brocades which by some means – I did not ask how – had got into her possession ...' To his credit, Baron Albert condemned the looting that went on after the Siege by the Europeans, and scolded Mary for accepting a gift of a piece of fabric.

Not long afterwards, Mary developed typhoid fever, and she had to leave Japan in the spring of 1901. She spent much of her time in Italy with the family of her brother-in-law, the Marquis Cavalletti. In Rome she was given an audience with the Pope, but Roman Catholicism had not provided all the answers she required, and later she flirted with Madam Blavatsky's cocktail of Eastern mysticism, Theosophy. Albert joined Mary in Italy in January 1902, from where they travelled back to Spa in Belgium, and thence back to Tokyo at the end of the year. Since 1898 Albert had become the doyen of the Corps, which gave Mary the leading social position amongst the Europeans.

★

If Mary had more than her share of exotic locations and prestige, her elder sister Ella was so immersed in domesticity at Lyonshall that when Charles Maddison Green was given a new appointment she was loath to move even a few miles. She wrote to her nephew Harry at the end of 1891:

> It is 11 years today since we came into our nice new Vicarage, and now we are going to leave it for a rambling old Rectory in Ledbury, a pretty little country town in Herefordshire. Still we are on the side of the Malvern Hills, in fact really *on* the hill. It is a great blow to us leaving Lyonshall, the children's only home, and I have lived here all my married life in this parish. Uncle Charles has been here 25 years! It is a great wrench uprooting, but we think it right to go, and that it will be advantageous to the family in some ways, though they will have to put up with only a small garden and no tennis ground.
>
> There is a splendid church close by the Rectory, with a peal of bells (I hope I shall not be deafened). Your uncle must keep a curate, as the population is between 4 and 5,000. He will have plenty to do as the parish has been neglected of late.

In his letter of acceptance to the Bishop of Hereford, Charles revealed: 'I should not be acting in a straight forward manner if I were not to add, that the value of the Living weighs with me at the present juncture. In justice to my family it must do so.'

Early in 1892, Alfred wrote to his son Harry: 'Ledbury is in lovely scenery, and is itself a most picturesque town, having numbers of those old-fashioned houses, gabled, with rafters of wood athwart the brickwork. Your Uncle Charles has bought the most picturesque of them all; not on account of its beauty however, but because it is next door to his own Rectory, over looked it, and was occupied by the *lowest* people in the place, whom he has got rid of.' The Rectory soon proved unsuitable for their needs, and they moved into St Katharine's House (Charles was Warden of St Katharine's Hospital), from where they continued to be the anchor the family so often needed.

Charles energetically planned a programme of restoration of his church which, although it was dedicated to St Peter, came to be known as St Michael and All Angels – possibly because Charles had got into a 25-year habit of using the name at Lyonshall. Roof timbers were replaced, large sections re-roofed, stonework refaced and re-cut, floors re-laid, vaults sealed, pews replaced with pew boxes, and the spire largely rebuilt. J. L. Pearson, architect of the neo-thirteenth-century Truro Cathedral,

Ella and Charles Maddison Green during their years at Ledbury,
Herefordshire.

was employed to finish the restoration of the fabric, and Charles Kempe designed ten stained-glass windows to enhance the newly restored building. Two other windows made in the William Morris workshop after designs by Burne-Jones were added later, one in memory of Charles himself. At the entrance to the north aisle is a bust of Charles and a tablet memorial to Ella and all their children.

At this time neither Andrew nor Jack had a base in England, and Jack and Aggie relied on relatives to take them in on their leaves. Jack had been moved to Trieste as Consul for the Provinces of Dalmatia, Carpiola and the Austrian Littoral. He and Aggie now had three children, and another was on the way, but his salary did not increase.[5] Trieste, at least, gave them convenient access to Italy and the Alps, and Aggie, using pseudonyms, began writing novels which were serialized in *Macmillan's Magazine*.[6]

Jack's predecessor, Sir Richard Burton, had been too busy with other interests to give much attention to the Consulate but, in contrast, Jack was soon embroiled in controversy. As usual he had no hesitation in taking up the cause of an underdog, in this instance a British subject of Greek origin, Mr Mangachi, who was accused of instructing his two sons, aged eleven and thirteen, to murder his mother-in-law.[7] In a less tragic episode, Jack became involved in setting up a British Seaman's Home in Trieste, as an alternative to the brothels and boarding houses. Jack thought he knew rather more about sailors than the Chairman of the Committee, Revd C. F. Thorndike, whose Rules he considered the result of 'narrow bigotry'. The acidic letters which flew back and forth between them were later printed and published in a booklet.

These quarrels, however, were not furthering his career, and in 1896 he consulted two separate astrologers. One, Alfred James Pearce, was a respectable, traditional astrologer and, having naval connections, a natural choice for Jack. As was common at the time, the tone of his predictions tended to be rather alarmist and of the fortune-telling style – Pearce warned Jack about days and months which were unfavourable for starting new ventures. Three years later, just before the century turned, there seems to have been little that *was* favourable about Jack's new appointment, but it turned out to have its advantages. At the age of nearly fifty he was again sent to one of the forgotten places of the earth: New Caledonia, in the Pacific Ocean. Jack was to be Consul to the Island and its dependencies, and would be based at the former French penal colony of Noumea.

Volcanic, mountainous and tropical, New Caledonia had until very recently been home to 9,000 French convicts and a further 4,000 former convicts who remained to pervade the island with a less than salubrious influence. The town of Noumea was described as similar to a little English town, though gay with cafes and taverns, but the large main square was a shadeless, open space. The low wooden houses were roughly built, like the shacks of Australian backwoodsmen, while the little shops displayed wares which were 'inferior in quality, and of a mixed description. Toys hung side by side with saucepans and boots; calicoes and hats were framed by jam and spirit bottles. The streets are badly kept and filthy; the roads outside the town have not been properly levelled, and the numerous bogs make travelling after dark very dangerous.'[8]

Jack's salary was increased to £800 a year, with a £250 allowance, but the climate was unsuitable for the children, so Aggie and the family stayed in France and Italy and spent holidays at Ditchingham. But Jack did, quite openly, take with him a French maid named Marie. Any evidence of Marie being Jack's mistress is circumstantial, but not unlikely.[9] Harry, when he dined with them in Sydney in 1901, wrote home that he 'was introduced to the Bretonne, a good little woman; they are the greatest chums'. The following year he met them again: 'The Bretonne is a good little soul and must be of the greatest use to him.' Jack may well have relied on her linguistic skills for his work, and perhaps she was also his housekeeper. He seems to have enjoyed Noumea and liked his job, despite telling 'bloodcurdling yarns about the . . . place' and giving Harry the impression that 'the inhabitants must be the scum of humanity'. Certainly he had developed such an antipathy to the Royal Navy that Harry could not even get him to come aboard his ship.

At Ditchingham, the gloom had lifted with the birth of a new daughter, Lilias, and with Rider's successive attempts to enter public life. After losing an election, he abandoned party politics, but he had his father's skill at self-promotion and he used his legal and writing abilities to become a useful member of Government Commissions and a producer of surveys and reports on agriculture and coastal erosion. Eventually, his speciality became the Empire, because, long after many people had begun to doubt its long-term desirability, Rider remained an idealist of British Imperialism. He managed to combine an agricultural socialism with Imperialist conservatism, seeing always the advantage of the spread of English institutions and the potential for small-holding in the great open lands.

Soon after the Jubilee celebrations of 1897, Imperial pretensions were both challenged and undermined by the second Boer War. Rider understood all the old conflicts which led to the uprising, although he could not have foreseen the immediate cause of the Jameson Raid. In his youth, Rider had found the Boers distasteful and, although the years had softened his views, he could hardly espouse their cause against England. But Alfred was of a very different mind. He actually believed the Boers were right to rebel against Imperial authority. He was in good company; Sir William Butler felt unable to command the British forces, and resigned.

Alfred was placed in a doubly difficult dilemma. For some years Rider had been giving Harry an annual allowance. Alfred's second son, Gerald, who seems to have been either rather dull or depressed by his life, had been at Cranbourne, but rather late in the day Alfred discovered that from Christmas 1897 to May 1898 he had attended only 71 out of 167 lectures, and had been absenting himself to pay attentions to a young lady. Immediate family action was called for. Rider provided £70 and some introductions to send Gerald out to South Africa. Harry went to see him off on the *Carisbrooke Castle* at Southampton, as did a certain Miss Vivian. Alice had relatives in South Africa, and it was intended that Gerald should find himself a job and make something of himself. With the Boer War coming so quickly on his heels, what he made of himself was a soldier.

Gerald was not a regular correspondent: his family only heard that he had had typhoid through Miss Vivian, and they may have lost touch after a while. When the war started he joined the Imperial Light Infantry and saw action, and then joined the First Regiment of Scottish Horse. To avoid the problems of finding forage the Army were using bicycles on the veldt. Gerald entered a Cyclists Section, enlisting with them on 16 February 1901. He died six weeks later, on 4 April.

A first-hand account of his death was sent to Rider via Rottingdean – Kipling's home – by a young man named J. Wentworth Sykes.

> We enlisted together and joined Cunningham's Column together, he as a cyclist and I as a trooper in the Scottish Horse. He as a veteran in the war, having served months, with Spion Kop and other battles to look back upon. I was a stranger from Tasmania who came across 'on my own', as the Colonials say . . . to strike a blow for my father's country. He was the first friend I made in the new land and we were mates to the finish.

Sykes related that, under a full moon, they had been ordered down a valley to draw the enemy fire so that another column could get through the pass. '"C" Squadron of the Scottish Horse with some 20 cyclists and a few scouts, numbering about 70 souls in all . . . were under the fire of the Kopjes round all day.' By about four o'clock, when the column had passed safely through the Nek, and as they began to return to camp, they were attacked by Boers who had crawled to within 300 yards under cover of the long grass. Sykes recalled that 'there was pandemonium . . . men calling on Christ and their comrades that they were hit.' The British casualties were nearly one in four, and Sykes tried to comfort the Haggards by telling them that 'Your nephew was shot through the heart and died instantly and of course painlessly . . .' Gerald was buried on the veldt on the morning of Good Friday.[10]

Arthur, who was in the militia, had gone out to South Africa with the Army Service Corps and was still in Johannesburg in May 1901. He didn't think much of the way things were being run and was glad that the war was winding up but, frankly, he dreaded coming home almost as much as staying on. In recent years he had been finding it difficult to make ends meet; he had tried his hand at mining speculation, possibly going out to the Klondike. He had had some small success with writing, but his books about life in the Army had the emotional simplicity of an Officers' Mess, and were not the stuff to make big sales. His collection of short stories, *With Rank and File: Sidelights on a Soldier's Life*, is interesting today as a source of contemporary attitudes and as evidence of Arthur's empathy with the common soldier. His novel *Comrades in Arms* is a prolonged tale of the friendship of men being betrayed by the perfidy of a woman – a common theme of military life. His literary exploits at least gave him the opportunity to frequent Douglas Sladen's famous salons, where the successful combination of whisky and actresses attracted not only the literati but also political and military notables.[11]

Devoted to his beautiful wife Emily, Arthur wrote to Ella: 'I do hope you would try and keep Milly from worrying about things so much.' The 'things' Milly worried about were financial problems; they had borrowed from her mother – which Arthur himself thought perfectly natural, but he knew he would return to England under the shadow of distaff disapproval.

Alfred could no longer pretend to be earning a living at all. What money they had came from Alice's family or from Rider and Will. It was not long before Harry was contributing to the family purse from his

Major Arthur Haggard in dress uniform with Egyptian campaign medals. He retired from the King's Shropshire Light Infantry and later joined the Bedfordshire Militia and then the Army Service Corps.

slim Naval pay. Alfred pottered away at scholarly translations from the Greek and Roman classics and at writing poetry – but none of it earned him a penny. He became increasingly involved in the Positivist meetings at Lamb's Conduit Street in London, and gave talks and wrote articles on such subjects as 'Comte's attitude to Socialism'.

While Alfred preached intellectually about socialist ideas, at home he remained entirely autocratic, and was increasingly unpleasant to his family. His politics did not, apparently, encroach on his ingrained sense of class: Harry was dismayed to learn that his parents were about to get rid of a pleasant governess because she had a slight Cockney accent. In contrast, Rider's personal humanism infused the next generation at Ditchingham, although he remained a singular Imperialist.

Bazett had caught malaria in Samoa, but he actually died of tuberculosis in 1899, after living for some time at a sanatorium at Parkstone, Poole, in Dorset. Julia, from whom he was estranged, did not come to his deathbed or his funeral in Ledbury. A bare twelve months later, she married her childhood friend Mr Lofthouse, through whose fortune she sailed like a tea clipper homeward bound.

Harry Haggard was serving on HMS *Prince George* when Queen Victoria, who had for so long orchestrated the loyalties of the European powers, died at Osborne early in 1901. The Queen's body was transported on the Royal Yacht *Alberta*, and from Spithead Harry wrote home about the 'pageant':

> It was a glorious day but rather cold. The guests came off about 1.30, had lunch and then we shifted into full dress and waited to man ship. Except for the Flagship we are at the extreme end of the line which at this end is double, the ships abreast being German. From this to Cowes there is an unbroken line of 30 ships, a distance of 8½ miles with a slight bend at one point to avoid a shoal.
>
> When the procession entered the line at Cowes all the ships commenced firing minute guns, ceasing as the yacht passed them. The *Alberta* carrying the coffin, was preceded by a double line of destroyers which were singularly effective, their black hulls gliding silently and slowly past, reminded one of dark robed monks like one sees abroad.

12

From One Generation to Another

When Alfred visited Will in Ecuador in 1893, he wrote: 'We had a festive dinner to the President of the Republic 2 nights ago, and the American Minister taking too much wine, flourished the champagne bottle, proclaiming the glorious Munro [*sic*] Doctrine in a mixture of Latin, Spanish and Yankee. Such a specimen of American diplomacy! Braggart, ignorant, vulgar, conceited and forward.'

Alfred's disdain characterized an Englishman's attitude to the increasing commercial influence of the Americans. The Monroe Doctrine, which had formulated the view that America wanted no more political interference from Europe, could only be guaranteed by the strength of the British Navy. Great Britain had no further ambitions in South America, and was content to maintain peace from naval bases on her Caribbean islands.

However, South American countries were still very much subject to the financial interests of Europe. British investment had led the field, but her exports were gradually being displaced by those of more attentive salesmen. Queen Victoria's relationship as grandmother to the Kaiser coloured British foreign policy to such an extent that few suspected Germany of harbouring imperial ambitions towards the often newly independent Hispanic countries. The United States was a more obvious candidate for distrust.[1]

After his father's death, Will made Bradenham his home in England, and enjoyed the convenience of a three-year posting in Tunis – at that time a pawn in the game of alliances which the European and Russian powers were playing. But in 1897 he was appointed Minister Resident at Caracas, capital of Venezuela, gateway to the Caribbean. Four years later Alfred's third son, Godfrey, aged seventeen, was sent out to work for Will as a preliminary to entering the Foreign Office.[2] And thus the stage was innocuously set for the drama which, though an entr'acte in itself, had repercussions which could be heard in Berlin and Washington, and even offered a distant marker to the First World War. It was Godfrey who, in retirement, wrote up his recollections of those peculiar events which are known to the world as The Venezuelan Crisis but might well be called the Haggards' Private War.[3]

Godfrey had been sent to an indifferent local school in Dorset, where caning was the order of the day, often followed by merciless reproval from his father. Their home in Charmouth was permeated by Alfred's temper and obstinacy, so that when Godfrey began to observe his Uncle Will at close quarters, he was neither surprised nor encouraged by what he saw.

Through Godfrey's eyes, the character of Will Haggard was a most significant element in the Venezuelan political conflict. This is supported by Miriam Hood in *Gunboat Diplomacy*, in which she accuses Will of 'obvious antipathy towards Venezuela and her people', as well as 'a complete lack of understanding'. This may be weighed against her own comments on the simple correctness of Will's judgement that Venezuela's poor international relations were the result of corrupt government; he may have been neither empathetic nor enlightened, but he was capable of being right. Rightness, however, is scarcely the business of diplomacy.

His thick-skinned attitude is well illustrated by one letter to a friend in 1898, in which Will wrote cheerfully: 'I do fear, however, that we are in for an epidemic of small-pox which will kill off the natives – mostly all unvaccinated – like rotten sheep.' Later in the year, after one of Will's private letters had been intercepted and printed, the local paper *El Tiempo* asked for his recall and the appointment of a 'more prudent, more diplomatic and less indiscreet Minister'.

Caracas was built high up in a valley surrounded by mountains, and her narrow streets were numbered east and west from the central Plaza Bolivar. The houses of adobe faced inwards on to courtyards, showing only plain low walls and grilled windows to the streets. The only route to the seaport at La Guiara was by rail, since the road had been destroyed by a dictator who was the principal shareholder in the railway.

Godfrey, having no *savoir-faire*, poor handwriting, little French and no Spanish, was initially no great asset either bureaucratically or socially. Immature, and isolated from his contemporaries, he became friendly with his sickly twelve-year-old cousin Rudolf. Will and Nitie did their duty by Godfrey, but they were not always kind, often speaking about him disparagingly in German, not realizing that this was a language which he *did* understand.

Godfrey described his Uncle Will as 'clever and companionable; a stimulating host; well-informed, though no intellectual; with a wide circle of acquaintances, some in high places'. Physically, Will was stocky but handsome – a fact of which he was well aware; and only his wife was permitted to trim his curly hair 'as he sat enthroned in a sheet with a hand mirror for sceptre'.

In middle-age, Will had the manner of a womanizer, or, as Godfrey put it, 'he had no end of a way with the girls which some of them liked, and others, my Aunt among them, did not.' Will was the kind of man who would be quick to help a woman find a wasp which had become tangled in her costume, and, admiring a mature beauty, would exclaim: 'By God, I'd like to come a cropper with that woman!' Godfrey added: 'I have seen my Uncle of a Sunday morning plunge deliberately like a footballer through the groups of young Don Juans which cluttered up the pavement corners making extravagant, even gross, compliments to ladies passing on their way to Mass.' Will's style of diplomacy was equally insensitive. Godfrey called him obstinate and contentious, with an inclination to sarcasm. 'To bring them up with a round turn' meaning 'to sharply deflect their course', was one of his favourite expressions, an attitude Godfrey was well-used to at home.

As the Fates would have it, in the opposing corner strutted President Cipriano Castro, 'as wild and stiff-necked a dictator as ever sat on a tyrant's throne'. Godfrey described him as a 'one-time cattle smuggler' from the foothills of the Colombian Andes, who had conquered Venezuela in 1899 under the guise of a revolution and stayed to become a 'scourge' to his people. 'He united considerable decision of character to complete ignorance, not to say indifference about every country but his own, which made him extremely difficult to reason with, the more so that he talked incessantly, a means of self-protection employed with success by other dictators since his time.'

Castro ruled entirely by terror; he and his entourage would ride through the streets of Caracas, clattering on the cobbles, and raising a clenched fist in salute. The Government's daily newspapers fed his vanity; a notably short man, his sexual prowess was vaunted unreservedly. Godfrey recalled that Castro's 'customs were frightful (here I am obliged to refrain); and as to manners he had none . . . the prisons were full of political suspects and Port of Spain in the off-shore colony of Trinidad was full of political refugees plotting in idleness and discontent . . . The "Calazbozo" at La Guarya where his choicest enemies languished had stagnant sea-water in the cells.'

Close by in Trinidad, the British Governor Sir Alfred Maloney hoped that Castro would be overthrown by Jose Antonio Matos who, having enjoyed the 'Trinidad fleshpots', took up arms against Castro in the eastern part of Venezuela. Sir Alfred's 'neutrality' looked anything but that to Castro, when it came to the export of arms across the Gulf and to giving safe harbour to the *Ban Righ*, a Colombian ship out of London which had been handed over to Matos and raided the coasts of Venezuela. Not only the British and Colombians supported Matos, for, according to Godfrey, 'our ambitious French colleague . . . was sending Matos daily over the French cable Company's lines a secret bulletin of Castro's troop movements . . . anyone but a perfect bungler like General Matos would have made something out of all this.'

Venezuela was largely undeveloped industrially, but its sparse rural population produced a significant coffee crop, and the strategic impor- tance of Venezuela to the Caribbean was obvious to all. Government corruption – successive Presidents simply amassed personal fortunes from the public coffers – and endless calls to arms had robbed the people of their income and placed the country in hopeless foreign debt, debt which was now being claimed by bondholders of many nationalities.[4]

Godfrey recalled:

> Again and again the talk I heard at the various 'days' held by the ladies of the diplomatic corps at Caracas would return to the topic of 'action' against the Government of General Cipriano Castro . . . To send cruisers, to seize Custom Houses against unpaid claims, to land bluejackets, to exact salutes in apology from a local navy – all that sort of thing was then a recognized part of diplomacy in Central and South America . . .

But Castro was the first to act; he began 'to capture, sink or burn British schooners plying with the mainland, marooning the crews on barren shores or deserted islands, and confiscating the cargoes whatever they might be – alleged contraband or not – thus levying a virtual blockade' on British communications and trade. Will's social connections and experience predisposed him towards Germany. He had been not only received at Windsor but entertained more informally at Sandring- ham. Not surprisingly he was close friends with the German Chargé d'Affaires, Baron von Pilgrim Baltazzi, who was 'shrewder and more reserved' than Will. Germany began to see that she might join forces with Britain, thereby gaining the use of British Naval bases from which to take action against Venezuela.

Will had been brought up with loud arguments which were resolved by slamming doors; his brother Alfred said of him: 'he would as soon quarrel as not'. Claims and counter-claims flew back and forth between the British Legation and the Venezuelan Foreign Office. Will's protests to the Venezuelan Government about the sabotage and burning of British vessels fell on deaf ears. In London, the Foreign Office was slow to respond, but Will hammered on and on. Godfrey remembered another player in the piece: Fombona Palacios, the Under Secretary of the Venezuelan Foreign Ministry, a malicious, sour man ready to stir up trouble by the use of a 'legalistic-casuistic dictionary' when wording his letters.

'We were driven at last to let them know that HMG might find itself obliged to close British ports to Venezuelan cruisers.' Castro practically suspended relations with Britain and, by June of 1902, Will Haggard issued an ultimatum: 'unless full compensation be paid promptly to the injured parties . . . they will take such steps as they may consider necessary to exact the reparation which they have the right to demand.' The action which would follow would be the seizure of the Venezuelan Navy, and a blockade of the coast to settle British compensation claims by proceeds from the Customs House.

Godfrey confidently pointed out that 'This was common and routine up and down the coast of Latin America and it worked perfectly well . . . You made a passing bow to the Monroe Doctrine by telling Washington what you were going to do and then you went ahead and did it, and everyone was the better for it.' Britain was trusted to withdraw her gunboats when the debt collecting was finished.

By August the Admiralty was being informed that Germany would like to join Britain's naval demonstration. German claims were only a fraction the size of Britain's, and they had lost no lives, yet no one at the Foreign Office stopped to wonder why Germany wanted to get in on the action. Miriam Hood points out in *Gunboat Diplomacy* that the Colonial Office was more sanguine, and warned that unilateral action would be preferable.

It was at a Council of War at the British Legation, attended by Captain Herbert Lyon of the *Retribution* and Commodore Scheder of the *Vineta,* that Germany first:

Will in 1910: Sir William Haggard KCMG, CB, Envoy
Extraordinary and Minister Plenipotentiary to Brazil 1906–14.

showed the cloven hoof. Our proposal was to capture the Venezuelan
gunboats by a *coup de main*; to hold them as hostages pending settlement,
and then give them back when it was all over (which in fact we did).
Scheder announced that he intended to blow his prizes up, crews and
all!

 . . . he was heard with indignation. It was explained that there was no
intention anybody should be *hurt*. This was just the usual debt collection
business: that was the way it was always done. Our ally listened with
reluctance . . . It was understood that he was acting on instructions.

In the family, the story goes that Will actually declared war on Venezuela for about half an hour and told the Foreign Office about it afterwards. If so, it would be interesting to work out when this would
have taken place.[5] The final ultimatums were actually delivered on the
afternoon of 7 December 1902, by Godfrey himself and his German
counterpart. Like some comic novel of parochial life, the Venezuelan
Minister of Foreign Affairs was discovered having a siesta when they
called at his modest home. He was somewhat bemused, the more so
since he could read neither German nor English. After the messengers
left he 'wandered out with them [the ultimatums] in the evening to the
Plaza Bolivar, falling in with my [Godfrey's] friend Goffart, the Belgian
Chargé d'Affaires, at a café'. The unsuspecting Goffart translated the
documents and, not having been party to what was afoot, got the shock
of his life – as well as a scoop for his own Government.

Inevitably Fombona drafted the reply, which was 'argumentative, prevaricating and unyielding' – giving, if it were needed, good justification
for action. 'What a different result there might have been with an Under
Secretary who could have swopped yarns with William Haggard over a
cigar. My uncle would have responded at once, human nature being what
it is, especially his human nature. But Fombona was narrow, tortuous and
anything but sociable.'

The members of the British and German Legations now prepared to
depart from Caracas by train. At the last moment Madame von Pilgrim
refused to leave, protesting that she was *enceinte*. Will, a man of some
experience in these matters, didn't believe her and, appalled at the inex-
pedience of Germany's ships bombarding the coast while her Chargé
d'Affaires sat holding his wife's hand in Caracas, he actually persuaded
the Baron to leave without her. The party then assembled at the railway
station to wait for the three o'clock train, assuming an air of innocence
that challenged the astonishment of the General Manager of the railway
and the Harbour officials.

La Guyara was not only dirty and smelly but was usually grilled to 100° from the heat reflected by the sun-baked rocks, so the staff of the British Legation gratefully boarded HMS *Retribution*, while the Germans were delivered into the hands of their own Navy.[6] After dinner the British settled down to wait for the fireworks and had a sing-song on deck, during which Godfrey tactlessly called for 'I fear no Foe in Shining Armour', which brought glares of disapproval.

In Caracas, the members of the British and German colonies who had been given no warning of the ultimatum bore the brunt of Castro's anger. Most of the British found asylum with the US Consul, but many Germans were arrested. 'We handed over the protection of British interests (and German interests) to the US Minister, Herbert Bowen, which was not without its humour considering the relations between our Legations.'

On board the *Retribution*, preparations were made for the 'cutting-out' expedition. Decks were cleared, guns trained on the two forts high up on the mountain-side, while the armed boats which had been preparing on the seaward side of the cruisers set out in double file across the quiet harbour. Uncle and nephew were now in the thick of the action, able to view with satisfaction the outcome of all the months of wrangling. '*Retribution* sent four boats with Maxim guns; but the Germans sent six so that the two best Venezuelan prizes fell to the *Vineta* and *Panther*. Our fellows tackled the *Margarita* and relieved her of enough machinery to disable her for some time, as well as of a dynamite gun and a pom-pom.'

Godfrey quoted from his own letter home:

> Soon tremendous crowds collected and shots went off, and one saw a steam engine rushing up the mountain side with the news to Caracas, but my suggestion to fire the 6-inch gun at her (she made a beautiful target) was not well received. The Fort then woke up too and began to train guns and things at us. I was up on the bridge when I heard the Captain [Lyon] yell out, 'Clear away the six-inch gun for'ard,' and I thought I was at least going to see a shot fired in anger. But they thought better of it on the Fort, though they could have sunk us I believe, and the Capn told me I needn't look so disappointed as I should have been the first person killed.
>
> The operation was timed to start at five o'clock. Not long afterwards as darkness fell the town began to buzz. Castro behind the mountain wall was wondering what he had better do. On our side there was less indecision; for about midnight, as we were feverishly cyphering away in captain Lyon's cabin, two explosions hit the welkin. The gallant

Scheder was blowing up his prizes [the gunboats *General Crespo* and
Totumo], as he said he would.

If the sound was not actually heard around the world, it was heard only
too distinctly in Washington, where it was assumed (wrongly) that the
crews had been blown up as well.[7]

The German Commodore then proceeded to land 125 men 'to rescue
the German Consul', and marched them through the streets like an army.
Godfrey believed there was evident intention to go to extremes and use
any excuse to get German troops on to South American soil.

> Five hours later a British party brought off such of the British residents
> as desired refuge. Dawn showed the waterfront lined with Venezuelan
> troops and some artillery; and the British Harbour Corporation managers,
> under siege by crowds ashore. Lieutenant Archibald Deas landed to
> rescue them under cover of the *Vineta's* boats. The Venezuelan Officer
> commanding the troops lining the shore stepped forward at the head of
> his men to prevent him. Deas rapidly brushed him aside and proceeded
> on his mission with such assurance and alacrity that – nothing happened;
> business-like action which saved a ticklish situation.

The Germans dug up a 360-year-old land claim to further support their
position and, while the *Retribution* sailed for Port of Spain, the Germans
bombarded forts along the coast.

Will never returned to Caracas, but Godfrey was inherited (along with
a damaged dining-room table) by Will's successor Henry Bax-Ironside,
an intriguing character who proceeded to demonstrate to the grateful
Godfrey a different kind of diplomacy. Will was awarded the order
of the Commander of the Bath, with a posting to the Argentine and
Paraguay.

The aftermath of the Venezuelan crisis still stirs up academic opinion,
and Godfrey was keen to point out the essential success of the action.
It should be said that no blockade was ever imposed:

> within five days of the seizure of his navy Castro . . . had accepted in
> principle our terms for discussion of pending matters by Mixed Claims
> Commissions in Caracas, and had paid up on the nail our claims for the
> injuries and acts of violence against us, classified as First Line. It seems
> he could not get the threatened blockade averted and his gunboats back
> fast enough; for he quickly guaranteed us the stipulated Thirty percent
> of the Customs duties to La Guyara and Puerto Cabello against payment
> by Venezuela of the amounts awarded by the respective Mixed Claims
> Commissions.

Godfrey argued neither for nor against the morality of Britain's actions, but he obviously took some satisfaction in the outcome: 'The Gunboat Diplomat had brought his opponent up with a round turn indeed!'

Will's aims were fulfilled, but there were weighty ramifications in the balance of alliances. Godfrey believed that Germany was hoping for some breakdown in the claims negotiations to give her the excuse to re-enter Venezuela on a more permanent basis. Meanwhile, Herbert Bowen was now ironically the Special Ambassador of Venezuela, accredited to come to terms with the blockading powers in Washington. He himself had drawn up the text of his instructions from Castro, by which he was to 'negotiate with the representatives of the Powers that have claims against Venezuela'. By sleight of pen, Bowen was in a position to insist that *all* powers which had claims against Venezuela should be paid. President Roosevelt, anxious to curtail the hated Anglo–German alliance, offered to arbitrate the question of whether the blockading powers were entitled to preferential treatment, i.e. to receive payment prior to the non-blockading powers. Instead, Bowen moved to get some aspects of the case referred to the Hague Tribunal, where he 'was careful to get himself appointed one of the Counsel as champion of the smaller "peace-loving" nations'. He admitted privately that his aim was to create discord between Britain and Germany – as well as, it seems, to get himself playing centre stage. The Hague Tribunal did decide in favour of the blockading powers – an unexpected outcome for all concerned. The claims themselves were made by individuals in Caracas.

'This decision of the Hague Tribunal,' wrote Godfrey, 'had some far-reaching results, since it implied that European armed intervention was now permissible under international law in countries of importance to the United States regarded as immune.' The United States annexed the Isthmus of Panama in 1903, and began to make it clear that it would shoulder more responsibility for policing South American states. The principal response, in Germany's case, was a formidable policy of ship-building which led to the Haldane 'appeasement' mission along the *via dolorosa* towards the First World War.

Will was the only one of the brothers who did not call upon Rider for financial help – in fact he took it as no compliment to be called Rider Haggard's brother, since he felt 'no need of reflected glory'. Rider increasingly became the source of welfare to his extended family. After a second trip to Noumea, Jack returned in 1904 to the bosom of his family to take up a new appointment at Malaga, which had the advantage of being close to home; his salary was an impossibly mean £600 a year. In Norfolk, Louie provided home and board for her nephew Andrew, as well as sending out clothes and provisions to Aggie. They remained firm and intimate friends, Aggie confiding to her all of Jack's fears of conspiracy among his colleagues.

Andrew was reported to be getting through his wife's money and, like Rider, had lost heavily on the stock market.[8] In 1904 he was moving up and down the Eastern seaboard of Canada and the United States and, in Boston, he met Ethel Fowler, an English widow from Whitestock Hall, Ulverston. Then he began to spend his time in British Columbia, where a gentleman who was fond of fishing could get by without too much cash. At first, in 1905, he lived in the Riverside Hotel on Lake Cowichan but a local man, Dan Savoie, built him a log cabin, to which he brought his new wife, Ethel, whom he had married in Boston on 22 January 1906.

Emily's fate is unknown – there is no record of her death or divorce in England. Perhaps Andrew was a little lax in the arrangements since, in March 1906, Harry wrote to his mother: 'It is a bad business about Uncle Andrew; I hope he pulls through. I have seen little of him but when one did meet him he seemed a very good fellow. It is a pity he disregards the conventionalities so completely.'

The new Mrs Andrew Haggard was a charming little woman and a popular figure in Cowichan, but the locals considered Andrew pompous and arrogant. Never one to let the grass grow under his feet, Andrew embarked on a whole series of French histories and biographies, but his novel *The Two Worlds* (1911), which contrasted the backwoods life of Lake Cowichan with the society of Victoria, was not well received. The plot relies heavily on two characters being able to materialize and dematerialize to one another, and on Rider's theme of eternal love. A most interesting document for what it reveals about the social life of expatriates, the book also hints at Andrew's underlying contempt for colonials.

Rider regularly sent Andrew moderate sums of money, but more draining and more irritating was his support of Alfred, who had given up any attempt to work.[9] In 1903, Rider wrote to Andrew:

> I am worried out of my life about Alfred – I have received 3 or 4 letters from him one after the other literally clamouring for £100. I sent an extra tenner to Alice (making £75 for the year, £130 in 1902) and he

only wrote back for another £100 . . . I have written to Alice to ask if it is true that they are about to 'lack food'. I suppose there will be a row, but I can't help it. His one idea is to come down on me – says he wants a season ticket to London 'to look for work' but that only means unlimited Athenaeum and cabs etc. I don't know what is to be done – it's kept me awake all night. He is the only fellow I know who not withstanding his abilities, can actually earn nothing at all.

When Godfrey returned to England from South America, he stayed with the Riders to cram for the Foreign Office exams, and he confessed the real state of affairs at home. A maternal aunt wrote to Louie:

> I am so glad that Godfrey has enlightened you as to Alfred's behaviour at home. He is a downright bully and poor Bea's life is not worth living. I am of course in dread of what may some day happen to Alice when she learns how their money affairs are . . . his misdemeanours have all been kept from her. I feel sure he would not spare her for a moment if he were in great difficulty, which must shortly come, and will very likely be the death of her. At the same time I cannot see how it is possible to separate them, as neither of them would consent to it for a moment – Alfred because his one chance of a home is through Alice and she for the loyalty she still has towards him . . . my family positively refuse to allow me to be put in the way of being subjected to his bullying . . . I fear too that there is no relief for poor Bea at present – her life is very sad and as you say almost unbearable – and she is behaving really nobly.

Louie seems to have had a reputation for intervening and sorting things out, and perhaps she did so on this occasion. 'Poor Bea' was deaf, and had taken on the role of prop to Alfred's and Alice's marriage; eventually she turned to Rome, dying from pneumonia at the age of thirty-five. Alfred wrote a heartbroken letter to Harry – apparently the only person to whom he could maintain an image of paternal affection.

When Jack died suddenly in 1908 from the effects of sunstroke, Aggie was obliged by Spanish law to bury him in Malaga, which she knew he would have hated. Aggie folded four flowers in his hands – one for each of their children – and pinned on his medal. His white coffin was draped with the Union Jack, and six Spanish peasants carried it to the mortuary.[10]

Aggie was faced with the task of raising her family with no pension and only her own annual income of £115. She wrote a poem called *Discipline*, which expresses the extremes of Victorian stoicism. The poem begins:

Curve for the scourge thy shoulder, bend thy neck to the yoke,
Bow thy back for the burden, welcome the falling stroke,
Hold, but with fear and trembling, the love that perchance may bless;
Earth's finer spirits are clothed with the raiment of loneliness.

Aggie was not one to avoid turning her hand to whatever she could, but it was Rider who helped with the bills, and it was not long before Ditchingham House became known as the Home for Stray Dogs. It was the unemotional Louie who, with tact, discretion and efficiency, organized the house to accommodate a constant flow of impecunious schoolchildren and youngsters. As far as the younger generation was concerned, Rider once wrote to Louie, 'I wish I were rich enough to look after the whole pack of them.'

Meanwhile, Julia Lofthouse lived 'in great luxury and is,' Rider complained to Andrew, 'I believe very wealthy. I heard of her the other day travelling out to Monte Carlo . . . playing bridge all day, she is devoid of any entertainment of her own and she won't pay her debts.' Not only did the Lofthouses owe Rider money, Lofthouse wrote Rider 'bugging' letters and Rider found himself having to pay Julia's butcher's bills in Bungay.

The bad feeling between the Riders and the Lofthouses was temporarily subdued by the engagement of Rider and Louie's daughter Angie to Tom, Julia and Bazett's son. The marriage of first cousins, although it consolidated family resources, had genetic disadvantages of which the Haggards were well aware, since there were already several precedents in the family tree. But this marriage was a love match and had the alluring possibility of a Haggard heir to Ditchingham. At about the same time, the Riders' second daughter, Dolly, travelled out overland across Russia to visit the d'Anethans in Japan and met a young naval officer, Reginald Cheyne, who was later to become her husband.

Dolly was able to see her aunt and uncle when their prestige was in full bloom. Mary had endeared herself to the Japanese by her energetic fund-raising for the Red Cross during the Russo—Japanese War, and she was always a determined envoy for Japan on her visits to Europe. In 1910, however, Baron d'Anethan died of kidney failure, much to the grief of Mary who, when she returned to England, embarrassed her relatives by telling them in great detail and length of Albert's dying hours. She was left modestly well-provided for, and had received a personal gift from the Emperor of Japan, and she set off on the feckless, but no doubt

Baron and Baroness Albert d'Anethan on board the P & O *Oriental*
in 1908 with an unknown Japanese gentleman.

diverting, course of accompanying Julia to Monte Carlo, where reputedly she managed to dispose of large amounts of money, no doubt some of it Rider's. Mary was a formidable figure in middle age, very large of bosom and with a loud voice. She was given to telling risqué stories, during which any children present would be quickly ushered out of the room, much to their disappointment.

Arthur's fortunes were little better than those of his brothers. He had met Edith McCaul in Johannesburg, and became deeply involved with helping her to found the Union Jack Club, which still exists near to London's Waterloo station. However, in 1907, once it was established, he resigned the secretaryship and went on to start a Veteran's Club and Employment Bureau to provide accommodation and new opportunities for servicemen in London. Rider thought it a rashly ambitious venture without capital, but Arthur's enthusiasm was unbounded.

Of the many calls on Rider's purse, perhaps the saddest came from Lilly Archer. Lilly had joined her husband in East Africa, where her brother and his wife lived in a house invitingly called the Gin Palace.[11] During their separation, Francis Archer had contracted syphilis, from which he died in 1907. Lilly, herself now infected, returned once more to England and to the charity of Rider and her brother. She lived with her unmarried sisters at the Red House at Aldeburgh, where her son, Geoffrey, visited her on leave and played golf on the Aldeburgh course. Later, when the disease took a stranglehold on her health, she moved closer to the sea at 1 Wentworth Terrace, where she died in 1909. She is buried with her sisters in Aldeburgh churchyard.

Our Stilly Woods of Oak

It was indicative of the times that many members of the new Haggard generation had entered the services. The Navy claimed Will's son Hal, Alfred's son Harry, and Arthur's son Geoffrey; Bazett's son Mark was an officer in the Welch Regiment. For all the young people, Bradenham was still the family home – some of them had lived or stayed there, and most had happy childhood memories of playing under the beech tree or in the plantations. Some could remember being taught to shout by the old Squire, or the serious conversations held with him while sitting in the men's privies at the top of 'Philosopher's Walk'.

During Will's final appointment, as Minister Plenipotentiary in Brazil, he let out Bradenham Hall to a succession of people.[1] Rio de Janeiro was a pleasant enough posting for Will, although the climate was not the best for consumptives: his eldest son, Rudolf, had been confirmed as tubercular. But Nitie knew and liked Brazil, and her wide circle of friends extended beyond the stuffy world of diplomacy and monarchists. Will had a considerable staff under him, including Ernest Hambloch who, in his memoirs, described Will more favourably than had Godfrey and appreciated the Minister's dramatic anecdotes: 'Haggard in spite of his gout and aches, was always full of energy, though he was often most erratic.'

Will enjoyed his quarrels and feuds but, in his cool relationship with his Consul-General, there was a deeper-seated antipathy. Sir Roger Casement, though sociable and voluble, was self-consciously Irish, humourless, and actively if not openly homosexual. It is surprising there were not more fireworks. In hotel registers, Casement was in the habit of describing his profession as Irish Consul-General. Hambloch commented,

Of course, Haggard, our Minister, got to know of this . . . but he merely classified it as one of Casement's 'unaccountabilities'. He [Will] was

looking at some books of Casement's on our shelves in the Consulate
one day after Casement had gone on leave. 'Look at this!' he said,
pointing to a life of Kossuth, 'always feeding on stuff of that kind. Bound
to be unbalanced. The poor chap is in a constant state of revolt. Makes
himself ill. He'll never settle down.'

And, of course, he never did. Years later, when Casement was tried
for treason, Will wrote to Hambloch:

> I attended his trial and saw him condemned to be hung. He never would
> have been if it had not been for his damning diary – for he had many
> friends among the 'powers that be', and, moreover, they were afraid of
> the Irish party in the U.S., whom happily the diary muzzled. He behaved
> like a gentleman in Court when he was condemned and throughout the
> trial, during which he was allowed every latitude in virtually appealing
> to the Irish–Americans.

Behaving like a gentleman had become the single most important
virtue for the Edwardian upper classes. They punted upstream from the
dark eddies in which the Victorians had bobbed, and skimmed along
softer, lighter waters. But there were dangers in the shallows, and it was
in the early twentieth century that the certainties of Imperial rule lent
an unearned arrogance and racial confidence to a new generation.

In this atmosphere, Aggie's younger sister, Marjorie Barber, suddenly
became what we might call a cult figure. Marjorie's career as a nurse in
the slums of London had been curtailed by illness – possibly spinal
tuberculosis – and she attached herself to the family of Mrs M. E. Dowson, a writer on the subject of Mysticism. Marjorie was acutely psychic
and said that, in the slums, she had 'learnt to love Death and understand
very little about life'.

Often in a haze of morphia or opium, pressed on her by Mrs Dowson,
Marjorie wrote religious stories before producing her masterpiece,
The Roadmender, which enjoyed such overwhelming popularity that it
was reprinted repeatedly for more than twenty years. Written on her
deathbed, *The Roadmender* is a ramble through the Sussex countryside
as well as a ramble through meditative reflections upon the mysteries
of life.

The Dowsons had rented Mock Bridge House on the Cowfold Road
near Henfield in Sussex, and Marjorie spent her last two summers there.
At Cowfold there was an old Carthusian monastery, from which she
drew her theme that a simple roadmender had as much vocation as a

monk, and that in nature the roadmender might observe as much about the workings of the Almighty as might any religious person.

The Roadmender's appeal may be attributed to its lack of intellectualism and to its emphasis on the individual spiritual experience. Marjorie's descriptions of the byways and characters of the Sussex villages are notable as early signs of the Edwardian nostalgia for a past way of life. The English countryside, especially the countryside close to London, was changing rapidly under the influence of mechanized agriculture. The impact of the book was so great that, by the 1920s, the London, Brighton and South Coast Railway issued a travel brochure which featured the 'Roadmender's Country', highlighting specific villages between Horsham and Arundel as objects of pilgrimage. Marjorie herself had died in 1901, leaving Mrs Dowson as her literary executor – which must have been galling for Marjorie's sister, Aggie.

If Rider quipped that the only place he liked in London was Liverpool Street Station, he was in truth depressed on the one hand by the squalor and degradation of urban life and on the other by the countryside, impoverished by the defection of the rural working class. The revolution in agriculture had caused not only a social upheaval on a scale unprecedented in human memory, but also a spiritual malaise. The nouveaux riches had amassed large country estates as playgrounds, while the role of the old landed gentry as responsible trustees had been undermined and eroded.

In Rider's eyes, the strength of the nation came from its close association with the land, and with nature. A culture which did not have agriculture as its base was a culture in danger of degeneration. No simple traditionalist, he was well ahead of his time in his withdrawal from blood sports, while his appreciation of the importance of maintaining the spiritual equilibrium between man and nature is in line with the whole environmental movement of the later twentieth century.

Out of these perceptions, Rider developed his passion for Imperial consolidation. He wanted to get people back on to farms – in Canada, Australia and New Zealand. Like most people of his time he viewed these countries as 'empty'. This was the gravest mistake of the period; like the United States, these countries had once been home to migrant people who were now reduced by genocide to scattered groups of defeated native peoples.

Rider had very clear views about settlement in the colonies – despising speculators and opportunists – and he discussed these with men of similar outlook, such as Roosevelt and Selous. At the same time he foresaw the almost inevitable rise of Asia and the decline of Europe. It was to offset this decline that he so fervently preached the consolidation of the existing Empire.

While there are areas where Rider's ideas overlapped those of Socialism, they were never rooted in Marxism, and he abhorred the Bolsheviks. His was always a humanistic approach and he never attacked the social order. He did not foresee the enormous revulsion against class which Socialism would produce, although once the dole was introduced he noted the difficulty in getting servants.

In the years leading up to the First World War, Rider made a substantial personal contribution to public life as well as transforming himself into a figure of international influence, but his popularity continued to rest on his writing. In the New Year's honours list of 1912 he was awarded a knighthood and, two weeks later, he was asked to sit on the Royal Commission on the Dominions set up to inquire into the state of trade within the Empire. It was his most important opportunity to contribute to the future.

Much to his friend Kipling's pleasure, Rider first visited India and Ceylon. This was followed by a tour of Australia, which Rider thought ripe for extensive settlement. In 1914, Louie and Lilias accompanied him to South Africa for a sometimes sad and sentimental journey through all his old haunts, which Lilias described in detail in *The Cloak That I Left*. Most significant was his distaste of racism and his condemnation of the treatment of the defeated Zulus.[2] He thought the situation was so critical that he wrote a report for the Government, and it is interesting to realize that the question of whether or not black men had feelings was under serious debate. Rider was firmly convinced both of their feelings and of their long memories, and he warned the English government: '. . . it will be found that no single blow or curse, or humiliation or act of robbery or injustice has been overlooked . . . For these in some shape, probably one that is quite unforeseen, an hour of reckoning will surely strike. It is not possible in this or any other human affair, continually and with intent to sow the wind and always escape the reaping of the whirlwind.'

Rider was in Newfoundland when war was declared and, after several days mulling over the implications, he gave a speech which Edward Harding described as 'in the very worst taste', adding, 'But Haggard prides himself on his diplomacy!' Rider had not escaped the family failing.

His 'trumpet-call' speech to rally the Canadians behind England had the flavour and syntax of a sermon: 'The Angel of Death appears in a dawn of blood; the Armageddon, which has so long been foretold, has at length fallen upon us . . .' Rider can scarcely have anticipated the incompetence and degradation of the First World War, but no doubt he did understand that war had nothing to do with good taste.

The Royal Commission was rapidly disbanded, effectively dismissing several years' work and curtailing any significant influence Rider may have had. He suggested that the Royal Colonial Institute send him to visit all the colonies as an Honorary Representative, to promote the possibilities for the settlement of ex-servicemen when the War ended. While Rider was welcomed for himself as a writer, the reaction of a Canadian official in London to his public role was indicative of the fact that times had changed. In a series of exchanges between Sir Harry F. Wilson, the Secretary of the Royal Colonial Institute, and J. Obed Smith, the Assistant Superintendent of Emigration for Canada, it becomes clear that Rider's activities were seen as an uncalled-for interference. Smith pointed out indignantly:

> I am under no misconception regarding Sir Rider Haggard's proposition, but quite fail to understand why there should be any attempt to educate the Canadian Government and our Department on business which has been their public duty for so many years, and which has received their particular attention since the war started. I do not quite see what advantage there would be in you discussing the matter with me, so long as neither the Home Government nor the Canadian Government have invited the assistance of any outsiders in connection with business which is obviously the first duty of this Department.

When Wilson wrote a letter of reconciliation and invited Smith to a farewell luncheon for Rider before his departure, Smith wrote back:

> It is not necessary that Sir Rider Haggard should be in complete agreement with the . . . points named in my last letter. The Canadian Government is entirely supreme on, at least, the first and third, and if I could bring myself to believe that the Royal Colonial Institute would find the cost of transportation for ex-servicemen after the War, I should be glad to attend a luncheon in honour of any member of the Institute.

Smith was also horrified to find that the Royal Colonial Institute had been applying to Canadian firms for money to sponsor Rider's trip: 'The . . . arrangement surpasses anything I have supposed could happen in connection with such a matter, and I would strongly recommend the Council to reconsider their whole attitude in this proceeding, if they wish to retain the record of the Royal Colonial Institute, which I have had something to do in building up.'

Wilson admitted defeat, and declined to discuss the matter further with Smith, but he did ask him if he intended to come to the luncheon. Smith had the last word:

> I could not, as an officer of the Canadian Government, attend the Luncheon you propose, under the circumstances, and as a Fellow of the Institute my regard for propriety prevents me from accepting the invitation of the Council to the Luncheon to be given by your Council to Sir Rider Haggard.
>
> I note your observation that no useful purpose will be served by continuing this correspondence but I must be allowed to say that should occasion arise, this Department will not hesitate to do so at any time.
>
> I have the honour to be, Sir, Your obedient servant, J. Obed Smith.

Although Rider undertook the inquiry, little came of his efforts. The time for amateurs had passed, though the Haggard brothers had not realized it. Andrew kept sending to his nephew Harry ideas of 'impossible inventions' for Naval use by which he hoped to make a fortune. 'He and his collaborators have already settled what their shares of the profits are to be,' wrote Harry irritably. Arthur pressed on with his Veteran's Club, sometimes getting Andrew and Mary to help with fundraising and he, too, annoyed Harry with his tedious reporting of minutiae.

Their myopia could not blind them to the devastation of the war. Bazett's son Mark was the first to die in September of 1914. He had led a charge against German Maxims until he was mortally wounded and carried away by his servant, who was awarded the Victoria Cross. Mark's last words, 'Stick it the Welch', were used on recruiting bills all over Norfolk (presumably through Rider's energetic promotion).

Bazett's son Richard never recovered from head injuries and had to be kept quietly at Ditchingham, where eventually he fell into the River Waveney and drowned. Bazett's son Tom was deeply shocked, and could not return to normal practice for some years.

Jack's daughter Joan lost her fiancé and never forgave Aggie for prophesying the event. Jack's son Andrew was shell-shocked into a nervous breakdown.

April 1915. Jack's daughter Phoebe married Alfred's son Dan. Left
to right: Jack's son Andrew, Phoebe, Dan, Cazalet (the best man);
seated: Sir Henry Rider Haggard, Jack's daughter Joan.

Arthur's son Geoffrey was captured when his submarine was destroyed
off the Dardanelles, and he spent three and a half years in a Turkish
prison.[3] His brother Lance, of Princess Patricia's Light Infantry, died at
Passchendaele on 30 October 1917. Harry wrote to his mother: 'I had
an unpleasant contretemps. Dined at the Riders [in London]; he, she, &
Lilias there. I had heard nothing of it and those queer people said not a
word. At 10 p.m. who should walk in but Uncle A. [Arthur] looking
very miserable; to say when the memorial service was to be held, & I
had to ask what had happened!'

Lilly's son Eustace Archer, in the King's African Rifles, was wounded
in France and West Africa. Rudyard Kipling's only son died in devastating

agony. Charles Longman, Rider's publisher, lost his son. The son of Greiffenhagen, illustrator of so many of Rider's books, was posted missing, presumed dead. The Old White Hunter himself, Frederick Selous, died in action in East Africa in 1917.

Will's son Hal was on Dover Patrol in 1917, in charge of one of the gun turrets which were loaded at night in case of action. In the course of discharging them a faulty shell exploded and falling steelwork shattered Hal's leg, which was amputated below the knee.

War was not the only despoiler. Charles Maddison Green, who had retired in 1908 to Malvern, died in 1911 after an operation. Ledbury church bell was tolled daily from the Tuesday of his death until the Friday of his burial, when a muffled peal was rung as the hearse made its way through the shuttered streets. His son Roland Maddison Green, who had been unsuccessfully pursuing investments in Argentina, died in Mendoza in 1918.

Max Western, Cecilia's husband, died in 1913, leaving Cissy to endure another three years of madness. After thirty years at St Andrew's Hospital she died of cancer of the liver in 1916 while staying at the Hospital's seaside house, Bryn y Neuadd Hall, in North Wales. Harry wrote: 'Poor Cissie – I did not know she still existed – I never remember seeing her.'

Alfred, who had been suffering from bladder problems, died from the effects of an operation in 1916, and was buried at Bradenham.

Will's eldest son, Rudolf, succumbed to tuberculosis at the age of twenty-five in Arcachon in 1914. Rudolf had loved Bradenham – which his younger brother Hal did not – and this, together with Hal's injuries, may have influenced Will to act as he did in 1917. No doubt Will's character made him intransigent once he had got the idea into his head. One way or another, he caused the most almighty and permanent rift in the family, while at the same time removing the symbol of its unity: he decided to sell Bradenham Hall.

This was to be the last quarrel.

Will had retired from the Diplomatic Service in 1914 and been duly awarded his knighthood. His relationship with his children was not good. In late 1917 or early 1918, having persuaded Hal, who cared little for worldly goods, to break the entail on the property, Will placed the estate with a land agent, and an advertisement with a photograph soon appeared:

SPECIAL ANNOUNCEMENT

This fine Norfolk Hall (Only Ten Bedrooms) with 140 acres for only £2,500. Originally the home of the Haggard family and the birthplace of Sir Ryder [*sic*] Haggard. A great Chance for Modernisation. Beautifully toned red brick, facing full south, over-looking its stately timbered park. Two drives, Adam's style hall, three fine reception rooms (one panelled), ten bedrooms, bathroom, good offices. All ground floor level. Centuries old gardens with beautiful timber, two fine old walled kitchen gardens, sporting woodlands. Two cottages, stabling, garage etc. An Expenditure of a little over £1000 would make the property a Most Charming Place, and with a market value of at least £6,000. Centre of West Norfolk Hunt. An hour's run to Newmarket and favourite Coast Resorts. A CHANCE SELDOM PRESENTED. Sole Agents Bentall, Horsley and Baldry, Brompton Road SW3.

At first, the remaining brothers were stunned; in June of 1918 Rider wrote to Andrew, in a tone of resignation.

I am very glad that I did not know he was actually selling it, since then one might have felt it to be a duty to try to save the place for the family which would have stripped me bare. For doubtless it would have returned no interest, even if the capital remained safe. I don't know who has bought it but I fear it may be one of these speculators who are going about the country, who will cut down the timber and sell off the farms for what they will fetch, though of this I'm not sure. Nor do I know what price he has got. Don't think, however, that I am criticizing Will, who I daresay has done what he thought wisest for himself and his family. Still, after 120 years or so it is a sad business though after all, what does it matter? Still one had hoped that Hal might have married someone with a bit of money and kept the place on. But I doubt whether he cares for it either − certainly not as Rudolph did. So that's that and exit Bradenham and . . . our name from Norfolk.

But, as the summer drew on, it became clear that Will hadn't finished yet. The auctioneer, George Cubitt of Norwich, was to preside over a three-day sale of the contents of the Hall on 26 to 28 August. All the paraphernalia of their youth, as well as many heirlooms, were to be picked over and sold off piecemeal. Rider went over to Bradenham the day before the sale and ate his lunch under the beech tree, and 'nearly wept'.

Will kept the family portraits and the plate, but no private arrangements were made, nothing personal was saved − even the family hatchments were abandoned – and Rider was forced to send an agent to the sale to buy up those items he wanted.

The Catalogue for the Sale includes a Library of 3,000 books, a Lely portrait of the Duchess of Norfolk, watercolours of St Helena, Imari plates, Nankin dishes, chandeliers, Eastern hangings, Benares brass, Chippendale tables and bookcases, a Hepplewhite drawing room suite, Sheraton cabinets and bookcases, guns, telescopes, swords, mahogany and oak furniture of every description, trunks, chests, screens, cabinets, lacquer and papier mâché; and from outside, everything from a tennis marker to fruit nets to man traps. The whole place was stripped bare. Will was selling not only their inheritance but the substance of their memories.

Afterwards, Rider wrote to Ella in a state of fury, having been told by his agent Bullen that the sale was 'run largely on my name' and, as a result, the prices went sky high and beyond Rider's purse. Bullen had bid '£70 for the tall clock but went for £100 – how *could* Will sell it?' He did manage to salvage 'the 3 cornered chair in which our father always wrote, also his table and writing apparatus (all of which Will abandoned)'.

To an irate letter from Ella Maddison Green, Rider replied on 2 September:

> Will and co can't have upset you more than they have me, also Louie and Lilias. My temper is permanently damaged! However, I have picked up several things of sorts (went round the Norwich dealers shops on Saturday). Amongst others I got that leather covered blotter inscribed 'W. Haggard from his Aunt Venning, St. Petersburg.' Also I think I have bought your bed – if so I will send it you, but until things are delivered I really don't know for sure.

A few days later, Rider wrote to Andrew:

> Will refused to give up the Nelson washstand to the Jack family, with the result that he has caused what I believe will be a permanent family split with them, Joan is furious and Andrew says he will never speak to his Uncle again. Louie wrote and told him that it would, she was sure, cause 'much bitterness' but it had no effect.[4]
>
> As regards the sale of the Estate – the matter was carried through with the greatest secrecy – even Sydney Jones, W.'s own lawyer, did not know that it was done till it had been completed.

It transpired that the estate had indeed been sold to a speculator who was only interested in the timber. The great Bradenham oaks – the pride of the Old Squire – were all that was wanted. What a tremendous irony, that a family who had made such a fortune as merchant bankers in timber should have been sold out on that very commodity. With his instinct for the mystical essence of life, Rider had written a novel way back in 1888, *Colonel Quaritch VC*, in which the oak trees of a threatened estate became symbolic of the strength of the family and their preservation is essential to its survival. The people must be at one with the land.

As the full significance of what Will had done began to be felt, Rider protested to Ella that Will might have taken advice and sold the farms and timber himself, and still kept the house. It began to emerge that it had not been finer feelings that had made Will secretive. He was afraid that if the family knew about the sale, they would lean on Rider to buy it, forcing Will to take less money than the market value of £18 per acre. Rider commented bitterly, 'so Will has got a mess of potage for his birthright!'

Later, he wrote to Ella: 'It is enough to make our Father and Mother turn in their graves and personally I shall never get over it.'

Whatever had been their hopes and aspirations for their children, Mr and Mrs Haggard would certainly have expected the estate to remain at the core of the family. But, as Mr Haggard wrote in 1887 when he was commissioning Carthew's book on West Bradenham, 'the whole history of the family well represents English Life.' Ironically, despite their obsession with discovering a Danish ancestry to clarify their Englishness, the Haggards were of very mixed blood – French, Jewish, Indian and Slav at the least. All that was typically English was not racial but cultural: their rise through trade and the professions to the status of landed gentry. That was certainly the story of hundreds of other families. And so was the sale of the Estate. The scything of the heirs in the First World War, the introduction of death duties, and the changes in agriculture meant that, all over England, old country estates were up for sale and the whole pattern of life was changing.

The Haggard history did not finish in 1918. Like so many other families they have adapted to a new order but, in losing Bradenham, they lost the landscape of stability and self-definition which bred that boisterous, energetic Victorian generation, and allowed for the collecting of the letters and documents which are the basis of this story.

Epilogue

After the war, Rider bought North Lodge, in St Leonards on Sea, for the winter months. The house, which straddled the road, had once belonged to Cecil Rhodes's sister — Rhodes had used to sleep on the roof. When Andrew returned to England in 1920, he and his wife lived in the little Paygate cottage attached to the house. Later, Rider sold the house to Sir Frederick and Lady Jackson on their retirement from East Africa — they had married late in life and had no children.

St Leonards was a popular spot for ageing colonial gentry; Mary d'Anethan settled at 64 Sedlescombe Road, and she and Andrew's wife, Ethel, ran a bridge club. Andrew disposed of most of his papers before he died in 1923. His coffin was covered with a Union Jack, and the pallbearers were all military men. Among the mourners at the nearby Hollington Church-in-the-Wood was a Miss Haggard who was reported to be his daughter. Mary lived on until 1935, and she is buried in the same churchyard. Many of her personal belongings were lost in a shipwreck, but her obituary mentions a second volume of memoirs which she was preparing, to be called *Jotted Down*: alas, it is no longer to be found.

Ella Maddison Green, who aged to become 'a terrifying lady' who ruled with a rod of iron, returned to Ledbury and died in 1921. Both she and Charles are buried in Lyonshall churchyard with their lost babies, and their memorials are in Ledbury church. Ella's extensive papers are one of the cornerstones of the family history, many of them transcribed by Jack's son Andrew.

Arthur died in 1925 and was cremated at Golders Green, his ashes and those of his wife being brought to Spexhall church in Norfolk. His descendants live on in Australia, but there are few remaining papers. Jack's son Andrew recalled one typical incident: 'On one occasion when we were both staying at Ditchingham and we were walking back from church he [Arthur] gave me a shilling. It does not sound anything very remarkable but I had not had a penny to bless myself with for weeks and to me that shilling was untold riches, so much so that the glint of that coin as it changed hands has remained with me for the last seventy years.'

Not long after Arthur's death, Rider died from post-operative exhaustion. He was cremated, and his ashes were buried at Ditchingham parish church. Louie lived on at Ditchingham until 1943, long enough to know the truth of Rider's comment in 1919: 'This Peace Treaty is made in fading ink.'

Will had destroyed all his own letters to his parents in 1911, but thankfully he had distributed to his brothers and sisters their own letters which had been preserved at Bradenham. He died in Mentone in 1926 at the age of 80, two years after Nitie who was buried near their home at Sittingbourne, Kent. Hal spent the rest of his working life in the Admiralty and, unlike Will, proved himself a loving father.

Aggie preserved many of her own and Jack's letters, which now form a substantial collection in the Rhodes House Library. She lived to be a hundred – fifty-two years as a widow – and did not die until 1960, by which time she was crippled and bedridden. Many of her poems were published privately.

None of Cissy's three surviving daughters married, but one became a Deaconess. Maximilian Western's scrapbook of newspaper cuttings has survived in the family.

Alfred Thacker fell on hard times, despite Rider's attempts to get him a billet in Rhodesia. He came up before the magistrates on at least one occasion, presumably for drunkenness. He had no known children, and retired to Woodbridge in Suffolk. Jack's son Andrew had the foresight to ask him for his reminiscences.

Geoffrey Archer had an outstanding career in Colonial administration, and became Governor of British Somaliland between 1914 and 1922, Governor-General of Uganda during 1923–4, and Governor-General of the Anglo–Egyptian Sudan in 1925–6. Wilfred Thesiger remembers staying with him. After a disagreement on policy, Geoffrey retired early, spending many happy years hunting in Kashmir before settling in Cannes – where, no doubt, he was regarded as a remarkable curiosity from the past, since he did not die until 1964. A romantic to the last, he requested that his body be cremated at Marseilles and thrown to the winds at the gateway to the port.

Lilias continued the tradition of family hospitality at Ditchingham, and she matured into a noted countrywoman and writer on country matters, much respected and cherished in Norfolk. She also established the collecting of an oral tradition of history with her best-loved books, *I Walked by Night* and *The Rabbit Skin Cap*. Her sisters' children preserved many of Rider's papers and other family letters.

Harry, who had served all through the First World War, became Chief of the Submarine Service between 1926 and 1930, and eventually reached the heights as Admiral Sir Vernon Haggard KCB – thereby proving that Alfred's creative abilities had not *all* fallen on stony ground. Alfred's and Harry's papers have been preserved, and they bear witness to the steadfast moral guidance which Alfred offered his son through his early days in the Navy.

And what of the riddle that was Rider Haggard? As Rider well knew, everybody loves a mystery, and it is his own inscrutable quality that continues to fascinate people. There are so many facets to his life, and so many collections of papers remain to be researched, and some yet to be rediscovered, that studies will continue to be made of his life. Of his own writings, his Zulu novels may be re-interpreted in the light of the new South Africa, and several of his historical romances are ripe for re-working into new media. His writings on agriculture and rural life will continue to be sources for research.

Of that other aspect of his personality – his psychic sensibility – one can only speculate. Was there some genetic factor in the family which, actively in the case of Cissy, less so in the case of Rider, led to a disturbance of the psyche?

From Rider's 'Commonplace Book' of 1882, Godfrey copied this passage:

> Do you know, I think that when I die, I shall find my little child waiting for me, and we two shall together wait for one who is our soul, for you know that in heaven each shall be with the one most beloved and desired.
>
> You must not think that these are idle dreams or fancies: they are not. I have made these things a study, and you do not know what comfort and strength it gives me.
>
> I believe that death is only the completion of the first little round in life, the first short flight marking the end only of our seed-time . . . death is the grandest step in life. It solves all its enigmas, it is the fulfilment of which this existence is the prophesy, and to the wise and pure it opens the shining portals of an endless day.

If the date of transcription is correct, this passage was written several years before Jock's death. Did it refer to the baby who died in South Africa? Or was it a sentinel of the coming tragedy? Christianity had bred in Rider a certainty of life after death. His creative imagination and second sight convinced him of the fact of reincarnation.

By intuition and experience he discovered that the surface of temporal reality was flawed. Time itself was not what it seemed. In his novels he demonstrated the power of the psychic imagination to reinterpret the material world.

Notes

Chapter 1: Gathered Here Together

1 William Henry Haggard (1757–1837), grandfather of William Meybohm Rider Haggard, bought Bradenham Hall so as to be close to his friend from Cambridge, Mason of Necton. William Henry Haggard married Frances Amyand, sister and heir to Thomas Amyand of Twickenham House, Middlesex. The Twickenham estate was inherited by William Meybohm Rider Haggard's brother, James Haggard of Pinehurst, Bournemouth, Hampshire, who lived off the income. Twickenham House is now a hospital.
2 Burke's *The Landed Gentry*, Essay on the Position of the British Gentry; 1862. The Revd John Hamilton Gray, Vicar of Bolsover, stated the case (in suitably flattering terms) for the apotheosis of the English Gentleman from country landowner to unofficial aristocracy.
3 The Haggard arms, which once adorned the east entrance to Bradenham Hall, have been removed by the current owners.
4 The Amyands of Moccas Court, Herefordshire, were of French extraction, which may have given them the reputation of excitability. The male line is now extinct.
5 The Haggards had longstanding connections with the Lyttons of Knebworth, Hertfordshire (see a letter of 1806 from William Haggard to his sister Fanny: HAG 148, Norfolk Record Office). The Bulwers of Heydon were neighbours to the Haggards at Bradenham.
6 In his autobiography *The Days of My Life*, Sir Henry Rider Haggard placed this incident when he was nine years old. However, since his daughter Lilias Rider Haggard recorded it in *The Cloak That I Left* as being at the time of Ella's wedding, he would have been a pubescent thirteen. Cornelia Brunner, who met and talked with Lilias, also places the incident at the later age and writes of its deeply sexual significance in her Jungian analysis of Haggard's life and work, *Anima as Fate*.

Chapter 2: No Wind Along These Seas

1 Jack saved a cat-o'-nine-tails from his Navy days, and it is now in the National Maritime Museum at Greenwich. Flogging was abolished in 1879.
2 Sir Robert Napier of Magdala (1810–1890), subsequently Commander-in-Chief in India 1870–6.
3 From an article on the Abyssinia expedition in *Country Life*, 16 January 1958, by Michael Bongell.
4 A supply of champagne for the officers was considered essential.
5 The Suez Canal was still under construction.
6 The Barkers of Shipdham gave Rider a copy of *Robinson Crusoe* for his birthday, and he became so engrossed in reading it that he refused to come out from under his bed to go to church.

Chapter 3: And All the Trees Are Green

1 The Heywards appear to have lived in Leinster Square, London, where the Haggards had a house for a time at no. 24.

2 Alfred was a prefect of Trevelyan House, Head of Form in 1862, and Head of Modern.

3 The following stanza illustrates Mrs Haggard's relish of violence in a noble cause:
> Afghans! no quarter grant: the long Jazail
> Is sure of aim – each bullet tells its tale.
> And ye, oh, holy Ghazees! ply the knife:
> Gash deep the prostrate, gash! in saintly strife!

The Kabul campaign was also notably represented in Lady Butler's painting 'The Remnants of an Army, Jellalabad January 13, 1842'. Lady Butler's husband, General Sir William Butler, played a leading role on the Imperial stage, and their books and memoirs are excellent sources for the period.

4 Evelyn Baring (1841–1917) later became Lord Cromer (choosing the title from his birthplace – his mother was a Windham of Felbrigg, Norfolk) and Consul-General in Egypt.

5 Sir Henry Wolff (1830–1908), diplomat and later MP, a friend of Alfred's uncle James Haggard, and probably also known to Will. Wolff's father was a Jewish convert who made the famous Mission to Bokhara in 1845.

6 Darjeeling was the favoured hill station for Calcutta.

7 See MC127 HAG 131, Norfolk Record Office; letter dated 31 August 1917 from Ellen Maria Haggard to her cousin Ella Maddison Green. The basis of the story is that a man named Torlassi (or Torlesse) married a begum (a well-born Moslem woman) and their daughter Eleanor married a Colonel Bond. Eleanor's daughter, Ellen Maria Bond, married Bazett Doveton and was Mrs Haggard's mother. Eleanor deserted Colonel Bond for another man with whom she lived in Paris, and *they* had a daughter, Amelie, who eventually married a man named Duval. These connections may account for Andrew and Alfred Haggard's interest in French history.

Ellen's letter states: 'All this I first heard from your brother Will and it was afterwards confirmed by my mother whom I asked about it. She naturally did not care to speak about her grandmother's unedifying past, nor the taint of black blood which she imported into the family, but she could not deny the facts . . .'

8 Charles gave meticulous care to the specification, and the resulting vicarage is a good example of Victorian domestic style. Despite the pleasantness of the exterior, the interior is austere and the passages dark. The study at the corner of the ground floor looks out towards the church and is provided with a discreet anteroom. The house is now privately owned.

9 Captain Amyand Haggard RN, 1849–1905, eldest son of Caroline and James Haggard, married Edith Maria Venning, daughter of James Meybohm Venning. Note the double connection with the Meybohms.

10 Sir Henry Bulwer, 1836–1914, third son of William Bulwer of Heydon. He was Lieutenant Governor of Natal, 1875–80, and Governor of Natal, 1882–5. His eldest brother was High Sheriff of Norfolk in 1883.

Chapter 4: Home-Born Ills

1 On his twenty-first birthday, Andrew received £100 from his godfather, the Reverend Parker of Saham Toney. Andrew told his nephew and namesake that he blew it all on a two-week spree in Paris, and 'had his money's worth of experience'.

2 From Sir William Butler's autobiography, written in 1911. Rider included Shepstone's character and views in *The Witch's Head*.

3 From *All Sir Garnet: A Life of Field-Marshal Lord Wolseley*, by Joseph H. Lehmann, Cape, 1964.

4 Rider used this material in *King Solomon's Mines*; he wrote home about it at Easter 1876.

5 The Schalchs lived at 44 Park Street, in suburban Calcutta.

6 At 106 Harley Street, London, lived Mary Stuart, a great friend of Mrs Haggard and a cousin of the Schalchs. Mary Stuart owned a substantial property at Charmouth, near Lyme Regis, and it is through this connection that the Alfreds eventually moved to Dorset.

7 Charles Carroll was a signatory to the Declaration of Independence, while his grandson, John Lee Carroll, became Governor of Maryland. The Carroll home in Washington was occupied at the time by the Russian Minister.

Years later, Andrew met Carrie in Quebec, and he wrote to Rider that he had a good idea how Carrie captured Will. Sadly, discretion prevented him from committing his thoughts to paper.

8 From an unknown Washington newspaper. The cutting is in the Norfolk Record Office.

9 2 Cambridge Villas, Richmond.

10 Rider's articles: 'The Transvaal' appeared in *Macmillan's Magazine* in May 1877, 'A Zulu War Dance' in *The Gentleman's Magazine*, July 1877, and 'A Visit to a Secocoeni Chief' in *The Gentleman's Magazine*, September 1877.

11 Rider expressed these views retrospectively in a letter to Jack, now in the Rhodes House Library.

12 Charlie Fitton had recently married Julia Venning, whose family had been in business with the Haggards in Russia.

Chapter 5: Youth Is the Time for Mating

1 In 'The Tale of Isandlawhana', from *The True Story Book* edited by Andrew Lang, Longmans Green & Co, 1893, Rider firmly puts the blame for the disaster at the feet of Colonel Durnford, who in the past had tried to avoid bloodshed and had been designated by the ungenerous nickname, 'Don't Fire Durnford'. Rider suggested the possibility that it was the memory of past failure that determined Durnford to engage the Zulus in the open rather than await the attack in the comparative safety of a *laager*.

Melmoth Osborn (1833–1899), who had been on Shepstone's staff, was Commissioner and Chief Magistrate of Zululand from 1880 to 1893.

Lord Chelmsford, Frederick Thesiger (1827–1905), vindicated himself at Ulundi but was replaced by Wolseley.

2 Cochrane's first two letters have been lost, but the third was written on 14 August 1879, and many others survive.

3 George Blomefield was a member of the Mason family of Necton, but he had taken the name of his kin – the same family as the Norfolk antiquarian Francis Blomefield.

4 Rider had been to stay at Ditchingham in December when they were first engaged, which his father had considered quite within the bounds of propriety. But Louie evaded Miss Hildyard, whom she easily dominated, and actually spent time alone with Rider, which was verging on the scandalous. Hartcup was horrified at the engagement: 'I can but reflect that a three Days acquaintance of the most accidental kind has sufficed to influence the future well being of your life. I sometimes fear that you think of nothing but your own enjoyment. I greatly hope that I may be wrong.'

5 The Westerns' works was located at what is now the site of the South Bank complex.

6 Cissy exhibited 'unreasonably jealous behaviour' towards her husband. Without some example it is impossible to interpret this statement. Information about her illness is taken from the 'Notes for Elizabeth Cecilia Western — St Andrew's Hospital, Northampton'.

Chapter 6: *The Ungirt Hour*

1 Mr Haggard enumerated the various monies which Bazett had received, which included £3000 since he left college, the marriage settlement of about £6000, and his allowance which had been reduced, two years previously, to £100 per annum for ten years; HAG 176, Norfolk Record Office.
2 On one of these walks, Jack and Rider discovered an old gibbet iron with a skull still inside it. The Squire exhibited the iron at a garden party, and it is now on view in the dungeons of Norwich Castle Museum.
3 Napier Broome's advice (in a letter; Cheyne Collection) to Rider on his engagement read:

> I hope you have many happy years before you; but they cannot begin
> — take my word for it — until you get rid of your farm, your mill,
> your ostriches, and your Cochrane. No gentleman ever did any good
> in Natal, or ever will, and you will only waste your time and your
> money by engaging in the pursuit of mean whites and Dutchmen.
>   You may take this as you like now, but if you lay it by and read it
> ten years hence, or at any rate remember it, you will find I am right.

4 The Amhursts' private museum of Egyptian antiquities at Didlington Hall in Norfolk inspired not only the Haggards but also Howard Carter of Swaffham.
5 Valentine Baker had been convicted of indecent assault.
6 It was not until 1890 that Shepheard's was largely rebuilt with an Italianate frontage. Lady Butler gives a superb description of the street scene from Shepheard's in her *Sketch Book and Diary* (1909), pp. 34–6. Lady Butler added that this was nothing compared to 'diving into the old city' of Cairo, 'to find oneself in the Middle Ages'.
7 General Yusuf Shuhdi Pasha, 1839–1899, was a Circassian officer educated in Berlin. He accompanied Andrew on the Special Recruiting mission of 1883 which uncovered extensive corruption. In 1886, Sir Henry Drummond Wolff, at that time British High Commissioner in Egypt, appointed him Turkish delegate to the Sudan with a mission to re-open trade with the Sudan and peaceably prevent a Mahdist invasion of Upper Egypt. Opposition from Lord Cromer blocked Shuhdi's proposals. He subsequently became Governor of Cairo and Minister of War and Marine. A man of great physical and moral courage, Andrew wrote of him: 'I have never liked a man better or known a better fellow than that gallant old Circassian.'
8 The reluctance with which Charles approached Bazett's misdemeanours suggests they may have been sexual.
9 Thacker was so like Andrew that, when the latter was orderly officer but wanted to go to a party, Thacker would don his uniform and turn out the guard in the middle of the night.

Chapter 7: *Imperial Fire*

1 Sir John Kirk, 1832–1922, was the Agent in Zanzibar between 1873 and 1887 and, as such, was the virtual ruler during this critical period of European intervention. With the Omani rulers of Zanzibar, Kirk negotiated a treaty for the suppression of the slave trade in 1873.
2 Haggard's Oribi, a buck, was named after Jack.

3 Furious at this premature publicity, Admiral Hewitt refused to take Cameron with him to Abyssinia. Cameron had already kitted up for the trip, so he lent his camp bed to Andrew, who in turn lent it to Fred Villiers of the *Graphic* – 'who has it still' Cameron was killed at Abu Klea.

4 In his introduction to *Early Days in East Africa*, Lord Cranworth described Jack as 'spirited and erratic'.

5 The Arabs called Jack's birds 'barua ballosi', or 'the Consul's freed slaves'; letter from Jack to Will, 27 September 1884, Rhodes House Library.

6 Has the inscription survived? Andrew wrote his diary in a 'Collins Daily Scribbler' given him by Chamley Turner, and it was eventually returned to his Regimental headquarters in Berwick-on-Tweed in the 1930s, having been left by him in Vancouver. Chamley Turner drowned in the Nile.

7 Spasmodic stricture is a common symptom of chronic gonorrhoea – scarcely a surprising condition for a Victorian seaman.

Chapter 8: *Honour All Over the Earth*

1 Positivism was a philosophy developed by August Comte which has been called 'Catholicism without God'. It was introduced to England through the translations of a remarkable Norwich woman, Harriet Martineau.

   Alfred wrote for the British India Committee: *Europeans and Natives in India* (1883); *England and Islam, The Condition of the Indian Ryot* [sic] and *A New Departure in Foreign Policy* (1886).

2 Emma was the daughter of Charles Bailey, of Lee Abbey, North Devon. Although younger than Will, she was 'not so young as she was'. Her position and wealth, and the friendship of Bargrave Deane, a barrister and Recorder of Margate, were her recommendations to the Haggards.

3 The Sherd of Amenartas is in Norwich Castle Museum, although not on display.

4 *Anima as Fate*, p. 17.

Chapter 9: *Distant From the Seven Hills*

1 Nyleptha and Sorais were the two names Aggie had given to the rival queens in *Allan Quatermain*. She never seems to have doubted that the baby would be a girl.

2 Native life in Madagascar, and its effects on an English trader, are evocatively described in Aggie's novel *The Tangena Tree* (1889).

3 Aggie is said to have taken a shotgun to couples who copulated under the stilted house.

4 Emily Calvert, daughter of Edmund Calvert, of Walton-le-Dale, Lancashire. The family lived in Spexhall, Suffolk.

5 Harry's letters span the years 1888–1925. He entered the Navy, at Jack's suggestion and with the sponsorship of Squire Haggard's friend Edward Birkbeck. Harry's moral aspirations were based on Alfred's classical learning and the sentiments of Wordsworth's *The Happy Warrior*.

6 Richard Ellis of Greenwoods, Stock, Essex. His daughter, Dorothy Booker Ellis, married Alfred's eldest son, Harry.

7 From Brian Roberts, *Cecil Rhodes*.

8 Letter from Elizabeth Hocking to Ella Maddison Green; MC 127 HAG 139 (602x1), Norfolk Record Office.

Chapter 10: In Our Very Death

1 The drains at Ditchingham had long been under suspicion since three little Margitson sisters had died there in the 1840s. See *Too Late For Tears* by Lilias Rider Haggard.
2 From Godfrey Haggard's unpublished memoir, 'The Last Consul'.
3 Ouida was the pen name of Maria Louise Ramée (1839–1908). Bazett wrote a riposte to Julia, 'Objects of Pity or Self and Company'.
4 Will had been made Consul-General at Quito in Ecuador, which he described to Harry as 'the dullest place on earth . . . the people are dirty, drunken and dissolute.'
    A newspaper columnist had reported that Will had been commanded to Windsor before his departure with the comment: 'It is surely somewhat a waste of brains and money to exile so experienced a diplomatist to such a post as Quito, where there can be little or no work for him to do?'
    Years later one of Will's daughters wrote these disrespectful lines:

> A gay diplomatic society gent
> (Of names in this ditty I'm chary)
> 'mid circles exalted familiarly went
> Where the fool (or the angel) tread wary;
> And as with the fair, and the wise, and the great
> He freely discoursed on all matters of State,
> His autobiography can but relate
> (let nobody call him mendacious)
> How her Majesty listened both early and late,
> How the Queen was most gracious;
> Most gracious! MOST gracious!
> The Queen most exception'ly gracious!
>
> I marvel whenever I hear him descant
> On his theme in such sweet moderation
> At the tact and the wit that this Court hierophant
> Displayed in each nice situation;
> While crowned heads delighted to honour him so
> (of names I must ever be chary)
> His despatches sped home to a grateful F.O.
> And e'en the Prime Minister (whisper it low!)
> Was exception'ly compl*ementary*
> Said the P.M. 'Promote him! but where can he go
> To prove what we think of his merits? I know,
> Just the thing, the legation at distant *Quito*!
> What could be more complementary!'

5 Richard Meinertzhagen relates, in his *Kenya Diary*, that the KAR's officers took their black mistresses into the Mess.
6 The board included Sir Thomas Fowell Buxton, Sir John Kirk and General Sir Arnold B. Kemball. The Buxtons are a Norfolk family, Kirk had been Jack's superior in Zanzibar, and the Kemballs had Norfolk connections. Two generations later Brigadier Humphrey Kemball was brought up at Kirby Cane Hall (Bazett's old home) and married Margery Bickham, a grand-daughter of Ella Maddison Green.

Chapter 11: Many Roads Thou Hast Fashioned

1 Chamberlain was the first professor of Japanese at Tokyo University, and his book *Japanese Things* was published in 1890.
2 Mary sent Japanese orchids to Rider for the orchid houses he built at Ditchingham. Rider always wore a buttonhole – often an orchid.
3 Sir William was the brother of Sir Hercules Robinson, Governor of Cape Colony.
4 See Mary Fraser's *A Diplomat's Wife in Japan*, edited by Hugh Cortazzi. Her brother was the novelist Marion Crawford.
5 When Jack had been appointed Vice-Consul at Lamu, he and the other retired Naval officers had been given special permission to retain their Naval pensions. But when he was appointed to Trieste, the authority for this decision was questioned by the F.O. and permission was withdrawn. Jack was asked to repay the pension he had already received and money was deducted annually from his salary until his death, when the residue was extracted from his estate.
6 *Secret of Saint Florel*, May 1896–February 1897; and *A Philosopher's Romance*, May 1897–May 1898.
7 Jack was appalled at the complete lack of evidence but, despite his protestations, he himself was never called as a witness and the poor man was found guilty by a jury. Although, in the face of public horror, the death sentence was commuted, Jack found the long prison sentence equally disturbing.
8 A contemporary description from *At the Antipodes* by G. Venschuur, translated by Mary Daniels, London, 1891.
9 Jack annotated one of his astrological predictions about death, 'Marie', implying that she had died, either out in Noumea or upon their return.
10 Mark Haggard, Bazett's second son, also served in the war, and Lilly Jackson's eldest son, Francis Eustace, fought as a Lieutenant in the Norfolk Regiment.
11 In *Twenty Years of My Life*, (pp. 284–5) Douglas Sladen mentions both Arthur and Rider Haggard as being guests at his literary salons. There are also a number of letters from both Rider and Arthur with regard to literary organizations in the Sladen Papers in Richmond.

Chapter 12: From One Generation to Another

1 Godfrey cites, as an illustration of the extent to which Britain blindly patronized Germany, the official protocol on the Memorial Service held in Caracas for the Empress Frederick, mother of the Kaiser and daughter of Queen Victoria. The British Minister, Will Haggard, was instructed 'to *thank* his German colleague' for having organized it.
2 Godfrey failed to get into the Navy on account of his bad teeth. It was still considered necessary for sailors to have strong teeth in order to bite lead bullets.
3 Godfrey Haggard's unpublished Memoirs, 'The Last Consul'.
4 In 1898, Will was writing to the Marquis of Salisbury at the Foreign Office about a proposed scheme for the US to lend Venezuela ten million pounds on the security of the Customs, which would then be administered by the Americans in the interest of the loan. 'There would seem to be nothing intrinsically improbable in the scheme; for the United States have lately shown a disposition to establish a more tangible hold on these republics than that afforded by the somewhat vague pretensions of the Monroe Doctrine . . . the peace and quiet which ought to follow the introduction of a "quasi" US Protectorate would add enormously to their future receipts; for the natural resources of this country are simply boundless, and are as yet practically untouched . . .' 12 October 1898, FO 80.387.
5 The Foreign Office states that, owing to damage from white ants, the following

volumes had to be destroyed: 1900 January to June; 1902 September to December. This is interesting, since Godfrey, who was given the task of sorting out the Legation papers, remarked on their good condition and how he believed the pervasive cigar smoke of a previous clerk had proved beneficial to their preservation. Perhaps the white ants moved in afterwards – one is intrigued by their selection.

6 The Baroness von Pilgrim (when she had recovered from her 'pregnancy') left Caracas a few days later and both she and her husband headed for Curaçao.

7 Godfrey recalled that the Kaiser's words at the time of the Siege of Pekin were still fresh in everyone's minds: 'Just as the Huns a thousand years ago under the leadership of Attila gained a reputation by virtue of which they still live in historical tradition, so may the name of Germany become known in such a manner in China that no Chinese will ever again dare look askance at a German.' This speech gave rise to the derogatory usage of the name 'Huns' for Germans on the part of the British.

8 In 1891, Andrew mentioned to Rider that the McKinley Bill – a protectionist measure – was going to undermine his financial position. Emily's cousin, Captain John Chirnside CMG, lived at Werribee, Victoria, Australia.

9 Hearsay has it that Rider also paid off his brothers' various illegitimate offspring.

10 In 1922, Aggie arranged for Jack's bones to be brought back to England disguised as a sack of potatoes. He is buried hard by the wall in Bradenham churchyard.

11 Lady Jackson's photograph album of Kenya, dated 1905–11, is preserved in The Royal Commonwealth Society Library (Y03046A).

During the Sudanese Mutiny of 1897, Jackson was seriously wounded by a bullet which penetrated his lungs. See *With Macdonald in Uganda*, by Major Herbert H. Austin, London, 1903.

12 Sydney Higgins was responsible for the initial uncovering of Lilly's identity, an account of which was published in *The London Magazine* of February 1987, Vol. 26, No. 11. The Red House at Aldeburgh became the home of Benjamin Britten and Peter Pears. See also Sir Geoffrey Archer's *Personal and Historical Memoirs of An East African Administrator*, Oliver and Boyd, 1960.

Chapter 13: Our Stilly Woods of Oak

1 In 1909, the tenants were a family called Moxley, who invited a young lad called Leslie Hartley to stay during a holiday. That summer at Bradenham, L. P. Hartley stored up the experiences on which, as an adult, he based his book *The Go-Between*. There is a story that he found a girl's diary in which she confided her passion – could it have been Cecilia's?

2 Alfred took the same strong, anti-racist view, counselling his son Harry to see always the humanity beneath the colour of the skin.

3 See *Straws in the Winds*, by Commander Henry Stoker DSO, RN.

4 Eventually Will's daughters prevailed upon him to give up the Nelson washstand, and it remains in the possession of Jack's descendants.

Bibliography

PRIMARY SOURCES

Letters from the Norfolk Record Office; MC 127 and MC 133.
Letters from private family collections.
Newspaper reports, attributed where possible.
Items from the Rhodes House Library: letters of John George Haggard, Agnes Marion Haggard, Andrew Thacker, Maximilian Western; and the diary of Ella Doveton.
Letters from the National Maritime Museum, of John George Haggard.
Consular and Diplomatic Documents from the Public Record Office.
H. Rider Haggard Papers, Rare Book and Manuscript Library, Columbia University.
Letters from the Royal Commonwealth Society Files, by permission of the syndics of Cambridge University Library.
Letters from the Cheyne Collection.
The novels of Sir Henry Rider Haggard.
Royal Commonwealth Society MSS 4: Arthur Hunter's Scrapbook on Jackson and Archer.
Unpublished journal of the Suakin Campaign, Andrew Haggard C.P., transcribed by Peter Beard; by permission of the Regimental Archive, King's Own Scottish Borderers.
'The Last Consul': unpublished memoirs and notes, Godfrey Haggard.

GENERAL BIBLIOGRAPHY

Amyand, Arthur (1895). *With Rank and File*. Osgood McAlvaine & Co., London.
d'Anethan, Baroness Albert (1907). *It Happened in Japan*. Brown Lanham & Co., London.
d'Anethan, Baroness Albert (1912). *Fourteen Years of Diplomatic Life in Japan*. Stanley Paul & Co., London.
d'Anethan, Baroness Albert (1914). *The Twin Souls of O'Take San*. Stanley Paul & Co., London.
Archer, Sir Geoffrey KCMG (1960). *Personal and Historical Memoirs of An East African Administrator*. Oliver & Boyd, London.
Armstrong, H.B.J. (ed.) (1949). *A Norfolk Diary: Passages from the Diary of Rev. B. J. Armstrong*.
Barthorp, Michael (1984). *War on the Nile: Britain in Egypt and the Sudan 1882–1898*. Blandford Press, Dorset.
Berwick, John (Agnes Haggard) (1963). *Selected Poems*. Private publication.
Bird, Michael (1957). *Samual Shepheard of Cairo*. Michael Joseph, London.
Brunner, Cornelia (1986) [1963]. *Anima as Fate*. Spring Publications, Dallas.
Bryant, T. Hugh (1903). *Norfolk Churches*. Norwich Mercury Office, Norwich.
Butler, Sir William (1911). *An Autobiography*. London.
Cairns, William Elliott (1899). *Social Life in the British Army*. Harper Bros, London and New York.

Carthew, G. A. (1883). *A History of the Parishes of East and West Bradenham.* Private publication.

Clowes, Sir Wm Laird (1903). *The Royal Navy.* Sampson, Low, Marston & Co.

Cohen, Morton (1960). *Rider Haggard – His Life and Works.* Hutchinson, London.

Coupland, Reginald (1968). *The Exploitation of East Africa.* (Includes letters held in the Public Record Office: KP Xb 229–32.) Faber & Faber, London.

Cranworth, Lord (1939). *Kenya Chronicles.* Macmillan, London.

Cresswell, L. (1874). *Norfolk and the Squires, Clergy, Farmers and Labourers.* Simpkin Marshall.

Cromer, Lord (Sir Evelyn Baring) (1908). *Modern Egypt.* Macmillan, London.

Dewing, Rita (1972). *Bradenham: A Popular History.* Norfolk Record Office: MC 496/9, 794x8.

Dilke, Charles (1868). *Greater Britain.* Macmillan, London.

Duff, David (1974). *Whisper Louise.* Frederick Muller, London.

Duguid, J. (1874). *Letters from India and Kashmir.* London.

Duman, Daniel (1983). *The English and Colonial Bars in the Nineteenth Century.* Croom Helm, London.

Ellis, Peter B. (1978). *H. Rider Haggard – A Voice from the Infinite.* Routledge & Kegan Paul, London.

Fairless, Michael (Marjorie Barber) (1902). *The Roadmender.* Duckworth & Co., London.

Fairless, Michael (Marjorie Barber) (1931). *The Complete Works of Michael Fairless.* Duckworth & Co., London.

Farwell, B. (1973) *Queen Victoria's Little Wars.* Allen Lane, London.

Farwell, Byron (1986). *Eminent Victorian Soldiers.* Viking, London.

Fisher, H.A.L. (1927). *James Bryce.* Macmillan, London.

Flower, Newman (1950). *Just As It Happened.* Cassell, London.

Foss, Arthur and Kerith Trick (1989). *St Andrew's Hospital.* Granta Editions, Cambridge.

Foster, Joseph (1885). *Men-at-the-Bar: A Biographical Hand-List.* Reeves & Turner, London.

Fraser, Marie (1895). *In Stevenson's Samoa.* Smith, Elder & Co., London.

Freud, S. (1954). *The Interpretation of Dreams.* Trans. and ed. James Strachey. George Allen & Unwin, London.

Galbraith, John S. (1972). *Mackinnon and East Africa.* Cambridge University Press.

Haggard, Lt. Col. Andrew C.P. (1889). *Dodo and I.* William Blackwood & Sons, London.

Haggard, Lt. Col. Andrew C.P. (1895). *Under Crescent and Star.* William Blackwood & Sons, London.

Haggard, Lt. Col. Andrew C.P. (1901). *Love Rules the Camp.* Hutchinson & Co., London.

Haggard, Lt. Col. Andrew C.P. (1903). *Sporting Yarns: Spun off the Reel.* Hutchinson & Co., London.

Haggard, Ella (1857). *Myra or The Rose of the East: A Tale of the Afghan War.* Longman, Brown, Green, Longmans & Roberts, London.

Haggard, H. Rider (1926). *The Days of My Life.* Longmans, London.

Haggard, Lilias Rider (1951). *The Cloak That I Left.* Hodder & Stoughton, London.

Haggard, William (1857). *The Militia: Its Importance as a Constitutional Force.* Longman, Brown, Green, Longmans & Roberts, London.

Hambloch, Ernest (1938). *British Consul: Memories of Thirty Years Service in Europe and Brazil.* George G. Harrap & Co., London.

Hassall, Christopher (1946). *The Timeless Quest.* Arthur Barker, London.

Headlam, Cecil (ed.). *The Milner Papers.* Cassell, London.

Hibbert, Christopher (1979). *Victoria: A Biography.* George Rainbird, London.

Higgins, D.S. (ed.) (1980). *The Private Diaries of Sir Henry Rider Haggard.* Cassell, London.

Higgins, D.S. (1981). *Rider Haggard.* Stein & Day, New York; Cassell, London.

Hood, Miriam (1975). *Gunboat Diplomacy 1895–1905: Great Power Pressure in Venezuela.* George Allen & Unwin, London.

Howe, Sonia E. (1938). *The Drama of Madagascar.* (Foreword by the Rt Hon. Lord Lugard.) Methuen, London.

Hyman, Ronald (1990). *Empire and Sexuality.* Manchester University Press, Manchester.

Ingham, Kenneth (1958). *The Making of Modern Uganda.* George Allen & Unwin, London.

Jackson, Sir Frederick (1969). *Early Days in East Africa.* Dawsons of Pall Mall, London.

James, L. (1985). *The Savage Wars.* Robert Hall, London.

Jersey, The Dowager Countess of (1922). *Fifty-one Years of Victorian Life.* John Murray, London.

Johnston, Sir Harry H. (1923). *The Story of My Life.* Chatto & Windus, London.

Jung, Carl G. (ed.) (1954). *The Spirit In Man, Art, and Literature.* Routledge & Kegan Paul, London.

Keppel-Jones, Arthur (1988). *Rhodes and Rhodesia: The White Conquest of Zimbabwe 1884–1902.* McGill–Queen's University Press, Kingston and Montreal.

Kloss, C.B. (1903). *In The Andamans and Nicobars.* John Murray, London.

Lehmann, Joseph H. (1964). *All Sir Garnet.* Jonathan Cape, London.

Lockhart, J.G. and the Hon. C.M. Woodhouse (1963). *Rhodes.* Hodder & Stoughton, London.

Lutyens, Mary (1979). *The Lyttons in India.* John Murray, London.

Mackay, Margaret (1968). *The Violent Friend: The Story of Mrs Robert Louis Stevenson.* J.M. Dent & Son, London.

Manthorpe, Victoria (ed.) (1986). *The Japan Diaries of Richard Gordon Smith.* Viking Rainbird, London.

Marion, Agnes (Aggie Haggard) (1889). *The Tangena Tree.* Longmans Green & Co., London.

Mason, R. Hendry (1884). *History of Norfolk.* London.

McCourt, Edward (1967). *Remember Butler.* Routledge & Kegan Paul, London.

McLynn, Frank (1993). *Robert Louis Stevenson.* Hutchinson, London.

Meinertzhagen, Col. R. (1957). *Kenya Diary.* Oliver & Boyd, London.

Moncrieff, A.R. (1910). *The World Today. Volume V.* The Gresham Publishing Co., London.

Moors, H.J. (1910). *With Stevenson in Samoa.* Small, Maynard & Co., Boston.

Morris, Donald R. (1966). *The Washing of the Spears.* Jonathan Cape, London.

Morris, James (1973). *Pax Britannica – Trilogy.* Faber & Faber, London.

Mostyn, Trevor (1989). *Egypt's Belle Epoque.* Quartet Books, London.

Moulton, Edward C. (1968). *Lord Northbrook's Indian Administration 1872–6.* Asia Publishing House, London.

Nelson, Nina (1974). *Shepheard's Hotel.* Cedric Chivers, Portway, Bath.

Nowell-Smith, Simon (1958). *The House of Cassell 1848–1958.* Cassell, London.

Pakenham, Thomas (1991). *The Scramble for Africa.* Weidenfeld & Nicolson, London.

Palmer, William Scott (M.E. Dowson) and A.M. Haggard (1913). *Michael Fairless – Life and Writings.* Duckworth & Co., London.

Parry, Ernest C. (1885). *Suakin 1885, by an Officer Who Was There.* Kegan, Paul, Trench, London.

Pearsall, Ronald (1969). *The Worm in the Bud: The World of Victorian Sexuality.* Weidenfeld & Nicolson, London.

Pearsall, Ronald (1972). *The Table-Rappers.* Michael Joseph, London.

Pearsall, Ronald (1975). *Night's Black Angel.* Hodder & Stoughton, London.

Pearson, R. (1933). *Eastern Interlude: A Social History of the European Community in Calcutta.* Thacker Spink & Co., Calcutta.

Peters, Carl (1891). *New Light on Dark Africa.* Ward, Lock & Co., London.

Platt, D.C.M. (1971). *The Cinderella Service: British Consuls since 1825.* Longman, London.

Platt, D.C.M. (1972). *Latin America and British Trade 1806–1914.* A. & C. Black, London.

Pocock, Tom (1993). *Rider Haggard and the Lost Empire.* Weidenfeld & Nicolson, London.

Pope-Hennessy, James (1964). *Verandah*. George Allen & Unwin, London.

Powell, Violet (1978). *Margaret Countess of Jersey*. Heinemann, London.

Preston, Adrian (ed.) (1971). *The South African Diaries of Sir Garnet Wolseley*. A.A. Balkema, Cape Town.

Ray, Rajat Kanta (1984). *Social Conflict and Political Unrest in Bengal: 1875–1927*. Oxford University Press, Delhi.

Roberts, Brian (1987). *Cecil Rhodes: Flawed Colossus*. Hamilton, New York and London.

Rogers, Alexander (late Member of Council, Bombay) (1878–9). *Life in India*. Proceedings of the Royal Colonial Institute 1878–9, Vol. 10, p. 299.

Rotberg, Robert (1988). *The Founder: Cecil Rhodes and the Pursuit of Power*. Oxford University Press, New York.

Rouillard, N., ed. (1953). *Matabele Thompson: An Autobiography*. Johannesburg.

Russell, William Howard (1877). *The Prince of Wales Tour 1875–6*. Sampson, Low, Marston, Searle & Rivington, London.

Said, Edward W. (1993). *Culture and Imperialism*. Chatto & Windus, London.

Samkange, Stanlake (1978). *The Origins of Rhodesia*. Heinemann, London.

Sandison, Alan. 'A Matter of Vision: Rudyard Kipling and Rider Haggard'.

Sandison, Alan (1967). *The Wheel of Empire*. St Martin's Press, New York.

Sawyer, Roger (1984). *Casement: the Flawed Hero*. Routledge & Kegan Paul, London.

Saywell, John F.T. (1967). *Kaatza: The Chronicles of Cowichan Lake*. The Cowichan Lake District Centennial Committee, Sidney, British Columbia.

Scruggs, William L. (late Envoy and Minister Plenipotentiary of the United States of America to Colombia and Venezuela) (1901). *The Colombian and Venezuelan Republics*. Little, Brown & Co., Boston.

Shaw, George A. (1885). *Madagascar and France*. London.

Spiers, Edward M. (1992). *The Late Victorian Army 1868–1902*. Manchester University Press, Manchester.

Stevenson, Fanny and Robert Louis Stevenson (1956). *Our Samoan Adventure*. Weidenfeld & Nicolson, London.

Stevenson, Robert Louis (1995). *The Letters of Robert Louis Stevenson*. Volume Seven: September 1890–December 1892; Volume Eight: January 1893–December 1894. Edited by Bradford A. Booth and Ernest Mehew. Yale University Press, New Haven and London.

Stevenson, R.L., Osborne and Rupert Leigh. *An Object of Pity or The Man Haggard*. Privately printed.

Thacker's Bengal Directories. Thacker Spink & Co., Calcutta.

Theobald, A.B. (1951). *The Mahdiya*. Longmans, London.

Thesiger, Wilfred (1994). *My Kenya Days*. HarperCollins, London.

Trzebinski, Errol (1985). *The Kenya Pioneers*. Heinemann, London.

Welsh, David (1971). *The Roots of Segregation*. Oxford University Press, London.

Whatmore, D.E. (1987). *H. Rider Haggard – A Bibliography*. Mansell, London.

Wolseley, Field Marshal Viscount (1903). *The Story of a Soldier's Life. Volume II*. Archibald Constable & Co., London.

BOOKS WRITTEN BY HAGGARDS

(Denys Whatmore has compiled a full bibliography of the works of H. Rider Haggard. Below are listed books by other members of the Haggard family.)

WILLIAM MEYBOHM RIDER HAGGARD

The Militia: Its Importance as a Constitutional Force (1857)

ELLA HAGGARD (née Doveton)

> *Myra or The Rose of the East* (1857)
> *Life* (1892)
> Poems (unpublished)

WILLIAM HENRY DOVETON HAGGARD

> *The Vazir of Lankuram* (1882)

ALFRED HINUBER HAGGARD

> *England and Islam* (1876)
> *Counsels of a Mother* (unpublished)
> *Descent of Vernon Hugh Schlach* (unpublished)
> *A New Departure in Foreign Policy* (1886)
> *The Condition of the Indian Ryot* (1885)

ANDREW CHARLES PARKER HAGGARD

> *Dodo and I* (1889)
> *Ada Triscott* (1890)
> *A Strange Tale of a Scarabaeus* (1891)
> *Leslie's Fate* (1892)
> *Tempest Torn* (1894)
> *Under Crescent and Star* (1895)
> *Hannibal's Daughter* (1898)
> *Love Rules the Camp* (1901)
> *Thérèse of the Revolution* (1902)
> *Louis XIV* (1904)
> *A Canadian Girl* (1904)
> *A Bond of Sympathy* (1905)
> *Sidelights of the Court of France* (1903)
> *Sporting Yarns: Spun off the Reel* (1903)
> *The Regent of the Roués* (1905)
> *A Persian Rose Leaf* (1906)
> *The Real Louis XV* (1906)
> *Louis XVI and Marie Antoinette* (1909)
> *The Amours of Henri de Navarre and Marguérite de Valois* (1910)
> *Two Great Rivals* (1910)
> *The France of Joan of Arc* (1911)
> *Two Worlds* (1911)
> *Romance of Bayard* (1912)
> *Louis XI and Charles the Bold* (1914)
> *Women of France* (1914)
> *Women of the Revolutionary Era* (1914)
> *Staël* (1922)
> *Hugo: His Work and Love* (1923)

ELEONORA MARY D'ANETHAN

> *His Chief's Wife* (1897)
> *It Happened in Japan* (1906)
> *Two Women* (1909)

Fourteen Years of Diplomatic Life in Japan (1912)
The Twin Soul of O'Take San (1914)
Her Mother's Blood (1918)
Enter Caroline (1921)
Veronica (1923)
John's Penelope (1926)

AGNES HAGGARD
(née Agnes Marion Barber) Pseudonyms: John Berwick, Agnes Marion

The Tangena Tree (1889)
Secret of Saint Florel (1896)
A Philosopher's Romance (1897)
Poems (privately printed) (1963)

PHOEBE HAGGARD

Red Macaw (1934)
The Master's Children (1939)

AUDREY HAGGARD

The Double Axe (1929)
Little Plays from Greek Myths (1929)

EDWARD ARTHUR HAGGARD

The Kiss of Isis (1900)
Malcolm the Patriot (1907)
(using the pseudonym: Arthur Amyand)
Only a Drummer Boy (1894)
With Rank and File (1895)
Comrades in Arms (1895)
The Social Status of the Soldier in Connection with Recruiting (1896)

STEPHEN HAGGARD

I'll Go to Bed at Noon (1944)
Nya (1938)
Poems (1945)

VIRGINIA HAGGARD LEIRENS

My Life With Chagall (1985)

Index